Applied Criminology

Applied Criminology

Brian Stout, Joe Yates and Brian Williams

SAGE Publications

Los Angeles • London • New Delhi • Singapore

Editorial arrangement © Brian Stout, Joe Yates and
Brian Williams
© SAGE Publications 2008

First published 2008

SAGE Publications Ltd
1 Oliver's Yard
55 City Road
London EC1Y 1SP

SAGE Publications Inc.
2455 Teller Road
Thousand Oaks, California 91320

SAGE Publications India Pvt Ltd
B 1/I 1 Mohan Cooperative Industrial Area
Mathura Road
New Delhi 110 044

SAGE Publications Asia-Pacific Pte Ltd
33 Pekin Street #02-01
Far East Square
Singapore 048763

Library of Congress Control Number: 2007937341

British Library Cataloguing in Publication data

A catalogue record for this book is available from the
British Library

ISBN 978-1-4129-4731-2
ISBN 978-1-4129-4732-9 (pbk)

Typeset by CEPHA Imaging Pvt. Ltd., Bangalore, India
Printed in Great Britain by TJ International Ltd,
Padstow, Cornwall
Printed on paper from sustainable resources

CONTENTS

IN MEMORY OF PROFESSOR BRIAN WILLIAMS
1953—2007

ACKNOWLEDGEMENTS

The editors would like to acknowledge the guidance and support of Professor Brian Williams who, as a co-editor, provided a wealth of experience and advice in the early stages of this book. Brian's sudden and tragic death on 17 March 2007 has been a terrible loss to all who knew him. Our thoughts are with his family Suzanne, Adam, Sian and Simon.

We would like to thank all the contributors of the book for their diligence, patience and hard work. We would also like to acknowledge Caroline Porter from Sage for her useful advice, guidance and support throughout this project. Finally, we would like to thank our families: Cathy Wood and Callum Stout; Stephanie Hurd and William Yates.

NOTES ON CONTRIBUTORS

Jenny Ardley is Senior Lecturer in the Community and Criminal Justice Division at De Montfort University.

Rob Canton is Professor of Community and Criminal Justice at De Montfort University. His teaching and research interests include most aspects of probation practice, the ethics of punishment and working with mentally disordered offenders.

Annette Crisp is Senior Lecturer in the Community and Criminal Justice Division at De Montfort University and is involved in training police and community support officers.

Jane Dominey is Senior Lecturer in the Community and Criminal Justice Division at De Montfort University. She is programme leader of the Certificate in Community and Criminal Justice.

Tina Eadie is Senior Lecturer in the Community and Criminal Justice Division at De Montfort University, with teaching and research interests focusing on professional development within organizational contexts.

Hannah Goodman Chong is Research Fellow in the Community and Criminal Justice Division at De Montfort University. She has previously worked as a Probation Service Officer and as Project Development Worker for the Victims and Witnesses Action Group in Leicester.

Barry Goldson is Professor of Criminology and Social Policy at the University of Liverpool.

Jean Hine is Reader in the Community and Criminal Justice Division at De Montfort University.

Judy Hudson is Senior Lecturer in the Community and Criminal Justice Division at De Montfort University. She has particular interests in training and development in the community and criminal justice sector.

Hazel Kemshall is Professor of Community and Criminal Justice at De Montfort University. Her research interests include the assessment and management of high-risk offenders, multi-agency public protection panels and community responses to sexual offenders.

Charlotte Knight is Principal Lecturer in Community and Criminal Justice at De Montfort University. She is programme leader of the Masters programme.

Roger Smith is Professor of Social Work Research at De Montfort University.

Brian Stout is Principal Lecturer and Head of Division of the Community and Criminal Justice at De Montfort University.

Steve Tombs is Professor of Sociology at Liverpool John Moores University and Chair of the human rights charity the Centre for Corporate Accountability (www.corporate-accountability.org).

Azrini Wahidin is Reader in the School of Sociology, Social Policy and Social Work, Queen's University, Belfast.

Dave Ward is Professor of Social and Community Studies at De Montfort University. He has a particular interest in community and service user involvement in the social and community justice sectors.

Brian Williams was Professor of Criminology and Victimology at De Montfort University.

Jason Wood is Senior Lecturer in Youth and Community Development at De Montfort University. His research interests include community engagement in high-risk-offender management, and the ongoing development of Multi-Agency Public Protection Arrangements (MAPPA).

Joe Yates is Principal Lecturer and Criminology Subject Leader at Liverpool John Moores University.

LIST OF FIGURES AND TABLES

Figures

Tables

LIST OF ABBREVIATIONS

AYJ	Association for Youth Justice
BME	Black and Minority Ethnic
CJA	Criminal Justice Act
CJCS	Criminal Justice and Court Services
DoH	Department of Health
DTC	Duty to co-operate
EBPP	Evidence-based Policy and Practice
ESRC	Education and Science Research Council
HMIC	Her Majesty's Inspectorate of Constabularies
HMIP	Her Majesty's Inspectorate of Probation
HMP	Her Majesty's Prison
HSE	Health and Safety Executive
IPLDP	Initial Police Learning and Development Programme
ISSP	Intensive Supervision and Surveillance Programme
MAPPA	Multi-agency Public Protection Arrangement
NAYJ	National Association for Youth Justice
NETCU	National Extremism Tactical Coordination Unit
NIM	National Intelligence Model
NITFed	National Intermediate Treatment Federation
NOMS	National Offender Management Service
NPIA	National Policing Improvement Agency
OGRS	Offender Group Reconviction Scale
PACE	Police and Criminal Evidence Act
PBA	Probation Boards Association
PIP	Professionalizing the Investigative Process
POP	Problem-Orientated Policing
PSSO	Police Standards and Skills Organisation
RIPA	Regulation of Investigatory Powers Act
ROM	Regional Offender Manager
SFO	Serious Fraud Office
UCC	Union Carbide Corporation
VFM	Value for Money
VIS	Victim Impact Statements
VPS	Victim Personal Statements
YJB	Youth Justice Board
YOI	Young Offenders Institution
YOT	Youth Offending Team

1

APPLIED CRIMINOLOGY

Rob Canton and Joe Yates

The development of social scientific theory and knowledge takes place not simply within the heads of individuals, but within particular institutional domains. These domains, in turn, are shaped by their surroundings: how academic institutions are organised, how disciplines are divided and subdivided, how disputes emerge, how research is funded and how the findings are published and used. In Criminology, an understanding of these institutional domains is especially important for knowledge is situated not just, or not even primarily, in the 'pure' academic world, but in the applied domain of the state's crime control apparatus.

(Cohen, 1981: 220)

Criminology is a contested, contradictory and interdisciplinary discourse marked by constant incursion, interactions, translations, deviations and transgressions. Competing theoretical perspectives meet and sometimes they are able to speak to, listen to and understand each other, at others they appear not to share any common discourse. There is, therefore, no one definition of 'Criminology' . . . but a multitude of noisy, argumentative criminological perspectives.

(McLaughlin and Muncie, 2006: xiii)

Chapter summary

This introductory chapter explores what is meant by Applied Criminology: that is, Criminology in its applied form.

It is argued that Criminology should be applied to three principal questions:
- what is to be done about offenders?
- what is to be done about crime?
- what is to be done on behalf of the victims of crime?

It considers the historical development of Criminology as a discipline.

Some of the major movements and theories within Criminology are set out and the implications of applying these theories are explored.

Factors which shape the construction of criminological knowledge are critically considered. It is argued that all these factors have an important bearing on how Criminology is (or might be) applied and therefore how Applied Criminology should be understood.

The chapter concludes by considering the practice and policy implications of an Applied Criminology and outlining the contributions the various chapters of the book make to these debates.

Introduction

Over the last ten years there has been an increase in Criminology courses in universities and in the number of students on these courses, many of whom anticipate employment in the community and criminal justice sector. This growth in the number of students is integrally linked to the perception that studying Criminology will not only improve the 'employability' of students but also, in doing so, it will improve the functioning of the criminal justice system and increase its effectiveness. There is a sense, then, that the Criminology studied in the academy will (or should) be applicable in the field—to what are presented as the 'real world problems' of crime and criminal justice—a form of Applied Criminology.

The growth of Criminology taught in the institutional domain of the academy has also coincided with an increase in governmentally sponsored Criminology research. Whilst this reflects the prominence of crime and effective crime control in political debate, it also reflects a broader ambition to use 'evidence' from criminological research—especially in relation to what does or does not 'work'—to guide policy and practice.

This governmental commitment to researching criminal justice and evaluating its effectiveness has also been a significant factor in the growth of the monies made available to fund criminological research. Between 1998 and 2001, Tombs and Whyte (2004) observed that there was a 500 per cent increase in funding for research by the Home Office, much of which was aimed at commissioning criminological research. This is a significant investment and represents the government's interest in the generation of criminological knowledge. However, as we will stress, criminological knowledge and its production are not value free; nor is the extent to which criminological knowledge is meaningfully engaged and subsequently applied. Different criminological theories emerge from different contexts, are shaped by different forces and therefore have very different implications if applied. As this chapter, and indeed this volume, will illustrate, this is not as straightforward a process as it seems. There have been a number of developments, for example in policing and youth justice, which make bold claims regarding the extent to which criminological research and 'evidence' have been employed in informing the direction of policy and practice. Yet the extent to which criminological research has been employed to inform rather than merely legitimate policy is hotly contested, calling for a reappraisal of how Criminology has been engaged or 'applied' (see Hine, this volume).

This introductory chapter aims to set the scene for the rest of the book by exploring these issues. In doing this it critically appraises the forces which shape criminological understandings and considers the extent to which these understandings are—or could be—meaningfully deployed in guiding the policies and practices of criminal justice.

We identify three principal questions which Applied Criminology should address

* what is to be done about offenders?
* what is to be done about crime?
* what is to be done on behalf of the victims of crime?

and outline how the chapters which make up this collection contribute to these challenges.

It will be shown in this introductory chapter that these apparently simple questions are conceptually much more complex than first appears and that any answers to them involve political judgements as well as debates about effectiveness—or indeed what is judged as evidence of effectiveness. At this point, it is enough to note that unless Criminology illuminates these questions it is not easy to see **how** it is to be applied or **to what**.

The other chapters in this collection also address these questions. They apply Criminology to understanding crime and criminalisation, to responses to crime and offenders, to penal policy, to the needs and rights of victims and to understanding why certain conceptions of criminal justice have been prioritized over others. These chapters accordingly offer not only an overview of Criminology and the extent to which it has been meaningfully applied in respective parts of the 'field', but also contribute to debates around criminal justice—critically exploring the relationship between Criminology and policy and practice developments. The chapters in this collection do not all adopt a similar approach. Indeed in many respects they reflect the theoretical diversity of Criminology and the contested nature of criminological discourse. What the chapters have in common is that they critically engage with the manner and the extent to which Criminology has been meaningfully applied to the particular element of the field they address.

Garland defined Criminology as 'a specific genre of discourse and enquiry about crime—a genre which has developed in the modern period and which can be distinguished from other ways of talking and thinking about criminal conduct' (Garland, 2002: 7). He argued that this distinctiveness rests on Criminology's claims to be empirically grounded and scientific, its focus on the subject matter of crime giving its distinctive disciplinary identity. Others dispute that Criminology constitutes a discipline in its own right (Walklate, 2005). According to Lea, Criminology is not a discipline but is defined by its subject matter—crime, criminal law and the relation between the two—and it is to this subject matter that we now turn.

The subject matter of criminology

> Criminology is the body of knowledge regarding crime as a social phenomenon. It includes within its scope the processes of making laws, of breaking laws, and of reacting towards the breaking of laws . . . The objective of Criminology is the development of a body of general and verified principles and of other types of knowledge regarding this process of law, crime and treatment.
>
> (Sutherland and Cressey, 1955: 3)

Whilst its disciplinary standing may be contested, then, Criminology involves a critical and systematic study of crime and criminals, of their victims, of the institutions and practices of criminal justice and punishment, of crime management, treatment and ultimately of reduction. This definition of the subject of criminological enquiry is ambitious, committing Criminology to inquiry and interpretation in areas conventionally explored by psychology, sociology and philosophy, by law, politics and economics. Indeed this theoretical abundance, whilst reflecting the 'rendezvous' nature of Criminology, is both part of its intellectual appeal and the source of its most intractable disputes and the subsequent 'fractures' between differing criminological perspectives (Ericson and Carriere, 1994).

Common sense suggests that crime must be the stuff of Criminology. Yet the definition of crime and correspondingly the boundaries of Criminology are notoriously problematic. An accepted, but minimal, definition of crime stipulates that crime is conduct proscribed by the law and liable to attract punishment. However, this definition has its limitations: how, for example, does an 'act' become transformed into a 'crime' and why are some acts defined as crimes while others are not? As Christie observes 'Acts are not, they *become*. So it is with crime. Crime does not exist. Crime is created. First there are acts. Then follows a long process of giving meaning to these acts' (1998a: 121).

Is there something that all crimes have in common? A Durkheimian (1964) approach would suggest that the criminal law expresses a consensus about what is right and wrong, what types of behaviour should be legislated against and punished. Stealing, for example, is a crime because it is agreed to be morally wrong. A more critical perspective, however, sees crime as narrowly defined by governments who represent the interests of powerful groups in society rather than as a reflection of consensus. For example a Marxist perspective identifies how the process of criminalization can be used as an instrument of economic power to serve the interests of the powerful (Sheptycki, 2006). An anonymous protest about land enclosure makes the point eloquently:

> The law locks up the man or woman
> Who steals the goose from off the common;
> But lets the greater felon loose
> Who steals the common from the goose.

The perception of the criminal law as a formal codification of the consensus of values that binds a society therefore arguably neglects these important dimensions of power. Without an appreciation of these dimensions of power it is impossible to understand how certain acts become criminalized whilst others do not. This plainly raises questions for Criminology: if Criminology is restricted to the study of acts that the state defines as criminal, it is clearly at risk of having the terrain of its enquiry limited and confined to agendas defined and shaped by the state. Many criminologists insist, therefore, that they have the right and the responsibility to investigate other types of harmful conduct—for example, the wrongs done by states to their citizens, or the harms caused by powerful corporations, whose actions may not fall within governmentally defined criminality, but are never the less socially harmful (Schwendinger and Schwendinger, 1975)

The legal parameters of crime should not just be accepted as given: it is an impoverished and uncritical Criminology that forbids itself by definition from inquiring into the origins of laws, who decides what kind of conduct is so proscribed and with what consequences.

Some have accordingly been tempted to call for a shift away from crime as the subject of inquiry and to instead focus on *harm* (Hillyard and Tombs, 2005). This perspective argues that crimes should be considered in the much broader context of the many harms that threaten and damage people's lives, including the pollution of air, water or food, poverty, exploitation and abuse by powerful industrial and commercial interests, health and safety at work, stress and social exclusion. Some of these harms are, to be sure, technically criminal, at least in some circumstances, but it is not usually these that governments have in mind when they debate 'crime concerns' and many of these harms are not 'criminal' at all. It is also not these type of crimes or social harms to which criminological enquiry is routinely *applied*.

Crime impacts disproportionately on vulnerable and disadvantaged communities, who are also most at risk of other social harms and from the crimes of the powerful. Much crime too is intraclass—that is, committed by members of these marginalised communities against one another (Young, 1986). To insist that the crimes of the powerful and the processes of criminalization impact unfairly on disadvantaged communities is not to deny the harms of crime as conventionally understood. Criminologists have an ethical duty to consider these issues, especially if we are concerned with the application of this knowledge and how the insights of Criminology can support and serve these communities.

Law as oppression, law as liberation

The criminal law calls upon the state to protect people who are powerless against the predations of those who would exploit and abuse them, and to bring the perpetrators to justice when crimes are committed. It is therefore an instrument of liberation.

The criminal law represents the interests of those who have the power to impose their preferences on the rest of society and, in some jurisdictions and in almost all societies at some times, sustains injustice. It is therefore an instrument of oppression.

Applied criminology

This chapter—and indeed this whole volume—affirm the possibility and value of Applied Criminology—that Criminology which self-consciously and deliberately explores the insights of Criminology for their relevance and application to policy and practice.

Some theorists have associated Applied Criminology with a dilution of criminological theory and the process whereby Criminology has become depoliticized. That is, they have seen Applied Criminology as focusing primarily on improving the service delivery of the criminal justice system, dislocated from consideration of broader structural issues and the theories which examine these. This perspective sees Applied Criminology as purely 'technicist' (Cohen, 1985), focusing primarily on the effective workings of the criminal justice system, a system which targets the transgressions of the poor and the powerless, and in particular socially deprived working class adolescents (Taylor, Walton and Young, 1973).

However, we would argue that an Applied Criminology should go much further than this. Applied Criminology should have a critical edge, casting a discriminating, analytical gaze over the processes of criminalisation, crime enforcement, and the criminal justice system. Since crime is such a highly politicised issue, Applied Criminology should seek to expose the relationship between governmental agendas and knowledge production. That is how government defines crime, shapes the criminological agenda and influences the way in which Criminology is applied. An Applied Criminology has an ethical duty to do this; otherwise it risks being fully incorporated by the state and its intellectual integrity and analytical efficacy severely restricted. In this respect, to echo Christie's assertion regarding the role of Criminology, Applied Criminology should not be aimed at *problem solving* for the state but rather should also focus on *raising problems* (Christie, 1971 cited in Bottomley, 1979). Applied Criminology should contribute not merely to the smooth functioning of criminal justice but must raise questions regarding the direction of policy in the context of a broader socio-structural critique. Thus the 'emphases and methodologies of applied work' should be considered in relation to the 'economic, political and social conflicts of the time' (Sim et al., 1987: 5). In this context any attempt to understand what is meant by Applied Criminology requires an appreciation of the context from which criminological theories emerge, and of state power and its relationship with criminological knowledge production.

As Hudson has argued Criminology not only seeks to understand social control but 'is itself part of the apparatus of social control in modern societies' (Hudson, 1997: 452). Applied Criminology accordingly calls for an element of self-reflection—for example why does Criminology focus mainly on the poor and the powerless rather than the actions of the powerful—or in the words of Hagan (1994) the crimes of the 'street' rather than the crimes of the 'suite'? Why is it these groups who become the paradigmatic target to which Criminology is applied—whereas other groups do not? This focus clearly ensures that Criminology focuses on certain types of problems rather than others, generating knowledge of certain types of activities to the neglect of others. Tombs and Williams explore this issue in detail in their chapter in this volume, demonstrating that while crimes committed by powerful business interests cost far more than street crimes, they are much less likely to be the subject of research.

Whilst Criminology is plainly vulnerable to misuse to 'legitimate' policy and practice, especially when crime is such a volatile political area, we would argue that Applied Criminology is worthy of study for a variety of reasons. Indeed, so long as it retains its critical and analytical perspective, Applied Criminology can make important contributions to informing policy and enhancing practice, illuminating the three identified principal areas of concern—what is to be done with offenders?; what is to be done about crime?; what is to be done for (on behalf of) victims of crime?

Applied Criminology shows us that each of these questions is much less straightforward than it looks, concealing a number of deeper questions and themes. How are we to understand the processes by which some wrongdoers (but not others) come to be identified as offenders? What types of intervention are just and effective? What of 'potential' offenders? How good are we at identifying them? And what are the consequences of identifying them and the ethics of intervening (perhaps compulsorily)— not on the basis of what they have done but in anticipation of what we think they may do? Indeed what type of issues would be raised if we considered this type of pre-emptive intervention with corporate offenders rather than juvenile delinquents? Since so few crimes lead to conviction, can the criminal justice system influence levels of crime? If not, what can? Who is to count as a victim? Many of these issues are questions with which the chapters in this volume concern themselves.

Another important insight of Applied Criminology is to recognise that these three broad questions cannot be collapsed into one. This fairly obvious point needs to be pressed because penal policy has often seemed to treat them as a single question— a question to which the answer is *punishment*. Penal policy, at least in the past twenty years, has insisted that condign punishment—whether justified in the language of desert, deterrence or incapacitation—is the appropriate way of dealing with offenders, displacing the rehabilitative aspirations that characterized the earlier years of the 20th century (Garland, 2001). Again, conflating the first two questions, policy has typically responded to anxieties about the prevalence or seriousness of certain kinds of conduct by penalizing these through the criminal law. Yet at least arguably this rests on an exaggerated faith in the efficacy of deterrence and the educative force of criminal justice.

Punishment is also felt to be a unique vindication of the experience of victims. The possibility that victims may need other sources of restitution, support or closure has often been politically marginalised on precisely this pretext. The persuasive trope of the *scales of justice*—in which the claims and needs of victims are weighed against those of offenders—encourages the belief that a balance can only be struck when punishment is heavy. Yet investigation shows the position is more complex than this. Victims respond to the distress of crimes against them in different ways. Plainly it will depend on the victim and the crime. It is no doubt safe to assume that victims want the offences against them to be taken seriously, but this is not at all to say that this can only (or even best) be demonstrated through punishment—and certainly not through punishment alone. Annexing the matter of the needs of victims to the punishment of offenders, moreover, leaves stranded the many (majority) of victims whose offenders are not caught or punished.

The first point, then, is that failure to separate out these three questions leads to poor crime control and an approach to victimisation that will leave most victims unsupported and unsatisfied. It is next to be noted that these are all *normative* questions, which are not 'value free' but call for political and ethical judgements. We saw earlier that the choice of definition of *crime* and the determination of the scope of Criminology irreducibly involves political and ethical choices—for example whether to study crime (or even what type of crime) or social harm. Similarly, the three questions raise not only empirical and conceptual challenges, but also ethical problems.

Yet, as Matza argued, the 'correctional perspective' in Criminology—the priority to denounce and repudiate—increases the possibility of 'losing the phenomenon— reducing it to that which it is not'. (Matza, 1969: 17) In other words, the urge to suppress crime interferes with a proper understanding. This perspective too at least partly explains why so much of the criminological tradition treats offenders as objects rather than subjects, inquiring into causes rather than the reasons that are usually sought when trying to understand behaviour. There are ethnographic traditions in Criminology too (Hobbs, 2007) which attempt to discover what offending means to its perpetrators, the sense they make of their conduct, listening to their 'voices'. Whilst these perspectives have been marginal in Criminology they have made a considerable contribution to the understanding of crime and criminality (Yates, 2004). However, these perspectives bring with them the risk of romanticizing crime—another shortcoming against which Matza warned (1969). Matza's proposal was for an appreciative inquiry which takes seriously offenders' accounts of their own behaviour without collusion or romanticization.

If we want to know why someone has behaved as they have, we ask them and they will give **reasons** and **meanings** in their account—not causes. Criminology has not usually approached offenders in this way, losing a potentially rich source of understanding. This may be because we are reluctant to 'understand' conduct which it is psychologically and politically more comfortable to deplore.

Matza's insight plainly has very significant implications for Applied Criminology. If, in an enthusiasm to denounce crime, criminologists abandon a critical perspective, as they apply their understandings to the real problems of crime, criminal justice and victimization, they are at risk of misunderstanding, of irrelevance and even of aggravating the problems they are attempting to address.

Some criminological approaches and their applications

There are a wide range of criminological theories, which offer competing perspectives on crime and therefore have very different implications if applied to the field of community and criminal justice practice. To illustrate this, we now review some theories and explore the issues raised in their application.

The 'Lombrosian project' (Garland, 2002) attempted to determine what it was about criminals that made them different from others through the application of positivist methodology and the utilization of the tools of the natural sciences to identify 'L'Uomo Delinquente'—the 'Criminal Man'. Yet the aspiration to reduce crime significantly through gaining knowledge of its causes as discerned from a study of offenders gradually came to seem less plausible. The biological or psychological factors that differentiated offenders from others were elusive and in any case probably beyond influence. Meanwhile, the worth of the project was challenged by other modes of understanding crime. The 'Chicago school' investigated the ecology of crime and suggested that crime might be a function of social organization (or disorganization). 'Strain theory' found the origins of offending in the 'strain' between aspirations of affluence and the realities that prosperity was attainable by relatively few: crime was one possible response to this predicament. 'Conflict theories' regarded crime as a manifestation of tensions—typically class tensions—grounded in the social order.

For all the many differences in the theoretical preferences and political affiliations associated with these accounts, they have it in common that constitutional differences between individuals are taken, at best, to be just part of the story. Sociological approaches recognize that any account of offending needs an appreciation of the social origin and context of crime and therefore insist that crime is a product of the political and economic arrangements of society rather than the aberrant behaviour of a few individuals. Unsurprisingly, governments favour individualized explanations and normally reject accounts that involve critiques of social structure.

Again, if all that crimes have in common is that they are proscribed by the criminal law, it may seem implausible that there could be such a thing as 'the cause (or even causes) of crime'. To suppose that there could be would not only neglect the political contingencies of criminalization but the sheer diversity of conduct encompassed by the term *crime* (even in its most conservative definition).

> The list of 'notifiable offences' (see Nicholas, et al., 2005: Appendix Two) includes a very wide range of crimes—from fraud by a company director to abandoning a child under the age of two; from abstracting electricity to religiously aggravated criminal damage; from adulteration of food to treason. How likely is it that genetics, biology or psychology could uncover the 'cause' of such diverse conduct?

For other reasons besides, it was also seeming increasingly unlikely that any such causes could be discovered by a study, no matter how meticulous, of the characteristics of known offenders. Self-report studies and victimization surveys were demonstrating (as criminologists had long suspected) that the convicted and imprisoned criminals about whom so much knowledge had been accumulated were no more than a very small proportion of all those who broke the law—and could not be assumed to be (more probably were not) representative of the larger group.

Cohort studies—tracking the criminal records of everyone born in a particular week—further demonstrated that a much greater number of people acquired a criminal conviction than had been realized. Attrition studies, demonstrating the various points between crime and conviction where offenders disappeared from the process, tried to gauge the size of the iceberg of which convictions are the tip and suggested that, certainly for some offences, there were no more than two or three convictions for a hundred crimes. Self-report studies suggested that even this number massively underestimated the incidence of offending and it became plausible to assert that many—probably most—people commit a criminal offence at some point in their lives (for discussion and references, see Maguire 2007).

> Cohort studies show that a significant number of people acquire a conviction for a serious criminal offence. Attrition studies show that only a small fraction of offences lead to a conviction. Victim surveys and self-report studies confirm that the number of people who commit an offence is very large. If most people offend, where does this leave the search for a difference between those who offend and those who do not? And if the criminal justice system deals with no more than a small proportion of offenders, can it contribute much to a reduction in crime? If not, what strategies should be employed against crime?

As well as challenging the project of discovering the causes of crime, these insights call into question the relationship between offending and the criminal justice system. How can the criminal justice system make more than a very modest contribution to levels of crime if only a small proportion of offenders are apprehended and convicted? A conventional reply is to appeal to *deterrence*: the prospect of apprehension and penalty deters people from offending—a phenomenon that is less apparent to those in criminal justice practice who only encounter those who have *not* been deterred. Yet Criminology has advised us to be cautious here: it is not that fear of the consequences never deters, but that deterrence makes unwarranted assumptions about behaviour that exaggerate its potential. In particular, there is little or no evidence that increasing penalties for offences will reduce incidence. If there is an optimal level of punishment that would deter, no one knows what it is.

Another possibility is that the criminal justice system has an *educative* influence, affirming the values that bind a community in the repudiation and denunciation of crime that is represented by arrest, trial and punishment (Durkheim, 1964). The criminal justice system no doubt does have some such effect: one of the ways in which we learn the wrongness of conduct is by witnessing the community response to such behaviour. Yet while it may be important and morally educative for a criminal justice system to remain thus connected to the values of the society it is intended to serve, the implications for criminal justice and sentencing practice are far from clear. In particular, there is no evidence to suggest that there is any straightforward relationship between *levels* of punishment and public perceptions of wrongness (Walker, 1991).

In sum, then, it is increasingly being appreciated, that, as Garland puts it:

> It is only the mainstream processes of socialisation (internalised morality and the sense of duty, the informal inducements and rewards of conformity, the practical and cultural networks of mutual expectation and independence etc.) which are able to promote proper conduct on a consistent and regular basis.
>
> (Garland, 1990: 289)

all matters plainly beyond the remit or capacity of state agencies of criminal justice.

One way of describing this trajectory in Criminology is to say that it became increasingly clear that the question 'What is to be done about crime?' is not the same as the question 'What is to be done with convicted offenders?'

An appreciation of the social context of offending is a warning about the limitations of the criminal justice system. There may be a place for intervention with troubled individuals, but the socio-economic order, the distribution of opportunities, the way in which we arrange our affairs and order our lives constitute the context in which people will have their opportunities to offend or to desist and in which they will make their choices.

Rational choice and routine activity theories protested that offenders had been 'over-pathologized': offenders were rational calculators like everyone else (or at least no less rational than everyone else) who took opportunities on the basis of judgements about their own interests. These approaches argued that the 'causes of offending' were largely unknown, probably unknowable, and in any case beyond influence.

(How might the 'mainstream processes of socialisation' to which Garland refers be amenable to change?) It was therefore a mistake, theoretically and politically, to approach crime reduction through what Criminology thought it knew about the untypical minority of convicted offenders it studied.

For that matter, the criminal justice system could not do much with the few offenders with whom it did manage to engage. There was very little evidence to show that any particular mode of intervention was more successful than any other in reducing the chances of reconviction (Brody, 1976). Worse, Criminology, arguing that 'crime' could not be studied in isolation from the processes of criminalization and the practices of enforcement, adduced some arguments to suggest that criminal justice practice is as much part of the problem as it is a solution. Most obviously, the more conduct is criminalized, the greater will be the incidence of crime. Nils Christie (2004) has recently argued cogently that there is a significant sense in which societies can have as much crime as they choose: there are several possible responses to misbehaviour and incivility and, if the political choice is made to designate many of them crimes, then there will be more crimes and more criminals. There may be other ways—including more effective ways—of reducing the incidence of the unwanted behaviour.

Interactionist perspectives suggested that formal state interventions typically made matters worse by characterizing offenders in ways which change their own perception of self (leading often to 'secondary deviance' (Lemert, 1951)) and make other people react to them differently and negatively. At the extreme, Schur (1973) counselled *radical non-intervention*, 'leaving the kids alone'. It is well established that crimes are disproportionately committed by younger people and that the normal development is to 'grow out of crime' (Matza, 1969; Rutherford, 1986). It is doubtful that criminal justice interventions can accelerate that process, but they can slow it down—by removing people from the environment in which they must learn to live lawfully and the opportunities that they need to create and sustain law-abiding lifestyles. This is an issue which the chapter by Goldson and Yates in this volume considers in detail.

Labelling theory, moreover, challenged the very coherence of the traditional criminological project of understanding offenders in order to reduce offending. There was *nothing* about offenders that made them different from other people—the difference being, as Becker famously said, neither a property of the offence nor the offender, but a function of the response to their conduct.

Labelling theory affords an unusual example of the way in which criminological theory can be applied to practice. The policy of diversion from prosecution, especially for young people, and of decarceration drew on interactionist understandings of offending. Even now that these approaches have been qualified and compromised, labelling theory remains as a chastening reminder that intervention can make things worse, as often as it makes things better. The idea of early intervention is beguiling—and is regularly reaffirmed by politicians. The early identification of young people who are likely to offend and a timely intervention to prevent this seems a plausible and attractive policy. Yet labelling reminds us that this is an aspiration with a very poor track record.

One of the objections to radical non-intervention concerned the 'message' that it gave—to offenders, to the community and, especially, to victims. To do nothing in response to offensive behaviour was indistinguishable from indifference. Braithwaite (1989), while recognizing the potentially stigmatizing and exclusionary consequences of traditional punishments, felt that criminologists had drawn the wrong conclusion: punishment was often a proper reaction to wrongdoing but must be administered in a manner that would facilitate the reintegration of the offender into the community.

Rational choice perspectives and the recognition that criminal justice is just one (limited) aspect of the response to crime had helped to separate out the question of what to do about *crime* from the question what to do about *criminals*. The increased recognition of the importance of the victim is characteristic of contemporary criminological discourse (Bottoms, 1995; Garland, 2001). Awareness of the victim prompts a third question: what is to be done on behalf of *victims of crime*?

Applied criminology—frameworks for practice

Applied Criminology should be able to contribute to answers to the three main questions we identified earlier in this chapter. It therefore has relevance for policy makers and for practitioners working in the field of criminal justice.

Students who plan to enter into the field of criminal justice need to be equipped not only with a firm grounding in theoretical Criminology, what Cohen in the opening quotation refers to as the 'pure academic world', but also an understanding of how these theories relate to policy and practice in criminal justice—that is, how these criminological theories are applied. This is key to Applied Criminology and indeed what it has to offer.

Students must be able to engage critically with developments in the field in which they work. The field of criminal justice is a dynamic and ever changing and increasingly expanding landscape (Muncie, 1999). It is therefore extremely important for students who are to become practitioners to engage with these changes reflectively and critically. In order to do this it is not enough for a student simply to be equipped with a range of technical skills—they also need theoretical knowledge and the tools of critical analysis. For example it is not enough for students to merely learn about the relationship between a theory and policy and practice, they must be able to offer an informed critique of it. It is through these processes that practitioners can develop practice models and improve the services they provide.

The flow of ideas, moreover, goes both ways—not only should the academy influence practice, but practice experience and innovative policy debate must have their influence on the character and direction of Applied Criminology.

All of the authors in this volume apply criminological theory to their topic and consider the relationship between criminological theory and policy and practice developments. This includes a critical review of how criminological theory has been applied in this area of the sector; the extent to which Criminology has been meaningfully engaged, paying particular attention to the contemporary context and to Criminology's relationship with power; and the implications of their analysis for diverse communities, with particular regard to discrimination, oppression and injustice. The authors also discuss how Criminology might be applied and comment on some of its unrealized potential and how it might be deployed to enrich the quality of political debate and contemporary practice.

The relationship between criminological research and policy and practice is key to any discussion around *applied* Criminology. Indeed, it is this relationship which is presented as key in the 'what works' and effective practice agendas and it is at the heart of the relationships between the academy, the state and the apparatus of social control. This is central to all of the chapters in this volume. Hine in her chapter explores some of the contours of the relationship between criminological research, policy and practice in more detail. In particular Hine explores the development of Criminology and its relationship with governance illustrating how the current relationship between Criminology, research, policy and practice can be traced back to these historical roots. Hine also examines the notion of evidence-based policy and practice and the current dominant conception of these relationships, as well as the individual concepts of policy, practice and research. Thus, Hine critically explores the relationship between research, policy and practice which lies at the heart of any discussion of Applied Criminology.

This dialogue between Applied Criminology and practice should be especially productive in the area of diversity and anti-discrimination. Crime policy has sometimes spoken about *offenders, victims* and *communities* in ways that neglect their differences—as 'standard cases'. But, as Hudson insists, 'Once the subject of justice is given back his/her social context and flesh and blood reality, it is clear that difference is the standard case, and that differences are routinely irreducible.' (Hudson, 2001: 166). Since a reflective Criminology should explore and expose these differences, Knight, Dominey and Hudson look at Criminology's erratic engagement with (and regular neglect of) these issues and discuss the emergence of critiques to mainstream Criminology. They examine the implications of practising in a criminal justice system which reflects and reproduces inequalities of power.

Opposition to inequality and unfairness calls for self-awareness—an appreciation of how practitioners' attitudes and behaviour must themselves be a subject of reflection if personal and institutionalized discrimination is to be challenged. It requires knowledge— of structural and cultural patterns, institutions and practices that sustain these inequities. It also calls for understanding and professional competence, as well as for an ethical commitment to justice. All this is a central part of applied criminological studies intended to produce practitioners who will recognize and oppose injustice and who must be supported by their organisations in this endeavour.

Crisp and Ward look at the role Criminology has played in informing developments in police and policing and in doing so outline the challenges for policing in the 21st century, exploring the insights criminological theory can offer in informing policing practices. They also critically appraise historical developments in policing and look at the relationship between the police and local community. In doing this they pay particular attention to issues regarding race. The chapter concludes by arguing that the recent developments in the training of police officers provide an opportunity to reflect on the application of research and theory on policing operations and the relationship between the police and the community.

Prisons are a key part of the criminal justice system and in the UK are the ultimate sanction for criminal wrongdoing. Wahidin and Ardley in their chapter on prisons look critically at imprisonment, and illustrate disturbing trends in the use of imprisonment and also its social effects. They take a critical look at the functions of prisons paying particular attention to women prisoners and older prisoners. They critically explore issues relating to ethnicity and self harm utilizing case studies to illustrate these problems. They then move on to consider abolitionism, arguing that the abolitionist approach offers an alternative vision of how we as a society deal with wrongdoing—a vision which contrasts starkly with traditional models of penality.

Canton and Eadie apply consideration to the area of discretion and accountability. Practitioners are called upon to make decisions all the time and are often guided by regulations that are intended to constrain or even to determine their course of action. But how can rules accommodate diversity—not only the very many ways in which circumstances differ from one another, but differences among the people affected by the decisions? A regulation designed for a 'standard case' could lead to injustice in the real world of diversity. Yet if professionals make their judgements case-by-case, this could in itself lead to unacceptable inconsistencies, to favouritism, bias and arbitrariness.

Canton and Eadie propose accountability as the protection against such unfairness. They further argue that attention to individuality and respect for difference are important parts of the legitimacy of criminal justice practice. Confidence in the criminal justice system and compliance with its demands are enhanced when people are treated as individuals and with respect. Accountability should not be confined to the line management relationship, but should be extended to a much wider constituency—and not least to those affected by the decisions.

Evidence-based policy and effectiveness, as noted in the introduction to this chapter, have become key terms in the lexicon of criminal justice. The chapter by Goldson and Yates critically assesses recent constructions of 'evidenced-based' policy formation and their application within the context of youth justice in England and Wales since 1997. They argue that there is a lack of congruence between research evidence and current youth justice practice and therefore call into question the extent to which Criminology has been meaningfully applied in youth justice. They argue that a genuinely evidenced-based approach to youth crime and justice must transgress crude politicization of youth justice. Ultimately, this requires the depoliticization of youth crime and justice and the development of more progressively tolerant, human rights compliant, non-criminalizing, inclusionary and participative strategies. It is to this, they argue, that 'applied Criminology' must strive. In doing this they argue that Applied Criminology should be constructed as a form of critical intervention.

Community interventions are a key part of modern day criminal justice systems. The chapter by Smith offers an overview and historical development of community interventions—a key area to which government claims criminological research has been applied. Drawing on examples from the youth justice system, Smith critically engages with the ideological justifications which community interventions draw on, asking questions both about their rationale and the practical consequences and exploring their links with Criminology and research evidence. Thus Smith wrestles with the extent to which Criminology, in this respect, has been applied. In a similar vein to Goldson and Yates and Tombs and Williams, Smith argues that Criminology has a responsibility to offer a critical perspective, both in terms of honest and accurate evaluations of effectiveness, but also in terms of making normative judgements about the desirability and value of interventions.

Wood and Kemshall discuss accountability in the practice of working with high risk offenders in the community. Accountability is due to many groups—victims, communities, the several agencies involved in a multi-agency endeavour—and to the offenders themselves. This is not only a moral requirement, but conduces to compliance. They point to 'a clear relationship between an offender's acceptance of and compliance with restrictions, and the extent to which the decisions made are clearly communicated and justified.' No risk management strategy can ignore the response of the offender to that strategy.

One of the most significant developments in community and criminal justice, in recent years, has been the increasing influence of restorative justice. Stout and Goodman Chong in their chapter look critically at the influence restorative justice has had on criminal justice policy and practice. They explore the influence it has had on both adult and youth justice systems. In doing this they explore key issues relating to the role of the state and the role of community that are not only inherent to restorative justice approaches, but are also key issues in broader debates around criminal justice. In this way the chapter looks at how the themes and principles of restorative justice have been meaningfully applied via criminal justice policy.

In a similar manner to the earlier chapter by Goldson and Yates, the chapter by Tombs and Williams can also be seen as a critical intervention, this time into debates around victimology and corporate crime. Thus whilst the victimology movement within Criminology has focused on the needs and rights of the victims of street crime, Tombs and Williams turn the analytical gaze up to corporate criminals. In doing this they critically appraise the extent to which the needs of the victims of corporate crime are meaningfully engaged with by Criminology or met by a criminal justice system so heavily weighted towards dealing with the crimes perpetrated by marginalised groups. They outline how Criminology can be applied in a manner which mounts a critique of ideologically driven definitions of 'victims'. Again this chapter raises a number of pertinent policy and practice questions regarding how corporate criminals are responded to and how the needs of their victims are met.

Conclusion

This chapter has set out to explore what is meant by Applied Criminology and to assess the potential contribution of Criminology to practice. We have argued that an Applied Criminology should engage critically with the field and extend itself further than the narrow confines of the needs of government for research to inform the apparatus of social control. It should not merely be reduced to providing technicist alibis (Cohen, 1985), constructed around narrow and conservatively constructed definitions of crime, proffered by the state. Rather it should move beyond this—to engage critically with issues of broader social harm, of why certain questions are asked rather than others, why certain evidence is profiled whilst other evidence is not and how governmental agendas impact on criminological knowledge production. As Christie argues, Criminology should be a problem raiser rather than a problem solver for the state. This requires an appreciation of how criminological discourse is constructed and how government agendas have shaped the institutional domain of academic Criminology. As Cohen argues in the quotation at the beginning of this chapter—this is especially important for Criminology precisely because criminologocal knowledge is applied. The rest of the chapters in this volume in their own ways explore different aspects of this application

We have identified three central practice questions—what is to be done with offenders?; what is to be done about crime?; what is to be done on behalf of victims? We have suggested that these questions are distinct, even though sometimes insufficiently differentiated in political debate. All criminal justice practitioners are required to address one or more of these questions and the associated challenges for practice. Practitioners equipped with the insights and the critical and analytical skills achieved through the study of Criminology will be not only be more reflective: they will be more effective in their work, because of their understanding of the potential and the limitations of their practice. The critical knowledge and accumulated experience of thoughtful and reflective practitioners is a rich (and under used) resource that has great potential to enhance policy and practice progressively.

Key arguments

It has been argued that the forces which shape criminological knowledge production have an important bearing on how Criminology is (or might be) applied and therefore how *Applied Criminology* should be understood.

This chapter has argued that Criminology should be applied to three principal questions: what is to be done about offenders?; what is to be done about crime?; and what is to be done on behalf of the victims of crime?

It is argued that these apparently simple questions are conceptually much more complex than first appears and that any answers to them involve political judgements. It is also argued that Applied Criminologists should be *problem raisers* as well as *problem solvers* (Christie, 1971). At the same time, the chapter argues that Criminology does afford insights and understandings that will enhance the quality of criminal justice practice.

The chapter concludes by considering the practice and policy implications of an Applied Criminology and outlining the contributions the various chapters of the book make to these debates.

Further reading

Garland, D. (2002) 'Of Crimes and Criminals: the development of criminology in Britain' in Mike Maguire, Rod Morgan and Robert Reiner (eds.) *The Oxford Handbook of*

Criminology. 2nd edn. Oxford: Oxford University Press. This chapter (not reproduced in the fourth edition, but available on the companion website) offers an excellent overview of the development of Criminology and provides useful insights into the relationship between criminological knowledge production and policy and practice in community and criminal justice. McLaughlin, E. and Muncie, J. (2006) *The Sage Dictionary of Criminology.* 2nd edn. London: Sage is a comprehensive resource for students of Criminology. Rock, P. (2007) 'Sociological Theories of Crime' in Mike Maguire, Rod Morgan and Robert Reiner (eds.) *The Oxford Handbook of Criminology.* 4th edn. Oxford: Oxford University Press. This chapter offers a full analysis of the role of sociological theories of crime. Muncie, J. McLaughlin, E. and Langan, M. (1996) *Criminological Perspectives: a reader.* London: Sage. This includes readings from a range of key thinkers. Newburn, T. (2007) *Criminology.* Cullompton: Willan is authoritative, comprehensive and accessible.

2

APPLIED CRIMINOLOGY: RESEARCH, POLICY AND PRACTICE

Jean Hine

Grown-ups love figures. When you tell them that you have made a new friend, they never ask you any questions about essential matters. They never say to you, 'What does his voice sound like? What games does he love best? Does he collect butterflies?' Instead, they demand, 'How old is he? How many brothers has he? How much does he weigh? How much money does his father make?' Only from these figures do they think they have learned anything about him.

(Saint-Exupéry, 1974 quoted in Oakley, 1999: 155).

Chapter summary

This chapter:
- Places the relationship between criminology and the application of research and theory in a historical context.
- Considers the impact of criminology and the use of evidence on the development of policy.
- Highlights some of the key debates in criminological research, policy and practice.

Issues of crime, or 'law and order' are at the heart of government and governance, prescribing in law what is acceptable behaviour and what is not, and what to do when people contravene the law. Criminal justice is one of the most high profile areas of government policy, and arguably always has been. The discipline of criminology is inextricably linked with this aspect of government. raising the promise that criminology can affect the decisions of policy makers and the practice of the many professionals who work in the area. Indeed many criminal justice professionals receive training in criminology as part of their qualification for the job. But to what extent does the work of criminologists, particularly empirical research, actually influence the decision making of policy makers or the delivery of criminal practice? This is what is meant by the term 'applied criminology'. The notion of 'applied criminology' is however something of a tautology. The origins of the academic discipline are firmly rooted in the notion of application, particularly the aim of providing insights useful to policy makers in the management of those defined by criminal justice system as 'criminal'.

This chapter will address these questions and issues. A brief review of the history of criminology will show how aspects of the current relationship between criminology, research, policy and practice can be traced back to those roots. The notion of evidence-based policy and practice will be examined, with consideration of the individual concepts of policy, practice and research and the current dominant conception of their interrelationships. Some of the key debates in these areas are highlighted together with ways in which criminology has and has not impacted upon policy and practice.

A brief history of criminology

There is no single definitive account of the history and origins of criminology. The interpretation of past events and their significance reflects the social and political context of the time of writing as well as the perceptions of the historian. A significant modern commentator on this history is David Garland (2002) who identifies the, 1950s as the key period in the establishment of academic criminology in Britain. Criminology teaching in British universities began in the, 1930s, gradually increasing to meet the professional aspirations of the growing numbers of social workers and probation officers. Its growth and potential to influence increased dramatically in the, 1950s, soon after the end of World War Two. This decade began with a government commitment to the funding of criminological research; later saw the production of the first text book on criminology, the beginning of the British Society of Criminology, the establishment of the Home Office Research Unit, and the decade ended with the foundation of the Cambridge Institute of Criminology in, 1959. A government White Paper of, 1959 proclaimed that crime and penal policy would be based on research findings (Garland and Sparks, 2000). It had become in Garland's terms 'an accredited, state sponsored, academic discipline' which was both 'scientific' and 'useful' (2002: 2). What was, and is, understood by those two terms—'scientific' and 'useful'—changes over time however, as we shall see later.

Locating the origins of the academic discipline in the, 1930s does not mean that the topics of concern to criminology, or even the title of 'criminology' or 'criminologist' did not exist before that. Far from it. Garland agrees with others that as long as there have been social rules there has been interest and debate about how to respond to those who transgress those rules, but he argues the ways those actions were perceived then were theological, philosophical or even supernatural, but not criminological. He argues criminology as we would recognise it originated in the late 19th century with the work of Cesare Lombroso (1876) who aimed to establish a 'science of the criminal'. Although his methods and theories have long been discredited the notion of the science has continued.

What is criminology?

The term 'criminology' came into use in 1890 as:

> a neutral, generic term which avoided the partisanship implicit in the original term [criminal anthropology] and others—such as 'criminal sociology', 'criminal biology', and 'criminal psychology'—which competed with it.
>
> (Garland, 2002: 22)

The origins of the coining of criminology place it as a 'rendezvous discipline'[1] in that many disciplines are unified by the study of crime and issues related to it.

Since those origins the range of other disciplines incorporated under the criminological banner has broadened substantially, bringing together people from a wide range of backgrounds to study this one specific topic.

Paul Rock, in his *History of Criminology* (1994) acknowledges that there is a variety of ways of framing the history of the discipline. He opts for what he describes as a 'pragmatic' framework, describing the development of criminology as starting in around 1500. He presents five phases in the development of the discipline, each characterized by a different type of interest and style of writing, but all in their various ways drawing attention to the way in which crime and its various institutions were working (or not). The first and longest phase covers the period 1500–1750, when a range of individuals was writing about crime and criminals, many in some way working with the offenders of the time. The topics about which they were writing were not dissimilar to those of interest today.

Rock's second phase is the period 1750–1830 where he sees the beginnings of an organized criminology motivated by philanthropic aims. He references the work of Henry Fielding, a magistrate writing in the 1750s, whose titles included *An enquiry into the causes of the late increase of robbers* (1751). Sherman (2005) says that Fielding conducted the first criminological experiments leading to the establishment of the Bow Street Runners and eventually the police force that we know today. This was also the time when people such as John Howard were campaigning for change, using surveys and observation to support their campaigns. The third phase (1830–1890) is characterized by the state's acknowledgement of the value of 'expertise'. This was the time of industrial revolution with its massive social and economic upheaval, changing the face of politics and views about the role of government. It was also the era of 'science' with its optimism about the ability to know and predict all things and enthusiasm for observation, categorization and counting as the means of knowing. It was the start of 'rational' government which could be guided by 'science'—what we now understand as evidence-based policy making. This was the time when many statistical records began, including criminal and prison statistics. Medicine was viewed as the archetypal science, and the concepts of medicine (diagnosis, treatment, cure, prevention) were applied in relation to offenders. Applied optimistically it must be said, as although it was premised upon the notion that the problem of criminality was pathological and located within the individual, it also contained the view that all offenders could be 'cured'. Indeed the first professions to work with offenders, both in treatment and research, were doctors and psychiatrists (Rock, 1994).

The fourth phase of the development of criminology according to Rock was the period 1880–1960, when criminology developed as a distinctive academic pursuit, particularly in continental Europe. This was the era of the development of the 'scientific method' in the striving for criminology to be a 'positive science', the results of which could be confidently applied to the management and reform of offenders. As mentioned above, this is the period when substantial state support for the discipline begins.

---

[1] Attributed to David Downes in Rock (1994): p. xii.

The final phase from, 1960 to now Rock calls the 'institutionalization of criminology' (xix). The expansion of the universities and the discipline led to a new influx of criminologists prolific and innovative in their thinking and writing. Rock describes the criminology of the, 1970s as 'expansive, argumentative, exuberant, factious and open' (xix), and he should know, as he was part of that wave of radical young criminologists aiming to break away from the traditions of criminology and broaden its horizons, both theoretically and empirically. In many ways they achieved this end, with modern criminology being a wide ranging eclectic discipline that covers the traditional topics of the causes of crime and the management of offenders, but also addresses a wider range of issues such as the crimes of the powerful and takes a critical view of the role of the state and the criminal justice system. In this latter stage of institutionalization the embrace of the state can be seen as problematic as well as supportive. The discipline is now more directly affected by the whim of government, as highlighted in the, 1980s and, 1990s when the government of the day saw less value in the need for research and evidence and withdrew substantial amounts of funding for research, both in-house and external, causing a contraction of the discipline and crisis in some institutions. The crisis was subsequently reversed with the change of government in, 1997, to a government committed to the notion of 'evidence-based policy' backed by substantial investment in research, particularly in criminology.

The period immediately following World War Two is significant in understanding criminological history. Walters identifies increases in recorded crime, coupled with the economic crisis of that period of recovery as leading to a view that 'society needed to be protected by the criminal law' (2003: 25). Preventing crime became a highly political issue with economic and social consequences. This in turn fuelled the rapid expansion of criminological resources and research in the, 1950s, but research of a certain kind, steered by government towards addressing the issues that were of most concern to them—the causes of crime and how best to reduce it. Nowhere on this agenda was there any critical consideration of what is 'crime' or 'criminal', questions which started to be addressed during the more radical phase of criminology in the, 1970s. Although criminologists continue to debate what is criminal and should be defined as such by the law, empirical criminological research cannot play a role in decisions about what should be defined as criminal and sanctioned. These are essentially moral and ontological choices that cannot be informed by empirical work. They can however be addressed by theoretical criminology, and there is much criminological literature that does this (see, for example, Tombs and Williams, this volume), and the social construction of crime is an important issue for research.

So in this history, whilst we see much change we also see much that stays the same. Many of the historical themes of criminology continue to be highly visible today, at least in public and media discourse if not in academe. Young (2003) suggests that 'plurality of narrative' is the distinctive feature of current criminology, with a wide range of theories and approaches co-existing within the discipline. At the same time he argues that criminology should 'not have an amnesia with regards to the rich past of the discipline' (106): because criminology is concerned with the central problems of social order and disorder it is inextricably bound with social theory.

As criminology has drawn in a range of new disciplines there has been a growing interest in crime within many other disciplines, as wide ranging as feminism and town planning. The boundaries of criminology are becoming less clear. Knepper (2007) suggests that much social policy is designed to deal with traditionally criminological problems such as the reduction of crime, and that indeed this may be a better location from which to respond than criminal justice policy. Many criminologists may well agree with that view. This move to multidisciplinarity is reflected in the political arena too, with government increasingly seeing crime reduction and prevention as a cross-governmental project. The, 1998 Criminal Justice Act required local authorities to consider crime and its reduction within all of their policies and developments, and the local Crime Reduction Partnerships introduced prior to this Act require multi-agency participation. Increasingly, responses to crime are seen as a multi-agency responsibility, as demonstrated by the establishment of multi-agency Youth Offending Teams in, 1998 and more recently the multi-agency Public Protection Panels for dealing with high risk offenders (see Wood and Kemshall, this volume). The empirical research evidence for these moves is scant however, with high profile government enquiries being more influential. A recent history of the criminal justice system (Rawlings, 1999) does not include the word 'research' in the index, and rarely makes any mention of research which has directly impacted on developments in criminal justice. The work of Cyril Burt (1931) is mentioned in relation to the development of the juvenile justice system. Here the relevance is that the research identified a wide range of influences upon criminality, rather than led to change: 'it [crime] springs from a wide variety, and usually from a multiplicity, of alternative and converging influences.' (Burt, 1931, quoted in Rawlings, 1999: 125). Rawlings argues that over the last 300 years huge amounts of money have been spent on dealing with crime, and yet crime statistics have continued to rise, suggesting a failure of the science to deliver.

The impact of criminology on policy

Criminology has seen substantial changes over time as the social and political context within which it operates has changed: the role of criminologists has changed and is still changing. One thing that appears to be unchanging, despite the impact of individual pieces of research such as the 'What Works?' thesis (Martinson, 1974), is the limited direct effect of empirical research upon policy decisions. Many criminologists bemoan this apparent lack of impact. The great founding criminologist Radzinowicz observed 'in spite of the output of criminological knowledge, a populist political approach holds sway.' (1999, quoted in Garland and Sparks, 2000).

Although the impact of criminological research may not be as great as hoped for, some important decisions have been influenced by criminological opinion, such as the abolition of the death penalty (Garland and Sparks, 2000). Young lists a range of ways in which recent criminology has influenced political thinking, ranging from notions of the underclass to restorative justice and repeat victimization, arguing that 'it would be difficult to think of a period where criminology had greater influence'

(2003: 99). Another example of research which had substantial impact, though more for its methodology than its findings, is the Islington crime Survey (Jones et al., 1986), which led to the introduction of the British Crime Survey, now routinized into an annual government sponsored exercise. At the same time there are many examples of policy ignoring the advice of criminologists, for example suspended sentences were introduced despite advice to the contrary (Trasler, 1986). Some will point to government concern for victims of crime and the range of initiatives introduced to support them as an example of successful evidence-based policy, but Sebba (2001) would disagree. His analysis and review identifies the issues that led to these developments as disillusionment with the rehabilitative ideal and a move to a 'just deserts' philosophy, the feminist movement concern for female victims, and the advocation of restorative justice with its increased role for victims. At the same time he notes that research which indicated some of the needs of victims has been ignored.

Researchers in the United States have reviewed the impact of criminology on their policy decisions, the most ambitious being Sherman (2005). His review of 250 years of criminology talks about 'criminology's failures of use in creating justice more enlightened by knowledge of its effects' (115). He attributes this to the quality of the research rather than the policy process, despite the considerable growth in criminological research (this is a position hotly contested by other criminologists as we shall see later). His argument is that 'experimental' criminology is better 'science' than the 'analytic' research primarily conducted. He believes that experimental criminology will provide comprehensive evidence about responses to crime, and thus better policy—with an apparent faith that the good science will be automatically acted upon by policy makers. Nowhere does he consider the rationale of the policy making process which, as we shall see later, makes his aspirations difficult to achieve. He describes social science, which includes criminology, as being a 'critic' rather than his preferred 'inventor' (117). He does however acknowledge the need for 'analytic' and descriptive research to form the basis for experimental research, providing material from which to generate hypotheses to test, and does acknowledge the impact on policy of some theories of criminology, such as anomie and differential association. Certainly juvenile justice in the UK was influenced by labelling theory in the, 1960s and, 1970s. An earlier analysis of the late, 20th century (Blumstein, 1997) identified the changing relationship between policy and research over time, and also concluded there was limited impact of research on policy. This too saw experimental criminology as the most desirable for its ability to influence policy.

Research shows how political issues are the major consideration in the real world of policy making. For instance, Cavadino and Dignan (2006) undertook an international comparative analysis relating the level of imprisonment in a country to its political economy. They identified four types of economic regime ranging from the paternalistic to free market and found levels of imprisonment correspondingly ranged from high to low. This suggests that, knowingly or not, a particular regime brings with it a range of other values and approaches that lead to the different levels of imprisonment— 'the greater inequality in a society the higher the overall level of punishment' (451). Jones and Newburn (2005) explored the commonly held view that UK politicians import

US policies, and suggest that underlying this superficial analysis the key elements related to a strategy becoming policy are unpredictable in both locations.

The government view of the situation is that decisions *are* based on evidence. In a major speech on responding to social exclusion in September, 2006 the then Prime Minister, Tony Blair said:

> There is now a wealth of empirical data to analyse. The purport of it is clear. You can detect and predict the children and families likely to go wrong. The vast majority offered help, take it. And early intervention is far more effective than the colossal expenditure of effort and resource once they have gone wrong. This is the lesson from Europe, the USA, New Zealand and many other countries.
>
> (Blair, 2006b)

It is somewhat surprising that he does not mention evidence from the UK, despite the vast amount of research on the subject in this country, much of it funded by the government itself. The impact of criminological research might be expected to be most evident in government crime strategies, the most recent of which has just been released (Home Office, 2007a). It presents a wide-ranging programme of new and continuing initiatives to reduce crime, and lays claim to being guided by evidence. A scan of this document reveals that much of this evidence is government statistics and surveys and departmental reports. There are just three references that might be considered to be criminological research, although it must be acknowledged that departmental reports may have been informed by a wider range of research or by expert input from criminologists. This does demonstrate that official statistics if not research are important to modern government.

Evidence-based policy

The evidence-based policy process is generally presented as a relatively straightforward, instrumentally rational and linear process that involves the accumulation of evidence from evaluative research projects which is then subject to systematic review or meta analysis to identify the best way forward for policy. Policy makers are assumed to accept these findings and act upon them as the research suggests. This model has been critiqued on three levels: first, that the policy making process is not this simple or this rational; second, there are debates within and outside of criminology about the best kind of research to undertake to provide the body of convincing evidence; and third, the notion of systematic review is questioned as the best way of identifying a way forward.

The policy process

Policy making has been defined as 'the process by which governments translate their political vision into programmes and action to deliver "outcomes"' (Cabinet Office Strategic Policy Making Team, 1999, para 2.4 quoted in Nutley and Webb, 2000: 14).

Who the policy makers are is undefined, but they can be a diffuse range of people closely aligned with the policy making process, including politicians, officials and advisers. The reality is that a range of issues come into play when policy decisions are made, including values and ideology, public, media and lobby group pressures, risks and economics. Any of these could be more important in relation to a particular decision than the 'evidence'.

Research, evidence and policy

The complexity of the policy process is noted by a report of the House of Commons Science and Technology Committee (2006), which says:

> In considering evidence based policy, we conclude that the Government should not overplay this mantra, but should acknowledge more openly the many drivers of policy making, as well as any gaps in the relevant research base. We make the case for greater public investment in research to underpin policy making and recommend the establishment of a cross-departmental fund to commission independent policy-related research.'
>
> (House of Commons, 2006:3)

Despite acknowledging the complexity (see text box), the committee still held to the view that policy makers need more and better research. Several writers discuss the work of Donald Schön in this context (for example Parsons, 2002). Schön described a 'policy swamp'—a 'world of change, and full of complexity, uncertainty and ignorance' (Parsons, 2002: 45)—a world unsuited to the simple application of evidence by policymakers. Schön felt it more important to understand processes of change: 'the deficit was less to do with information than our capacity for public and private learning' (47), and 'evidence, in itself . . . cannot help us to resolve conflicts of value in an uncertain world' (49).

Tonry (2003) highlights the contradictions in the government's espoused commitment to evidence-based policy making whereby it maintains a policy of being seen as tough on crime when the research evidence shows that imprisonment (the generally accepted measure of toughness) is not the best way of preventing further offending: in fact quite the opposite. He analyzes the government proposals in the White Paper *Justice for All* and the, 2002 Criminal Justice Bill on the basis of available evidence and finds that most of the proposals go against that evidence. He suggests three reasons for this: placating the judiciary who want to be able to continue to sentence in their own way; 'stalemating' the political opposition so that they could not accuse the government of going soft on crime; and being wary of public blame should things go wrong. All are political drivers. Crime and law and order are highly politicised issues and the symbolic impact of responses to it can be more important than their actual effectiveness. The current view is that individuals are responsible for their actions and an appropriate response is increased control and surveillance of identified risky individuals. The preferred approach to crime prevention is situational rather than individual, and the need 'to provide intellectual legitimation for state policies [has] waned' (Haggerty, 2004: 217).

The ways in which evidence, and particularly research, can influence policy and practice are varied. Weiss et al. (2005) have undertaken much work over more than twenty years exploring the possible routes by which research evidence can influence policy. They suggest that evaluation is used in three main ways:

(a) *instrumentally* where research gives specific direction to policy and practice. This simplistic model of influence, which evaluators may like to see in an ideal world, rarely happens. It is difficult to find an example of a specific piece of research or evaluation that has led directly to a policy.

(b) *politically* or *symbolically*, where research is used selectively to justify pre-existing preferences and actions. These policies could have been decided 'on the basis of intuition, professional experience, self-interest, organizational interest, a search for prestige, or any of the multiplicity of reasons that go into decisions about policy and practice' (13). They argue this does not represent misuse of the research unless the findings have been distorted to fit the policy.

(c) *conceptually* providing new generalizations, ideas or concepts that are useful for making sense of the policy scene. Decision makers often find research and evaluation useful, even though no immediate action ensues. This is the most common, and arguably the most important route to influence as 'When evaluation findings percolate into the decision arena in direct and indirect ways, sometimes in the long term, they become the new common wisdom.' (14)

The nature of research/evidence

When the term 'evidence-based' is used, the 'evidence' is generally understood to be research, usually evaluative research. This conflation of the term 'evidence' with 'research' is a fundamental fallacy, for as we have seen research is just one of many kinds of possible 'evidence'. Evidence-based policy and practice (EBPP) was seen to be such an important development that the ESRC fund a UK centre to bring social science research nearer to the decision making process and explore EBPP issues (http://www.evidencenetwork.org/). As part of that initiative five models of the relationship between research and policy have been proposed.

Research and policy: five models

- *Research as knowledge driver* is where the research agenda is decided by researchers and supported by policy. In an extreme form policy can abdicate political choice in favour of experts know best. This can be a dangerous position for researchers.
- *Research as problem solver* is where policy shapes the research priorities that researchers follow, and these feed directly back into policy. Although much research is generated on this instrumental model, increasingly by charitable foundations as well as government departments, the direct feedback into policy happens rarely.
- *Interactive research* is a two way process. Research and policy are mutually influential and it is difficult to identify who influences whom.
- *Political/tactical research* sees policy as the outcome of a political process and the research agenda is politically driven. Research supports policy and there is a danger that the science is politicised.
- *Enlightenment research* maintains a distance from policy and its immediate policy agenda. Research affects policy indirectly, often providing a frame for thinking about a policy issue.

Young et al. (2002)

Enlightenment is Young et al.'s preferred mode, for two reasons. Firstly a view that it better reflects the reality of the policy process, and secondly that it better fits research aims to understand an issue or situation rather than provide a policy solution. Donald Schön would have agreed, suggesting as he did that 'the essential difficulties in social policy have more to do with problem setting than with problem solving, more to do with the purposes to be achieved than the selection of optimal means to achieve them.' (Schön, 1993: 138). This model is similar to the conceptual model of policy use of research advocated by Weiss (2005).

Controversy abounds around two research issues that have a bearing on its value as 'evidence'. The first is about the nature of the best kind of research that can 'evidence' policy decisions. The second concerns the role of government as the funder of much criminological research, in the process of which it not only determines the priorities for research but also frames the methodologies required.

Research: the gold standard?

Whilst many commentators talk about the 'irrationality' of policy making, and the way in which a wide range of influences come to bear on the process, there is at the same time, and somewhat paradoxically, a view that such irrationality would be overcome if the quality of the evidence were better. Writers such as Sherman (2005) and Farrington (2000, 2003) call for more experimental research, aspiring to the so-called research 'gold standard' of randomised control trials. Supported by the Home Office quality standards for research (Home Office, 2004a), this view presents a continuing link with criminology's beginnings. An example of influential research is the Cambridge Study which began in the, 1960s in the heyday of empirical positivist criminology and continues to actively influence policy decisions. A strength of this research is its long-term longitudinal value, with the most recent report (Farrington et al., 2006) following up the sample at age fifty. There are interesting findings about the unpredictability of futures within this report, and yet a key recommendation is the need to intervene in the lives of children deemed to be 'at risk' before the age of ten years, supporting current policy. This study is described by Downes as a project that 'embodies all the canons of positivism at its best' (1986: 197).

The 'positivist' approach does not acknowledge the role of values in research nor the way in which its requirements can frame the findings. For instance some statistical analysis techniques require particular ways of viewing the issues being researched, such as the need for binary categorization like offender/not offender. Law and Urry (2004) go further saying 'methods are never innocent . . . in some measure they enact whatever it is they describe *into* reality.' (403, original emphasis). This is perhaps most clearly reflected in the work of Farrall et al. (1997) who argue that 'fear of crime' is something that has been created by research that attempts to measure it. Another school of researchers who disagree that experimental research is the best approach argue for a realist research approach to provide an understanding of the mechanisms by which interventions may be effective (Pawson and Tilley, 1997; Sanderson, 2002). Knepper (2007) identifies four types of criminological research, each of which implies a different relationship with policymaking.

Four types of criminological research

- *Experimental* Sees science as the most reliable route to planning sound policy, focussing on problems identified by the government. It is based on the experimental method as described above: criminologists supply facts, policy makers make choices about values and priorities.
- *Crime science* Focuses on how crime is committed rather than why, and in particular promotes simple, practical ways of reducing opportunity for crime. Knepper likens this approach to that of industrial research, with developments being taken up by private as well as public interests.
- *Critical criminology* Takes a 'critical' stance towards criminal policy, arguing that criminologists should be problem raisers rather than problem solvers. This school has initiated a broader thinking about the notion of 'crime', including the study of white-collar crime, workplace injury and the illegal activities of multinational organisations.
- *Left realism* Defends social welfare and believes that criminologists should integrate themselves with the policy making process at the local level, conducting empirical research that can directly inform that process. Politicality is not only allowable, but desirable, and as its name suggests this type of research aligns itself with left of centre policies.

Knepper, 2007

Research: in the pocket of government?

Some researchers believe that the government has too much control over the research that is undertaken. Walters argues that 'to participate in Home Office research is to endorse a biased agenda that omits topics of national and global concern in favour of regulating the poor and the powerless' (2006: 6). He sees universities as colluding in a process of the 'commodification of knowledge' (Walters, 2003: 168). This is a view shared by Pawson who observes 'On a bad day the ivory tower can look awfully like a shopping mall.' (2006: 3). All agree that this position has been brought about by financial pressures on universities and growing numbers of academics competing for limited research funds.

Whilst all criminological research is political because 'crime is a category which is politically and not academically determined.' (Morgan, 2000: 76), it is also political in that it is substantially funded by government, and as such constrained by government priorities and requirements. Morgan argues, however, that the importance of such research should not be underestimated. Government funded research and more radical criminological theorizing have an essentially symbiotic, though often unacknowledged relationship: on the one hand researchers who undertake government research are able to use that experience and data more broadly: 'it is always open to an imaginative and critically minded researcher to view the data collected within a broader theoretical frame of reference; that is, once the ball has been picked up there are few real limits to the distance one can run with it.' (77), and on the other theorists often depend for their insights on the empirical data generated by the Home Office through their statistical systems, regular surveys or research projects. He describes these data as 'the clay and straw that make the bricks which both make for an accountable criminal justice system and permit it to be effectively challenged and analysed.' (77)

Systematic review

Systematic review is a technique that attempts to synthesize the results from large numbers of research studies. It is usually undertaken on outcome studies to identify which methods produce the best results. Meta analysis is a popular procedure for doing this, originating in medical research early in the, 19th century. It first began to be used in criminology in the, 1960s, though arguably the most influential study in the UK has been Lipsey (1995). This work identified that programmes for young offenders do have positive effects on reoffending, providing a push for the Probation Service *What works* project. A more recent and ambitious project is the Campbell Collaboration Crime and Justice Co-ordinating Group, modelled on the Cochrane Collaboration in medicine and health. An international organization established in, 2000, its mission is 'to coordinate, facilitate, assist and encourage the production, updating and accessibility of high quality systematic reviews.' (http://www.campbellcollaboration.org/CCJG/mission.asp).

A range of problems have been identified with systematic reviews, primarily to do with decisions about which evaluations are included/excluded and the impact of these decisions on the validity of the results (Mair, 2004). The quality of research to be included is assessed against the so-called 'gold standard' of randomised control experiments giving preference to quantitative over qualitative research. Pawson does not believe in evidence-based policy, describing evidence as 'the six-stone weakling of the policy world' (2006: viii). His view is that systematic review as currently conceived cannot provide the knowledge necessary for improving decision making, and proposes an alternative, realist model of research synthesis to build an understanding of the mechanisms and contexts within which things 'work'.

The Crime Reduction Programme: A Failure for EBPP?

In April, 1999, the United Kingdom Government began to roll-out the most ambitious, best resourced and most comprehensive effort for driving down crime ever attempted in a Western developed country. . . the UK turned to 25 years of accumulated crime research and experience to develop and implement a new and highly innovative programme.

(Homel et al., 2004: v)

Conceived as an evidence-based project, it began with a review of the existing research evidence (Goldblatt and Lewis, 1998) about the various ways in which crime reduction might be addressed: preventing criminality, reducing opportunities for crime, social cohesion in communities, policing, sentencing and intervention with offenders. Based on this evidence, 20 wide ranging projects were designed with the aim of generating 'a road map for guiding long-term investment strategies for the government in its continuing effort to drive down crime.' (Homel et al., 2004: v). The Treasury invested £250 million into the first three years, with ten per cent committed to comprehensive evaluation of the projects. Although designed as a project for the long term (ten years), the programme was ended after the initial three years, although some of the projects continued. The review identified two key reasons for this: firstly, a shift of focus from research and development to reducing crime; and second the establishment of regional government and devolution of management of the programme to the regions (Homel et al., 2004: vii). Both happened early in the programme, and both were significant political

---

Continued

The Crime Reduction Programme: A Failure for EBPP?—cont'd

developments that were deemed more important than the potential learning about crime. Both dramatically impacted upon the implementation and delivery of the various projects. My own experience as a principal investigator on one of these evaluations reflects the difficulties created for both implementers and evaluators by these politically shifting sands (France et al., 2004).

The impact of criminology on practice

Although decision making in policy and in practice appear very different, they are similar in needing to deal with complexity. Research evidence is just one of many factors to be taken into account. Evidence-based practice is about the learning from research being applied in practice on the ground. This could refer to practitioners individually identifying the lessons from research and incorporating them into their practice, but in reality this rarely happens. Practitioners are limited in what they can put into practice and how, and their options have become more and more limited as practice is increasingly proscribed by government policy. Most of the discussion around evidence-based practice focuses on policy makers making decisions about practice and how to bring about those required changes, though changing practice is often more about changing organizational practice than about changing individual practitioners. At the same time, the distinction between policy and practice is not always clear cut. Policy making and reshaping happens at a number of levels within an organization, and although the broad policy framework may be determined by a central government department, local managers and policy makers translate it for the local framework, and individual practitioners in turn shape policy in its implementation (Nutley and Webb, 2000: 15).

Evidence-based practice is often presented as being better than professional judgement but Hammersley (2005) argues that although they are different one is not always and inevitably better than the other. He discusses the difficulties of practice implementation: applying a finding based on groups to a particular case; that research cannot provide all of the information needed to make a judgement; that some practice problems do not lend themselves to the application of 'evidence'; that research findings are fallible; the difficulties of standardizing treatments in delivery, and standardization of under-standing by the recipient; and most importantly an oversimplified conception of causation within randomised control trials. He explains how judgement, although subjective, is not the same as bias, but that it is frequently treated as though it is. He also argues that methodological rigour is no guarantee of validity of research, and questions 'naive faith in experiment', concluding: 'While research can provide evidence about the consequences of various policies, on its own it cannot tell us what is the best thing to do, either in general terms or in particular cases.' (25)

Gray and McDonald come to a similar conclusion, arguing that the notion of evidence-based practice is 'conceptually narrow' and 'theoretically limited'. Aside from the problems of identifying what is meant by effectiveness in social work, they argue that the notion of evidence-based practice is premised on the false view that there is a formal rationality of problem solving in social work. Their view is rather that 'Social work is an incredibly complex series of activities undertaken in diverse, unstable, constantly changing social "spaces".' (2006: 14). The same is true of the practice of criminal justice professionals.

There is little written about evidence-based practice in criminal justice, although writings about social work provide relevant insights. A survey of social workers found substantial support for the idea of evidence-based practice, but problems in application. One reason was the difficulty of finding out what might be the best thing to do in any situation, exacerbated by a reluctance to be seen reading research, which was generally not construed as 'working' by colleagues and managers. Some practitioners do not accept that research knows better than them, and for others the blame culture prevalent in some organizations leads to caution in trying something new in case they get it wrong. Some practitioners feel they do not have sufficient understanding of research, and yet others suggest that the generalist structure of the profession makes it harder to keep abreast of relevant literature, especially where they do not have easy access. An important and frequently mentioned problem was lack of time, both to keep abreast of research and for the more reasoned decision-making process requirement (Moseley and Tierney, 2005).

The relationship between research and practice has a long history, and not always a comfortable one. From my own experience as a researcher working in the probation service there are several reasons for this. Practitioners can feel that their work as individuals is being scrutinized rather than policies and agency implementation of them; they are frequently the providers/generators of data but receive no feedback or report of the work they have participated in; practitioner priorities are not necessarily those of policy; and a common complaint is that research measures of outcomes are too blunt to see the impact of their work. These issues have only increased with the coming of the *What works* project, and sadly little other research now takes place in probation.

Conclusion

Criminology as a discipline is clearly flourishing, as witnessed by the increasing numbers of courses and students in universities, and by the number of books and articles published in journals. The wide and continuing interest of politicians, the media and the public make it unlikely that this will diminish in the foreseeable future. The health of the discipline is also demonstrated by the range of debates taking place within it and its diversification, both substantively and methodologically.

Research aims to produce knowledge that tests and develops theories and understanding, in accordance with principles and procedures designed to assure the trustworthiness of the results. For some this means a focus on methodology which, as Bottoms (2005) in his discussion of 'methodological sloppiness' has demonstrated, is crucially important. This does not mean that any particular methodology is better than any other. Whilst some researchers argue the importance of quantitative methods, many others argue the value of qualitative methods (see the quotation at the start of the chapter). More important is that the methods that are applied are appropriate for the questions being addressed. Some interesting recent developments are looking at crime, offending, the criminal justice system and desistance from offending, from the perspective of the offender (for example Farrall and Maruna, 2004, Hine, 2006). Qualitative methodologies are clearly good ways to address such questions.

One thing that is clear from research into the causes of crime, back to the earliest studies, is that there is no simple answer, even though successive governments continue to search for a 'magic bullet'. This complexity is compounded by developments in understanding not only how the choice of research method and topic is informed by values and beliefs, thereby framing what are seen as problems and, ultimately, what is found, but further that the process of social research is implicated in shaping the world that it is attempting to describe and understand. It is suggested that traditional research methods are inadequate to address this complexity and there is a need to develop new approaches (Byrne, 2005; Law and Urry, 2004). Some, such as Walters (2006), call for a more radical agenda: 'a criminology of resistance' (7).

Innovation in method is being fuelled both by the growing interdisciplinary and multidisciplinary interest in the topic of 'crime' and by expanding boundaries in terms of what can be explored under the label of 'criminology'. Some of the most significant impacts of criminology have emerged from critical theoretical reflection about the discipline and its topic of study. The most recent developments focus attention on areas not traditionally conceptualized as crime despite their substantial impact on numerous individuals. 'Social harm' is the name given to this area of study (Hillyard et al., 2004), which incorporates topics such as medical mistakes and financial misselling in an attempt to redress the neglect of these areas, some of which can be more damaging than the effects of 'crime'. This work comes close to a promotion of social justice rather than criminal justice, as discussed by Knepper (2007), who argues that the pursuit of social welfare and reduced crime involves challenges, dilemmas and obstacles, the most important of which are matters of justice. Criminology and social policy is embedded within larger moral priorities, ideals and principles (169). He also suggests that criminology can benefit from 'accidental criminologists', that is researchers working in other disciplines or areas who have an interest in crime in some way. The blurring of disciplinary boundaries engendered by these debates may well mean that, as Roberts suggests, 'the solutions to crime, social harm and injustice may lie outside the confines of traditional criminological inquiry' (2006: 3).

The application of criminological research and theory to policy and practice is an ethereal process, which many of us would argue is the best way for it to be, gradually building up a body of empirical knowledge and theory that filters into and shapes the thinking of those with the power and authority to bring about change—policy makers and practitioners.

Key arguments

- The discipline of criminology is in a healthy state and criminological insights continue to be sought by policy makers.
- The modern relationship between criminological research policy and practice can be traced in the history of the discipline.
- Political decision making is complex and evidence from research is rarely the prime consideration.
- The impact of criminology is often more theoretical than empirical, though the two are inextricably linked in developing new ways of thinking about crime and offenders.
- Issues of offending and responding to offending are complex, and researchers need to be methodologically rigorous and politically and ethically aware.
- Criminology needs to be innovative and to be open to insights provided by other disciplines.

Further reading

Garland (2002) and Rock (1994) both provide considered accounts of the history of criminology. For those interested in evidence-based policy the edited collection by Davies et al. (2000) provides both theoretical analysis of the issues and examples from a wide range of disciplines, including criminology. Pawson (2006) takes a more radical, and entertaining, view of the topic, analyzing the difficulties with the current approach and proposing an alternative. Two different perspectives on the relationship between politics and policy in criminology are provided by Morgan (2000) and Walters (2003), and suggestions for new ways of examining the issues are put forward by Knepper (2007).

3

'DIVERSITY': CONTESTED MEANINGS AND
DIFFERENTIAL CONSEQUENCES

Charlotte Knight, Jane Dominey and Judy Hudson[1]

'Diversity' as a concept and as a strategy for change can easily be hijacked by the imperatives of managerialism, losing its force as a means of promoting social justice, and becoming rather a means of achieving narrower organisational aims and objectives, which provide the surface appearance rather than the deeper essentials of diversity.

(Bhui, 2003:196)

Chapter summary

- The process of understanding the differences between us, in a society (United Kingdom) and a system (criminal justice) that affords some groups, or 'identities' differential access to power and opportunities.
- An overview of the history and development of the concept of 'diversity'.
- Some observations on how criminology has helped to inform and sometimes obscure the debate.
- An exploration of language and definitions.
- An overview of some of the issues related to managing, resourcing, teaching and learning in this area.

We hope this chapter will offer students of applied criminology, academics, researchers and practitioners working within the system, some suggestions and guidance on how best to navigate their own journeys through the intellectual discourse and into the pursuit of social justice and anti-oppressive practice, that we believe defines the concept of 'diversity'. As a group of academic staff, all of whom have practice backgrounds and a strong commitment to the development of knowledge and practice in this area, we have taken our own discourse and practice on the subject of diversity to inform this chapter. We are based in Leicester; a city where the term 'ethnic *minority*' is perhaps becoming a misnomer, given that in some wards of the city black and Asian people constitute a *majority*. Whilst we would like to believe that the multi-cultural nature of our city, campus and programmes helps us in our endeavours to be more inclusive and integrative in our debates

---

[1]With particular thanks to Lucy Baldwin and Alan Clark for contributing additional material and engagement in discussion with us about some of the key issues and concepts.

on diversity, we make no claims to have acquired a superior knowledge. This chapter does not offer definitive answers to difficult questions, but rather some guidance on the process by which meanings, understandings and actions might best be achieved.

The reason for the significance and importance of 'diversity' as a concept in the criminal justice system arises from the increasing body of research evidence, cited later in the chapter, which shows us that people as offenders, victims or staff can be treated differentially, and sometimes very badly, because of their membership of a certain group or community rather than, intrinsically, because of their behaviour, ability or circumstances. We suggest that it is an imperative for students, practitioners and academics to understand these treat-ment differentials and to be committed to changing the system that maintains them.

Our understanding of these issues and the history of different and 'diverse' groups within British society comes from a range of theoretical disciplines. It is influenced by values and the ideologies of powerful institutions that have a vested interest in maintaining the status quo. It is sustained by belief systems, both religious and non-religious, by political ideologies, by culture and by tradition. It is challenged, usually, by the groups themselves who, from their own personal experience of disadvantage and discrimination begin to collectively articulate this, and push for change to the status quo (Freire, 1972). It is rarely articulated or challenged by the powerful, who have a vested interest in retaining their position(s). Indeed, if left to the powerful, the knowledge and experiences of oppressed and disadvantaged groups would remain hidden. For example young people's voices, and those of other marginalized groups, continue to be silenced (Hillyard et al., 2004). It has, however, been championed by some movements within criminology, for example feminism and critical perspectives. Examples of where crimi-nology is being constructed as a form of critical intervention can also be seen in this volume (see chapters by Goldson and Yates, and Tombs and Williams).

Background to the discourse

Some of the most powerful forces for change in Britain began with the identification of the 'class struggle' (Marx and Engels: 1888) with challenges to the forces of capitalism. The struggle to abolish slavery in the 19th century and the history of colonialism, informs much of the 'Black Power' movement and our understandings of the impact of racism that continues today. Other movements—feminism, gay liberation, disability rights, have all started from the groups themselves becoming politicized and beginning to define their own experiences of injustice, disadvantage, oppression, and denial of access to goods, services and resources. This developing awareness and knowledge led to the discourses of challenge defined as 'anti-oppressive' (anti-racism, anti-sexism, etc.) in the 1970s and 1980s.

How criminology has informed the debate

We are concerned that whilst there has been a developing body of knowledge about issues related to 'diversity' the impact of this knowledge on legislation and policy has not always been as durable or influential as we might have hoped. During the 1980s growing concern about the differential impact of criminal justice policy on, in particular, women and black people, led to a growing body of research (NACRO, 1986, 1991, 1992, 1993; Heidensohn, 2006) and subsequent policy development. A new breed of 'radical' criminologists began building on the work of earlier criminologists, and in the chart below, we attempt to identify some of the links between these theories and their counterparts in 'diversity' terms today.

Table 3.1 Links between criminological theory and 'diversity'

Authors	Theories	Links with diversity
Marx (1888)	Marxist criminology	The exploitation of the working classes, power held in the hands of the elite
Durkheim (1893)	'Anomie'	Influence of class, poverty and
Merton (1938)	'Becoming deviant'	alienation from mainstream society
Matza (1969)	Delinquent subcultures	as reasons for predominantly
Cohen (1955)	Social Structure	working class youth committing
Cloward and Ohlin (1960)	Strain Theory	crime
Merton (1968)		The lack of structured and legitimate means for most people in society to attain what was indiscriminately held out to all as the ultimate goal – material wealth
Becker (1963)	Social process theories	How people interact, and can be
Lemert (1964)	Symbolic Interactionism	negatively labelled as part of a
Wilkins (1964)	Labelling Theory	process, determines who is likely to
	Deviance Amplification	offend and/or be apprehended
Taylor, Walton and Young et al. (1973)	Social conflict theory	Crime is a function of relative
Radical Criminology	Left realism	deprivation; criminals target the poor
Slapper and Tombs (1999)	Post-modern theories	Questions the focus of the criminal
	Crimes of the powerful	justice system on working class crime at the expense of corporate and white collar crime
Smart (1977)	Gender and Crime	Examines the gendered nature of crime
Heidensohn (2006)	'Race and Crime'	Examines how crime is 'racialised'
Bowling and Phillips (2002)		

Whilst 'diversity' remained an unnamed concept within the early theories, a re-reading of these texts identifies the themes of 'difference' from the 'main stream' both in the subjects' experiences of life in British society and in their 'identities' as primarily young (age), white ('race'), male (gender) and working class (class). Here we see the development of the Marxist analysis of how the powerful in society (capitalists and land owners) determine the laws and the norms of society and how those on the margins (young, working class) are pressed into conformity or identified as deviant.

Class continues to be a major explanatory theme for why it is that certain groups within society find themselves as 'defendants' in court where others are the magistrates and judges who deliver the sentencing. The same is true of 'race'. There continues to be a minority of black and minority ethnic staff in all ranks of the judiciary with none in the Lords of Appeal and Heads of Division. However, whilst 'race' and gender (a minority of women as defendants and in the judiciary) continue to be observably in operation in differential ways, class remains an uncomfortable topic of conversation for most practitioners, trainers and academics. Given that the definitions of class can refer to significantly different sorts of categories including income, occupation, lifestyle, values and/or geographical location, it is hard to find specific and current research evidence that maps class and crime (see Devlin, 1993).

Our own observations of court dynamics, based on many years of collective practice experience, bear out the fact that a majority of judges continue to be 'middle/upper class', most magistrates represent 'middle-class' lifestyles and values, and most defendants continue to come from the lower socio-economic groupings and/or are unemployed. Certainly, people with these characteristics are over-represented in prison. Yet, as critics of 'underclass theory' point out, people in every social class commit crime but the crimes of the powerful tend to avoid censure. Tombs and Williams (this volume) argue that victims also generally come from the most powerless groups in society.

> We continually return to the fact that power, for much of our recent UK history, has been held in the hands of white, able-bodied, middle or upper class, heterosexual men. Whilst theories of masculinity (Messerschmidt, 1997) offer some explanations for this, we have to ask what it is that makes this characteristic so durable.

So what is 'diversity'?

An understanding of diversity is central to any value system but 'diversity' as a concept is not straightforward. The history of our developing awareness of 'difference', of how certain groups of people in our society are treated less favourably and are subject to discrimination and oppression, has had a strong focus in criminal justice from the research described earlier. This has proved beyond doubt that black and Asian people of both genders experience racism at both individual and institutional level, and that white and black women are treated differentially. It is worth noting, however, that criminology took a long time to begin to think deeply about issues of both 'race' and gender in analyzing causes of, and responses to, crime.

We know much less about the experience of other discriminated against groups, for example, lesbians and gay men, transgendered people and people with a disability, although we believe we can make some assumptions from other research e.g. Oliver (1996), the Disability Rights Commission, Stonewall and the Equal Opportunities Commission,[2] and from first hand accounts from people in these groups. We would

---

[2] The Disability Rights Commission, the Commission for Racial Equality and the Equal Opportunities Commission were all merged into one body: the Commission for Equality and Human Rights (CEHR), in October 2007.

include mental ill-health as a diversity issue here, because of the stigma still attached to mental illness, and because the oppression experienced by minority groups can in itself increase their mental ill-health (Mind, 2007) and limit their access to resources. The report of the independent inquiry into the death of David (Rocky) Bennett found that black and minority ethnic communities are not getting the services they are entitled to from the National Health Service (Norfolk, Suffolk and Cambridge Strategic Health Authority, 2003).

High profile inquiries about the deaths of Stephen Lawrence in the community (Macpherson, 1999) and more recently Zahid Mubarek in prison (Keith, 2006) have continued to galvanize action in relation to debate and policy development around 'race' matters. So too has the development of 'black criminology' with its focus on the social construction of black offending (Dominelli, 2006). However, it appears to us that many organizations within the community and criminal justice sectors have made slow progress in relation to understanding what is meant by 'institutional discrimination', which in our view is about failing to value diversity. We suggest a number of reasons for this.

Firstly, whilst politicians and policy makers can use the language of diversity in speeches and in policy, a real grasp of its meanings and implications lies in under-standing it on both a personal *and* a structural level. Those who generally have a better grasp of the importance of diversity as an 'identity' concept have often, but not always, been on the receiving end of discrimination themselves and have learnt through painful journeys of personal discovery, understanding and awareness. In order to begin to understand the experience of a black person, a white person needs first to understand their own 'whiteness' and what it means for them and the society in which they live. Similarly, in order to understand what it means to be gay or lesbian, a heterosexual person needs first to examine their own sexuality. These can be uncomfortable and challenging journeys to make, but failure to do this allows those with power to continue to assert their authority as decision makers whilst fail-ing to take into account the experiences of the 'subordinate' groups who are the subject of their decision making (Heidensohn, 2000). We also acknowledge that the production of knowledge as a research enterprise can be similarly constrained and legitimized by the frameworks imposed by those with the power to set the agendas.

Secondly, the evolving use of language to define the territory of the debate is ambiguous. In some respects the use of the word 'diversity' allows for a more positive connotation to be placed on minority groups, a valuing of their difference, than has sometimes been the case historically. However, 'diversity' is also a bland term, and in its attempts to homogenize and simplify the issues, it risks concealing the interrela-tionship between power and disadvantage that our knowledge of discrimination and oppression highlights. We have begun to lose the more explicit language of the 1980s and 1990s of 'anti-discrimination',' anti-racism' and particularly 'anti-sexism' and 'anti-heterosexism' which clearly recognized the exercise of power that could lead to disadvantage, and the need to challenge and transform the circumstances that created it. We cannot claim that such explicit language was necessarily transformative and indeed some of the discourse at that time was too narrowly focused and counterproductive.

Nevertheless, using the term 'diversity' can be a way of avoiding detail and failing to name the challenging issues that need to be resolved.

Valuing diversity may seem an easier objective than combating racism or overcoming homophobia but it is only in paying attention to detail that diversity policies are translated into practice. Historically, criminology has endeavoured to find 'grand' and 'objective' theories of deviance to explain offending behaviour and this has led to a failure to acknowledge the subjective and individual experiences of offenders.

Thirdly, good diversity practice can cost money but failure to address diversity, particularly in relation to staffing, also has a cost. There are financial costs in terms of loss of productivity if a work force is not working to its full potential because workers are feeling alienated and undervalued. Additionally there are the costs of industrial tribunals and compensation claims as a result of experiences of unlawful discrimination.[3] For organizations which do not embrace diversity issues for their staff the costs can be huge. The loss of talented staff because they have suffered harassment or discrimination or are not able to work flexibly, means additional financial costs in recruiting, inducting and training new staff.[4] Staff sickness can increase and stress related absenteeism (of which harassment and discrimination could be a major factor) can cause over £10 billion losts to UK employers each year. Harassment and discrimination at work is not only 'bad for business' but it is also against the law. In a recent tribunal (2005) the first case settled under the Employment Equality (Sexual Orientation) regulations resulted in a £35,000 payout to the employee (Stonewall, 2007).

In some ways the private sector has recognized and addressed this more proactively than the public sector. High profile appeals by individuals within the banking and the legal professions against dismissal on the grounds of sexism, or racism or homophobia are not good for business and have led to considerable change in these sectors. Conversely, recognizing the significance of diversity can sometimes be profitable; for example, the 'pink pound'. However, whilst this more 'opportunistic' recognition of costs and benefits of diversity may be relevant and appropriate to the private sector, what about those who have no 'consumer' power? We know that offenders as a group are frequently the most inarticulate, the least able to negotiate and bargain, the least likely to complain about poor service and the most disenfranchised. They are rarely involved in their own research and their views are infrequently sought in evaluations undertaken on the 'effectiveness' of a range of interventions.

Definitions and terminology of 'diversity'

Most organizations within the criminal justice system offer definitions of diversity related to inclusive practice and business effectiveness (e.g. Home Office, 2001a). However, Bhui's statement at the beginning of this chapter argues that the term has

---

[3]Clements and Jones, 2006:17 provide statistics on costs; for example, the average award for race discrimination cases is £26,660.
[4]Estimated average to be between £5,000—£10,000 (Clements and Jones, 2006).

been hijacked by the imperatives of managerialism and misses the deeper essentials. We believe that discussion around language and definitions of key concepts used within the debate about diversity is an imperative for identifying these 'essentials'. Such language is dynamic and evolving and we need to be constantly checking our understanding of the language used, not for fear of being accused of 'political correctness',[5] but because we owe it to the minority groups who are themselves working out the implications of the labels used to define them. We take the view that those who struggle with oppression should have the right to determine the language that defines them. Thompson refers to the concept of 'conscientization', which he defines as: 'helping people understand the extent to which their position is a reflection of broader cultural and political patterns . . . it can help people to stop blaming themselves for their predicament' (Thompson, 2003:223).

Whilst we should take our lead from these discourses we should 'own' the definitions we choose to use, based on reading and reference to current campaigns, and be willing to update them as new knowledge arrives (British Council, 2007). Crude attempts to 'censure' language in the workplace without an explanatory framework and opportunities for discussion can lead to resentment and hostility.

One of the particular challenges relates to the constantly changing nature of the terminology. The term 'Black' as a political concept was widely used during the 1980s and 1990s. 'Black' was the political colour of opposition in 1960s England following the American politics of representation during the civil rights era. The 'Black Power' movement gave voice most obviously to African Americans and African/Caribbeans in Britain, but also established the principle of self-empowerment and offered a model for political action for other disempowered groups. Historically, the term 'Black' was used as a political concept that identified the common experience of racism amongst all groups of people whose skin colour was not 'white'. Within some of the larger criminal justice organizations, unionized groups of staff formed under the umbrella of 'Black', for example the Association of Black Probation Officers (ABPO) and the National Black Police Association (http://www.nationalbpa.com/). However, whilst the term 'Black' offered unity and solidarity to beleaguered groups of staff, it provided insufficient explanations of difference within 'Blackness' and implied a homogeneity that did not exist. Thus we saw the emergence of groups such as the National Association of Asian Probation Staff (NAAPS), and the increasing use of the term 'Black and Asian' to indicate the differences between 'Black' meaning those of an African–Caribbean origin, and 'Asian' meaning those with origins in the Indian sub-continent.

---

[5]Political Correctness (PC) refers to language and ideas that are explicitly inclusive, avoid making assumptions about identity and reflect the preferences of the groups themselves (for example: fire fighter not fireman, partner not husband/wife). Critics of political correctness argue that it leads to outcomes that no-one wants (e.g. the loss of the traditional celebration at Christmas for fear of offending those of other faiths) and stifles debate about important aspects of public policy (because it is not possible to question issues such as the place of women in the workforce or the race of street robbers). We would argue that the use of language is important and that the development of more careful and inclusive language plays a part in creating a culture where diversity is valued.

More commonly now the term 'ethnic minority' or 'Black and minority ethnic' (BME) is to be found in reports and inspection papers (for example: HMIP, 2007). [6]However, the use of these terms seems to convey the message that white people have no 'ethnicity' and they continue to be a relatively inadequate description of widely different groups of people with differing life experiences.

> The Parekh Report on the future of Multi-Ethnic Britain resists the use of the term 'ethnic', explaining that all people belong to an ethnic group. Its preference is for using the terms 'black, Asian and Irish' or 'black and Asian' with Asian referring to all Asian countries and regions, not to Bangladesh, India and Pakistan only (Parekh, 2002: xxiv).

Bradby's research, based on the health service, identified a confusion between the terms 'race' and 'ethnicity' that is clearly still evident in the criminal justice system today. She argues that for the last 50 years social and biological scientists have been demonstrating that race does not exist in scientific terms, however its continuing retention as an 'analytical concept' allows the focus of effort to produce resistance to racism. Nevertheless, the fear remains that to use the term without explanation is to continue to afford a false status to a concept that in fact is just an ideological construct (Bradby, 1995).

We believe that the common ground in any definitions of diversity should be the experience of discrimination, although recognize that this too is problematic in terms of who defines the discrimination and its variable significance for different groups and individuals. A strong theme throughout Hall's book on 'Hate Crime' (2005) is that the foundations of 'hateful' expressions are entirely normal to the human condition. However, making the difficult connections between the underlying reasons for the commission of 'hate crime' and the underlying resentments or resistances of some staff to understanding and working with 'difference' amongst their service user groups may prove essential if we are to make progress in this area. Whilst individual offenders can cause immense damage to individual victims, the damage caused by workers who exercise their prejudice in a discriminatory way can be more pervasively damaging. The targeting of resources to address the underlying causes of particular forms of hate crime is critical for these reasons.

Visible and invisible differences

Whilst 'visible' difference, particularly in relation to 'race' or 'skin colour', is perhaps the most obvious way in which discrimination impacts, many other aspects of identity which are less visible, or only visible in particular circumstances, or to those with greater knowledge, can lead to discrimination and incorrect assumptions can be made. For example, an ability to distinguish between a Catholic and a Protestant will be

---

[6]We explore some of the difficulties in current 'terminology' later in the chapter.

critical to an inhabitant of Northern Ireland, but the distinction will be much less apparent to other 'external' groups. Yet such distinctions have been core to the operation of prejudice and discrimination in Northern Ireland for decades. A white male living in England may be assumed to be English, Church of England or non-religious, when in fact he may be Irish, from the travelling community and Catholic. In the culturally rich society of contemporary Britain it is interesting that we continue to make assumptions based on what is visible. These assumptions may have a significant impact on the individual's experiences, identity, access to services, view of society and indeed of themselves, and at times on their mental health.

> The need to strive for conformity in appearance as well as behaviour is one of the key ways in which heterosexuality is maintained as a 'norm' at the expense of alternative expressions of sexuality in our society, and 'differently abled' people are pushed to the margins. The 'invisibility' of certain groups, for example gay men, and lesbian women, can lead to a different form of discrimination linked to the suppression of their identity and the denial of the means to live a meaningful and fulfilling life.

We could make links back to the Lombrosian project (Jones, 2006) of defining people by their physical characteristics, and associating 'criminality' with 'odd' or 'abnormal' physical characteristics. Also the incidence of mental ill-health is higher within gay and lesbian communities arising from their need to hide, deny and conceal core aspects of their identity (Mind, 2007).

The 'invisibility' of particular areas of difference has led to the omission of many relevant issues in policy making and service provision both in social policy and in relation to the criminal justice system. For example it is only with the passing of the Civil Partnership Act (2004) that same sex couples are allowed the same visiting rights and access to information within prisons as heterosexual couples. However this only applies to those who take the risk of being open about their sexuality in a potentially volatile setting. The Government uses the figure of between five and seven per cent of the population as being gay and lesbian, and Stonewall (Stonewall, 2007) accepts this as a reasonable estimate, although of course no hard data exists because no national census has asked people to define their sexuality. Some forces within the police service are now asking for this information from all new applicants to the service and if such a policy spreads to other criminal justice organizations then identification of real numbers may become easier (Gay Police Association, 2005). Whatever the actual figure it is apparent that in almost every social and professional setting heterosexuality is assumed, thus placing non-heterosexual individuals in a potentially isolating and discriminatory position. Furthermore they are then faced with the 'choice' of whether to 'come out'; this leads to immense pressure around choices of personal disclosure in order to receive access to services, to avoid discriminatory conversations and to receive the acknowledgement that those in the heterosexual world take for granted.

The process by which 'invisible' differences are made more visible is a complex one, and requires sensitive and thoughtful handling. A young gay man may be encouraged to identify his sexuality to the pre-sentence report writer, but may fear that inclusion of this fact in the report might lead to prejudicial treatment elsewhere, for example in the prison system, should he receive a custodial sentence. However, a failure by the report writer to identify his difference could lead to the suppression of crucial facts related to his criminogenic needs or to the circumstances of his particular offence.

Similar arguments relate to other 'invisible' communities such as Irish people, travellers, people with dyslexia, Jewish people and the 'invisibly disabled' such as those with diabetes, epilepsy and hearing difficulties, although some aspects of these identities may be more visible in certain situations. Research has highlighted the influence of invisible social identities (Clair et al., 2005) and the importance of influencing policy making and provision of services.

Multiple identities

We acknowledge that all people have more than one and sometimes 'multiple' identities. Some people are, however, multiply advantaged by their social identity, others are multiply disadvantaged, and for others it depends on the situation and circumstances. We live in a complex world and people look for simple solutions where there are none. The racism of a white woman worker may be inappropriately challenged via the medium of sexism from her black male manager, and the young gay Muslim man struggling with the homophobia amongst his own 'community' will also be looking for support against the Islamaphobia of his white neighbours. Whilst, as indicated earlier, racism assumed a hierarchical position in the list of oppressions in the 1980s, that position has softened with the increasing knowledge of the oppression of other groups.

Case Study

Andrew is an 18-year-old white gay man who has committed two offences of criminal damage, one of wounding, and has one previous conviction for an assault. The probation officer writing his pre-sentence report is concerned that he is at high risk of receiving a custodial sentence for the offence of wounding. She is not initially aware that Andrew is gay. Puzzled at the apparent lack of motive for the assault and criminal damage she pushes him to tell her about any relationships or 'girlfriends' he might have. He reacts angrily to this telling her she has no idea about his life and the pressures he is under to conform to his family's expectations of him.

The probation officer subsequently explores with Andrew potential alternatives to custody including unpaid work through a community sentence. Andrew's response to this is that he won't work with any 'Muslims', as they are all 'terrorists' and would beat him up for being gay.

Offending and diversity

Good practice in the area of diversity and discrimination ensures that offenders are dealt with on the basis of the crimes that they have committed, the risks that they pose and the needs that they manifest. However, as identified earlier, there is evidence to show that this is not always the case and that some groups of offenders find themselves either over or underrepresented in various parts of the criminal justice system or are dealt with unfairly or ineffectively. We have to acknowledge the extent to which criminology has been complicit in this process.

> Criminologists are paid to research street crime, and to create knowledge regarding these forms of crime, which is subsequently used to control these groups. As Hudson (1997) argues, criminology does not just study social control, it is a part of it. Criminology, by focussing on the poor and the powerless (see Walters' 2003 critique of the racist undertones in the work of Lombroso) colludes in this process, and we need therefore to think critically about the relationships between power, criminological knowledge production and policy.

There are a number of places to look for information and analysis of these trends. As indicated earlier, official statistics about crime are not a straightforward and uncontested source of information (for example, see Coleman and Moynihan, 1996) but they certainly provide a starting point. Section 95 of the Criminal Justice Act, 1991 placed a duty on the Secretary of State to publish information considered necessary to enable those working in the criminal justice system 'to avoid discriminating against any persons on the ground of race or sex or any other improper ground.' Section 95 reports are available on the Home Office website and provide reasonably up-to-date statistical information about the position of Black and Asian people and women as suspects, offenders, victims and workers in the criminal justice system.

As part of its research programme, the Home Office has also published a number of research studies that look specifically at diversity issues and seek explanations for the patterns to be found in the statistics. For example, in Home Office Research Study 277, Calverley et al. (2004) tackle the subject of Black and Asian offenders on probation and analyze information about their criminogenic needs, their experiences of supervision and their contact with other criminal justice agencies. Hedderman and Gelsthorpe (1997) discuss the sentencing of women and explore the extent to which men and women do receive differing sentences even allowing for differences in their offending. They conclude that courts are reluctant to fine women offenders and, as a consequence, women are more likely to be discharged or placed on supervision than men in similar circumstances.

Another source of information, debate and guidance about good diversity practice can be found in the work of the inspectors of the criminal justice agencies: Her Majesty's Inspectorates of Prisons, Constabulary and Probation. These three independent bodies report on the work of the criminal justice system and identify both good practice and areas of weakness. There are a number of examples of inspection reports that touch directly on issues of diversity and discrimination. For example, in 2004, HM Inspectorate of Prisons published 'No Problems – Old and Quiet: older prisoners in England and wales'. This report investigates the circumstances and treatment of older people in prison, identifies many areas of poor and unsuitable provision and makes a number of recommendations to improve practice.

The report 'Embracing Diversity' is the last in a series of three on the theme of community and race relations undertaken by Her Majesty's Inspectorate of Constabularies (HMIC, 2003b). It considers the extent to which the police service is responding to the challenge of policing all communities and recruiting, training and supporting staff that reflect the diversity of local communities.

As introduced earlier in the chapter, some key developments in the way that the criminal justice system manages complex diversity issues have followed from investigations into serious incidents such as the deaths of Stephen Lawrence and Zahid Mubarek.

Stephen Lawrence, a young Black man, was murdered in London in April 1993. His attackers have remained unconvicted. Many aspects of the investigation of his murder and the treatment that his family and friends received from the Metropolitan Police have been the subject of grave official censure. The public inquiry into these events made far-reaching recommendations impacting on all aspects of criminal justice practice and highlighted the concept of institutional racism which it defined as:

> The collective failure of an organisation to provide an appropriate and professional service to people because of their colour, culture, or ethnic origin. It can be seen or detected in processes, attitudes and behaviour which amount to discrimination through unwitting prejudice, ignorance, thoughtlessness and racist stereotyping which disadvantage minority ethnic people.'

> (Macpherson, 1999)
> (Stephen Lawrence Inquiry, (1999: s6.34)

Zahid Mubarek was murdered by his cell-mate at Feltham Young Offenders Institution near London in March, 2000. In his report into the death, Mr Justice Keith outlined many omissions, errors and examples of poor practice that had contributed to the murder. He makes wide-ranging recommendations, dealing with, for example, the management of mentally disordered prisoners, arrangements for cell-sharing and assessment of risk. The report also recognises the importance of religion as a diversity issue. Recommendation 86 reads:

> Without suggesting in any way that the Prison Service should be regarded as institutionally infected with religious intolerance, thought should be given by the Home Office to recognising the concept of institutional religious intolerance, along the lines of the definition of institutional racism adopted by the Stephen Lawrence Inquiry.

> (Keith, 2006)

Campaigning groups and voluntary organizations have also had an impact on the way that the criminal justice system responds to the concerns of minority groups. For example, the Prison Reform Trust has produced an information book for disabled prisoners aiming to provide advice about rights, benefits and sources of support (Prison Reform Trust, 2007). The website of the organization Press for Change (Press for Change, 2007) publishes a number of reports and documents that deal with the needs of transgender offenders and prisoners.

In direct work with offenders the importance of 'responsivity', which means that 'interventions should be delivered in ways which match the offenders' learning style and engage their active participation' (Chapman and Hough, 1998:14), is a critical feature of good diversity practice. The aim is to increase the motivation of offenders to change. 'Pro-social modelling' (ibid: 16) by the supervising probation officer in terms of punctuality, respect and honesty is similarly important.

A good example of this is not making assumptions (based on 'visibility') about people when inter-viewing them for the first time; for example using the term 'partner' allows the person to disclose if they are in a same sex relationship, thus enabling more open discussion. Similarly the use of the term 'partner' in reports to courts and other organizations reduces the possibility of further discrimination on the basis of their sexuality. In terms of learning disabilities and educational achievement it is good practice not to assume that offenders will be able to complete agency forms in the interview.

In a climate of managerialism, targets and National Standards (2005) within the National Probation Service, it is often seen as too difficult to challenge the interpreta-tion of policy for offenders who have different needs. There are examples of excellent practice by staff who have challenged agency policy by, for example, obtaining taxi fares for disabled offenders to reach the office, and bus fares for pregnant women, even though they live within the boundary where offenders are expected to walk to the office. It is important to empower those offenders who may have suffered discrimination previously and take action to combat any oppressive organizational policies. As well as challenging perpetrators of racially motivated offences or domestic abuse, practitioners also need to be enabled to work with victims of abuse and crime.

Case Study

Chris is an Offender Manager in a Probation Office who supervises a caseload of 50 low to medium risk offenders. One of Chris's clients, Eesha, is Asian, female and has experienced domestic violence and abuse as a child. In one supervision session she is visibly shaking and when asked why, informs Chris that she is very anxious when waiting in reception as the other people are predominantly white, male offenders, some of whom she knows have committed offences against women and children. Chris reassures Eesha that this matter will be taken up with the team manager and they will write to her before the next appointment about how the matter can be addressed. At the next team meeting it is agreed that women offenders will be offered the choice to attend appointments on Tuesday mornings and Thursday afternoons (with a facility for evening appointments). It is also reiterated that in line with good practice no offenders should be kept waiting in reception for more than ten minutes.

Managing and teaching diversity

As already argued, it is important to have a diverse workforce, particularly in the criminal justice sector, to represent all sections of society. This builds up trust in an organization, for example Allen (1998) highlights research that shows the importance of having black role models in professional and academic positions. Research in higher education found that minority ethnic people were suspicious of organizations where most of the academics were white; leading them to question their commitment to racial equality (Modood and Acland, 1998). The Race Relations (Amendment) Act,

2000 places a general duty on public authorities (including higher education institutions, Police and the Probation Service) to actively promote race equality. Recent progress has been made in the National Probation Service and by 2003 11.2% of probation officers were drawn from minority ethnic groups (Morgan, 2006). However, as with other agencies, the senior grades remain predominantly white.

It is important in all organizations for staff to have training in diversity issues; and particularly for teachers in higher education who are preparing people to work in the criminal justice sector. Training should cover the legal framework and what constitutes discrimination and knowledge of the key policies in organisations. Training also needs to value difference and diversity (Daniels and Macdonald, 2005). It should aim to raise awareness and should centre on changing attitudes, beliefs and views about groups that are different from the ones with which staff may normally associate. It should challenge what people have learned previously in terms of social learning theory and conditioning.

Core Elements of Diversity Training

- Knowledge about the legal framework and key organizational policies
- Facts and knowledge about different groups in society and the impact of discrimination on them
- Issues of power – the powerful and the powerless
- Experiential learning to engage with the personal feelings, values and perceptions of participants
- Methods and processes for running such training takes into account people's differing learning needs
- Use of a 'Diversity Workbook' such as those developed to assist students training to be probation officers/probation service officers
- Development of a personal action plan for anti-discriminatory practice

---

In many sectors of the criminal justice system some training on diversity issues is now provided. According to the Home Office (Home Office, 2007b) all new recruits to the police service, both police officers and administrative staff, are trained in communicating with people from diverse 'racial' groups. They also meet representatives from minority ethnic groups to discuss their experience of policing and what can be done to improve community relations. The Metropolitan Police (Home Office, 2007c) encourages staff to register their knowledge and/or membership of a community, which languages they speak, what life skills have been obtained as a result of their ethnic origin, sexual orientation or religion, and what their hobbies entail. Greater Manchester Police has a childcare voucher scheme to help with the balance between childcare responsibilities and work. South Wales and Greater Manchester police deploy gay officers to break down barriers between police and attendees at gay pride events. For further information see Rowe and Garland (2007), 'Police diversity training: a silver-bullet tarnished?'. They cite Foster, Newborn and Souhami (2005) who show that diversity training has reduced the use of racist language in the police force. However, diversity training cannot on its own confront structural issues within the organization.

It is important on all training and educational programmes that the different experiences of female, black and minority ethnic, lesbian and gay and differently 'abled' students are taken into account. Literature relating to different perspectives should be referred to; for example Chigwada- Bailey (1997) on black women's experience of the criminal justice system and Spalek (2002) on Islam, crime and criminal justice. It is also important to examine ethics and values and their relationship with work as a professional in the criminal justice setting. Using ethical frameworks (Banks, C., 2004) students can identify what theories they are drawing on to resolve dilemmas. It is important to use consultants or representatives from local agencies, such as lesbian, gay and bisexual support groups or trainers with different perspectives or world views (Clements and Jones, 2006). The importance of reflective practice (Schön, 1983 in Clements and Jones, 2006: 48) and inspiring students to consider different perspectives is paramount. Savin-Baden (2000:148) in her discourse on problem-based learning notes the importance of encouraging 'critical contestability'. Any form of education, but particularly diversity training should encourage students to think critically about accepted norms and practices in the workplace. Savin-Baden and Howell-Major (2004: 32) also discuss Freire (1972) and Mezirow's (1990) work on transformational learning where the aim is to change ideas, perspectives and pre-existing knowledge.

It appears to us that there are different 'orders' of training and policy development; some are primarily 'technical' and 'pragmatic' responses to diversity. The wider, conceptual issues require a much more thorough and experiential form of learning and there is an argument that this should and must be located within a higher education framework.

Conclusion

We have endeavoured to set out some of the discourse around the debates on 'diversity' and to unpack what it means for students and practitioners. We are concerned at the gulf between the political and policy driven use of the term, and the reality of its implementation within a practice setting. We have acknowledged the difference between the critical and reflective thinking arising from personal journeys exploring difference (supported by research evidence) and the pragmatic and more bureaucratic responses. Whilst both are needed we would argue that it is the former that ultimately will transform the workplace, whilst the latter might sometimes be misapplied or held up as examples of good practice whilst attitudes and behaviours remain unchallenged. We acknowledge that we have not answered the question why certain groups have been able to hold on to power at the expense of others. However, through the application of theory and the recognition of the relationship that criminology has with power we can identify that much of this is held in place by centuries of tradition, custom and law, and that change will inevitably be slow. We are, however, heartened by evidence of some very good practice emerging.

So how should both students and practitioners try to understand and make sense of the meanings and implications of this term 'diversity' for both their academic study and their potential work as practitioners? We suggest some guiding principles:

Guiding Principles

1 Good diversity policies and practice, informed by theory, should be viewed as an essential feature of all aspects of criminal justice policy and practice. This should be supported and sustained by strong management and monitoring procedures.
2 Training about and awareness raising of diversity needs to be complemented with an understanding about power and disadvantage.
3 Diversity can only be understood if the 'abstract' knowledge and evidence is combined with 'personal journeys' and 'subjectivism'.
4 The changing nature of language is a critical and necessary part of understanding diversity and demonstrating our growing awareness.
5 Whilst criminology has been slow to engage in some of these debates it can help to bring the evidence together and place it in a criminal justice context.

Key arguments

1 Diversity as a concept requires a commitment to increasing knowledge, understanding and self-awareness
2 'Diversity' is informed by different criminological perspectives but can only be really understood through an awareness of how power operates
3 Diversity as a concept can be used superficially, to address business effectiveness, or at a deep level to promote social justice
4 Effective criminal justice policy and practice requires us to understand the significance of diversity in an integrated way and to have a commitment to managing and teaching it within all criminal justice organisations

---

Further reading

For further exploration of the concepts of diversity and offending read Gelsthorpe and McIvor's chapter on 'Difference and Diversity' in the *Handbook of Probation* (2007). Lewis et al.'s (2006) 'Race and Probation' is quite a comprehensive text on 'race' and offending and Calverley et al. (2004) present important research findings. To pursue the themes of institutional discrimination read the Macpherson and Keith Reports on the deaths of Stephen Lawrence and Zahid Mubarek. Heidensohn (2006) writes in a contemporary context about gender and justice. We have been unsuccessful in tracking down any texts that directly link disability and crime, and sexuality and crime, but would recommend Oliver (1996) and the Stonewall website (http://www.stonewall.org.uk/) for further reading.

4

POLICING THE COMMUNITY IN THE 21ST CENTURY

Annette Crisp and Dave Ward

There is little dispassionate, thought-through, public examination of just what it is we are here to do in the 21st century—to fight crime or to fight its causes, to help build stronger communities or to undertake zero tolerance, nor of how these things should be done or what priority each should have or what we should stop doing.

(Sir Ian Blair, 2005)

Chapter summary

- Although its origins are grounded in the community, British policing has, driven by events, policy and strategy, developed many facets, some of which strain this relationship.
- Criminological insights point towards the efficacy of a community orientation. There are indications that the Government's Police Reform programme is taking this into account.
- Increasing diversity in the make-up of society, in social relationships and in the police service itself, presents a serious and continuing challenge for both policing practice and for the management of the service.
- Training reforms have a key part to play in developing an effective and responsive service capable of meeting the divergent and fluctuating challenges of the early 21st century.

This chapter will outline the challenges for policing in the 21st century, with consideration for the recent historical context and the insights of criminological theory. It will argue that the recent developments in the training of police officers provide an opportunity to reflect on the application of research and theory on policing operations and the relationship between the police and the community.

Recent police history

There has always been a strong tradition of community based policing in Britain, stretching back to the roots of the police in society itself. The link between the police and the community it serves has historically been strong. However, the 1960s brought structural changes of profound significance. Forces were amalgamated in order to develop greater efficiency and professionalism, a process which significantly strengthened national government's control and boosted the powers of the chief constables, enabling their use of operational discretion at the expense of the local community's direct control of local policing.

At the same time internal corruption scandals and gathering social, political and industrial dissent and unrest through the next two decades led to confrontations with political demonstrators and striking workers. The police force began increasingly to be perceived by the public as a bureaucratic, detached, insensitive organization willing to condone corruption within its own ranks but determined if necessary to use extreme force towards the public to uphold the law.

> The anti-Vietnam War demonstrations outside the American embassy in London in 1968 served to undermine public support for the police. Media coverage showed police horses charging down demonstrators and police wielding truncheons chasing groups of confused but generally inoffensive-looking demonstrators.

This trend gathered momentum in the 1980s during which Thatcherite policies for industrial and economic restructuring led to confrontations with the trade unions, reflected most rancorously and, at times, violently in the miners' strike of 1984. The police found themselves playing a significant but supporting role to unpopular government policies and, to fulfil the demands made upon them, working increasingly at a national rather than local level.

According to Reiner (1992: 769):

> Local accountability to police authorities has atrophied. It is being replaced by a degree of central control amounting to a de facto national force. Thus accountability has been transformed, rather than simply reduced. What is clear is that the perceived lack of adequate local accountability has been a major factor undermining police legitimacy in recent years.

Key events such as the Brixton riots, caused indirectly by Operation Swamp 81, which targeted Black youths in the capital, and the Toxteth riots in Liverpool, which again emerged out of community reaction to poor police practice in relation to the 'suss' laws, overshadowed positive aspects of policing and brought a spotlight on the police force as racist and lacking in community understanding.

The Broadwater farm riots in Tottenham were seen by some as a turning point. The deaths of PC Keith Blakelock and Cynthia Jarret sent shock waves throughout communities and the police alike. The socially deprived had been neglected by government's free market policy and, as its agents, the police were seen as—and increasingly felt themselves to be—alienated from the community.

The police **force** began to appreciate that it needed to reconceptualize itself to become a police **service** and to learn to more fully engage with its customers; the diverse and multi-ethnic communities it serves.

What this means and how to do it, in the context of its statutory obligations to detect and prevent crime and maintain law and order, has been the challenge the force has had to face and wrestle with over the past two decades. It remains unfinished business.

This task has been further complicated, since 9/11, by the rise and fear of transnational terrorism.

Policing and criminological theory

In his 2005 Dimbleby Lecture, Sir Ian Blair argues that there is little reflective, public debate about the role of the police (see quotation at the start of this chapter). Blair highlights a particular predicament. The mass media and political expediency appear to influence disproportionately policing policy and subsequently much of what officers are expected to undertake. However, we can draw from criminology more considered ideas as to what directions policing policy and practice might fruitfully take.

Criminological theorists of the right such as Murray (1990), would, for example, argue that, as criminal behaviour is part of an individually rational enterprise, the costs of potentially being caught by appropriate policing methods should outweigh the benefits. Control theory as proposed by Hirschi (1969), would furthermore propose that citizens have a general consensus of beliefs linked to societal values which become reflected in the idea that legislation develops for the benefit of the majority—those that abide by the law. Thus deviant behaviour, being 'chosen' by the individual, is properly the subject of societal mechanisms of control and sanction in which the police are at the forefront. Under this perspective the role and actions of our police, whose conduct is linked to maintaining the value set of the majority, is inherently closely aligned to the community they serve as they are protecting the interests of the 'mass'. This would suggest that the role of the police should not simply be detached as mechanistic law enforcement and social control but be substantially linked to proactive community-focused policing measures.

Interestingly, a left theoretical perspective as identified by proponents such as Young (1979) can lead to similar conclusions. For example, the 'left realists', while recognizing the structural factors that may lead to offending, stress the damage that offending does to working class people and their communities and would advocate policing approaches that would recognize and engage with these, pending wider policy changes to tackle the root causes of crime. They, thus, differ from the more thorough-going Marxist position (Hirst, 1975) which would see the police as an incorrigible obstacle to structural change, as agents of the existing dominant and oppressive order. Furthermore, within feminist and anti-racist perspectives as proposed by Millet (1977) and Bowling (1998), there is scope for engagement with policing and its institutions. The purpose is to overcome and change attitudes and practices which have oppressed and disadvantaged women and minority groups both as members of the police service and as recipients of its actions (see Brown, J., 2000 and 2005). Overall, then, the signposts are towards public and community engagement.

Embedded within the current Government's reform agenda for the British state is the theory of 'social capital', as articulated by the American sociologist Robert Putnam (2000). As such it has influenced thinking about policing. Social capital looks at 'bonding' and 'bridging' capital, enabling people to secure benefits as members of social networks, as a feature of communities and nations. The aim is to develop community cohesion by, for example, achieving the primary objective of developing more bridging capital within minority ethnic communities—against the straining benefits and the purported drawbacks of bonding capital in those communities.

Such concepts lead to incorporation, within the role of the police, of community and neighbourhood policing initiatives. These move the police into activities previously viewed as more the business of workers in the social welfare and community development fields. Arguably the 'iron fist' and 'velvet glove' then become blurred in the day-to-day practice of social control. For example, the authors have observed community support officers in some areas to being used increasingly for covert intelligence gathering rather than community engagement and reassurance, a trend reinforced by the Government's performance targets for the police.

Essentially Putnam (1993) defined social capital in terms of four characteristics which enhance cohesion:

- the existence of community networks
- civic engagement (participation in these community networks)
- local identity and a sense of solidarity and equality with other community members and
- norms of trust and reciprocal help and support.

However, as Hawton et al. (1999: 34) note, this may be a rather romantic view:

> In reality, communities are not always comfortable homogenous entities. They are crosscut by a variety of divisions—race, gender, and class—and contain a multitude of groups whose interests may conflict with each other. In the most divided communities, these conflicts may be played out violently or through such behaviour as racial harassment.

Indeed, recent societal concerns over the terrorist threat have polarized public opinion against certain members of society, identified primarily by their faith and race. Thus groups, which have already identified themselves as outsiders, sense they are disenfranchised and now, additionally, find themselves vilified and specifically targeted for surveillance and precipitate intrusion as potential perpetrators of terrorism.

A Metropolitan Police Authority report (2006) has noted:
Asian communities feel threefold victimhood: they are equal victims of the bombings; they are victims of the backlash in terms of racially motivated crime; and they perceive themselves to be victims of racial profiling in terms of counter-terrorist policing.

Thus, whatever might be the theoretical signals, policing, like so much public policy, is in practice driven by events and less rational and discernible forces.

Criminologists have also identified different models of policing, and these will be discussed in the next section. Within these models, all of which currently exist and, indeed, operate side by side, can be seen the ebbs and flows and intermingling of public expectation, government policy and the self-interest of the police service itself.

It is evident that they do not necessarily sit comfortably together but that there would be too high a political and professional price to pay in surrendering or overprioritizing any one of them.

Key models of policing

Community policing

Community policing was introduced as a reaction to the 'crime fighter mentality' of the 1970s, and as response to the public reaction to initiatives such as Operation Swamp in 1981 and the subsequent recommendations by Lord Scarman's enquiry (Scarman, 1981). It demands a policing attitude that emphasizes community support for and cooperation with the police in their role of preventing crime. It additionally stresses a police role that is less centralized and more proactive. Driven by the Crime and Disorder Act 1998 this process is manifest in the recognition that, whilst remaining a professional organization, the police are a *service* with responsibilities to local communities. As such they are authorized and encouraged to develop a more intimate relationship with those they serve and to exercise their discretionary power as opposed to the enforcement requirements of performance focused policing.

This is seen as positive by Leigh, Read and Tilley (1996: 200): 'Types of police involvement in a community focused role resolve many of the critical issues that have formerly dogged the police as public servants; such as aspects of fear, suspicion and respect for community values'.

Community policing can be viewed as a return to policing roots.

Zero tolerance policing

Addressing community issues from another angle is 'zero tolerance policing'. This approach is based upon 'broken windows' theory of Wilson and Kelling (1982), who argue that: 'One un-repaired broken window is a signal that no one cares, and so breaking more windows costs nothing'.

By focusing policing on 'quality of life' issues the resulting impact intends not only to improve the environment and reduce crime overall but in so doing to build bridges with the community.

In supporting the principles of this theory, much has been made of the practical examples provided by the work of Bratton and Knobler (1998) in the USA, and others, including former Detective Superintendent Ray Mallon of Middlesborough, whose crime reduction claims and subsequent influence over local crime reduction gained him the title of 'Robocop'.[1]

---

[1]According to Reform as a result, between 1994 and 1996, the total of reported crimes fell by 27 per cent, thefts of vehicles fell by 56 per cent and domestic burglaries fell by 31 per cent.

This process, however, is to its critics not without cost in, for example, escalating the significance of minor misbehaviour and prematurely criminalizing minor, often young, offenders, who might otherwise desist in the course of growing up. Worse, it may draw away attention from and allow for the escalation of more serious crimes.

Lott (2000) criticizes zero tolerance policing for inconsistent results and, in revisiting the initial claims, Harcourt and Ludwig (2006) find: 'No support for a simple first-order disorder/crime relationship as hypothesized by Wilson and Kelling, nor that broken windows policing is the optimal use of scarce law enforcement resources'.

Intelligence-led policing

Intelligence-led policing, also known as proactive policing, proposes that the aim of policing should be its involvement in a cycle of proactivity which focuses upon the securing and management of intelligence to generate target areas for the strategic management and application of police practice.

In the UK, the National Intelligence Model (NIM) thus engages with four elements or 'products', defined as analysis, intelligence, knowledge and systems.

In essence they establish identification of targets (offenders or offences), advise on the development of intelligence, initiate related crime-pattern analysis and develop both tactical initiatives against targets and partnerships with other agencies.

Criticized by Sir Michael Bichard in his 2004 report in the wake of the Soham murders (Bichard, 2004), NIM has been subject to review because of the fragility of both the data and processing systems upon which it depends.

Professional policing

The professional model of policing tends towards detachment from the community in favour of attention to specialized aspects of performance and process in fighting crime and the exclusive authority of the police professional. This style of policing was very popular in the 1970s but was challenged by strategies which favour the community as public disquiet with this detached approach grew.

In essence the key components of the professional policing model are tools such as the Policing Performance Assessment Framework (PPAF), Professionalising the Investigation Process (PIP) and National Occupational Standards. It necessarily links to a reduced emphasis on the social service function of police, with resources and strategies directed towards crime control. Limits are placed on police discretion which may be perceived by the public as an over-emphasis on the legal authority of the police and on following guidelines.

A Big Brother Society?

Centralised, procedure-driven police departments promote a certain distance between police officers and citizens.[2] Although a quick response to calls for service may be made possible by technological advances and innovations such as CCTV, rapid response units and centralized

Continued

A Big Brother Society?—cont'd

command, the office-based procedures which accompany the monitoring and processing of offences remove officers from the streets to undertake 'administration'. Although these may represent aspects of strategies to deter and respond to criminal activity, they can 'spill over', into what the public perceive as a 'Big Brother' society where all movements are observed [3] and a police force operates behind predominantly closed doors, be they mobile (speeding, siren-wailing, squad cars) or increasingly centralized fortress-like operational centres.

The New Labour government's focus on managing the public services, including the police, through performance targets has reinforced this model. The need to place a tick in the appropriate box of performance, in particular meeting targets for arrests, has not only created tensions with alternative policing approaches but also with other parts of the criminal justice system. According to the former Chair of the Youth Justice Board, Professor Rod Morgan[4] this has meant effectively criminalizing some members of the community to ensure that arrest targets are met. Certainly at a 'beat' level it provides officers with fewer opportunities to use discretionary powers.

Problem orientated policing (POP)

Goldstein's (1975) theory of problem solving involves the police acting to resolve problems in the community rather than just simply responding to calls. POP, it was suggested, would enable officers to move beyond incident response towards endeavouring to control or resolve the root causes of particular instances of recurring crime or disorder. Under this model officers should examine the long- term implications of the situation or problem by, for example, analyzing patterns of offending in an area and interviewing residents to determine the reasons for an area becoming a scene of offending. As a result of such analysis and investigations, plans involving (where appropriate) other public and voluntary organizations could be put into place aimed at preventing further criminal activity.

Neighbourhood policing

The government has recently committed its police service to 'neighbourhood policing' initiatives. This model is based on the notion of local priorities being identified by local people as the issues that need to be dealt with in their area and police and partners working together to tackle them.

The focus of this model is the drawing together of communities and agencies to resolve local problems (National Policing Improvement Agency, 2007). Strongly emphasized is

---

[2]The result of increased use of car patrols as opposed to foot patrols.
[3]According to Liberty Britain is monitored by 4 million CCTV cameras, making us the most watched nation in the world. There is one CCTV camera for every 14 people in the UK. If you live in London you are likely to be on camera 300 times a day.
[4]Rod Morgan (26 January 2007) BBC Newsnight 'Government targets for bringing offences to justice are having "perverse consequences" by swelling prisoner numbers unnecessarily'.

police officers visibly spending time within neighbourhoods getting to know local people, understanding their views of their problems and needs and building a policing response accordingly. It is seen as a particularly important and appropriate approach for creating good relationships and effective policing in multi-ethnic areas (HMIC, 1997) and is intended to counter the negative consequences of perceived detachment and alienation associated with the professional model outlined above.

Private policing

Up to now, the picture presented of British policing is of an institution, for the most part controlled and directed by central government and responsive to its policy imperatives. However, in the USA more decentralized and localized democratic institutions have allowed the formation of a diversity of policing bodies grounded in local municipal structures or, indeed, private organisations. At the public level, such diversity has largely disappeared from British policing, only remaining residually by way of the railway police (the British Transport Police), the Parks Police and the City of London force. In recent years the private sector has made a considerable comeback to assert its presence through a rapid expansion of the security industry.

There is inevitably a tension between commercial pressures and a public service. Measures linked to profit and loss have to be met—although some would argue that the introduction by government of targets and performance indicators, with associated penalties and rewards, has had the same effect in the public sector.

Shearing and Stenning (1983) have linked the growth of uniformed private security to the post-World War Two boom in property ownership. It is not surprising perhaps that in the UK of the 1980s this linked to the Thatcherite insistence on the positive values of the free market as opposed to the inadequacies and inefficiencies of public services. While private security firms are taken for granted in the protection of commercial property and in the movement of money and high value products, they have come to be hired privately to patrol residential neighbourhoods.

As Wakefield (2004: 531–2) suggests:

> 'By resorting to private methods of order maintenance rather than relying on assistance from the police, property owners are better placed to ensure that policing strategies within their territories complement their profit-maximisation objectives'.

As a matter of policy, privatization has also entered the public aspects of policing. The Posen Review (1994) examined the most cost effective methods of delivering core policing services and assessed the opportunities to 'release resources currently absorbed by peripheral non-essential tasks or by finding more cost effective methods of delivering core tasks'. Thus, responsibilities such as court security, electronic surveillance through CCTV and some aspects of road traffic management have been contracted out.

The Police Reform Act (2002) embedded the concept of 'extended policing role partnerships'. Under this legislation, chief constables were permitted to authorize discretionary powers to be held by local authority employed neighbourhood wardens on accredited schemes and, in parallel, to develop within forces the new role of the Police Community Support Officer. Thus, in addition to the contracting out of services to be undertaken by private security, decentralization has introduced a more community focused aspect to service provision.

Loader (1999) examined the impact of 'consumerism' on the services expected of the police. He contends that the commodification of policing and security can fruitfully be theorized and investigated in terms of the impact of the spread, more generally, of a consumerist culture. He argues that while there may be limits to the spread of commercially-delivered policing and security, the introduction of a 'consumer attitude' and a mixed market in this field has created a space for the development of modes of policing increasingly shaped by citizens acting through new democratic forms.

Policing in the 21st century

The past few years has seen an unprecedented spate of government enquiries, Green and White Papers and legislation geared towards reforming and 'modernizing' the police. There is even a special government website (www.policereform.gov.uk) devoted to the topic. The thrust of the reform agenda as set out by government is to increase community engagement, strengthen accountability and modernize the workforce.

The Government's Vision for the Police

In early 2007 the then Home Secretary, John Reid, outlined his vision for the police (Home Office, 2007d: 2):

I want a police service which is:
- *Trusted and respected everywhere: which serves locally and protects nationally* Trust is the bedrock of policing and the police act with the consent of citizens and communities. Trust drives effective policing and, in turn, generates respect.
- *Accountable and public facing* Many police operations will be out of the public view, but the delivery of neighbourhood policing must be driven by public need and expectations.
- *Collaborative, working in partnership with other forces and authorities and with other partners* Jointly many things can be achieved that cannot be achieved alone. More and more, the need to work with other forces and agencies to identify and solve problems will come to the fore in order to tackle the local and national challenges we face.

In this section we will draw upon the key models of police activity to present a framework for contemporary policy and practice and for understanding its role at this juncture in the 21st century.

Bowling (2005), in reviewing aspects of policing in the Caribbean, has developed the categories of *Bobby, Bond* and *Babylon* to identify key dimensions of policing practice in that region; community policing, intelligence gathering and armed response. We believe they can be equally apt when applied to expectations of officers in the British context.

Bobby?

Community policing has always been perceived as the badge on the helmet of British policing, so much so that the British brand of community policing and public engagement has been exported worldwide.

Community policing in its purest form is composed of two main strands; community partnership and problem solving, in other words knowing a community sufficiently well in order to be in a position both to support it and protect it against threats to its well-being. Similarly, according to Kelling (1988: 2–3), the role of the police in this setting is: 'to stimulate and buttress a community's ability to produce attractive neighbourhoods and protect them against predators', a goal which all parties can agree upon and share.

Oettmeier (1992) describes this process as being part of the functional continuum of policing—reactive, proactive and co-active, with the co-active function being key to the success of community partnerships. Consultation should, it is suggested, be one of the more straightforward aspects of a community relationship.

Jones and Newburn (2001) explored aspects of police public relationships in more testing circumstances when investigating relationships with 'hard to reach groups'. Contrary to the principle of co-action this research suggested that:

> A clear and explicit statement of the objectives of consultation is somewhat rare both in the police service and within community groups. It is often assumed that the purpose of consultation is self evident and unproblematic. The research suggested that police and community participants in consultative mechanisms approached them with different general objectives.
>
> (Jones and Newburn 2001: 9)

The Strategic Plan for Criminal Justice 2004–2008 and a wealth of additional Home Office generated reports (e.g. 2004b, 2007d) and papers have sought to embed the ethos of partnership working both within official organizations and within the community. However, criminal justice organizations and the police service remain widely distrusted, according to social commentators and researchers.

Dunningham and Norris (1996) found that the prevalent distrust of police, detected by the Lawrence Inquiry within BME communities, was much more widespread.

Expressed vividly, their view is that:

> crime is facilitated as well as repressed; criminals are licensed to commit crime rather than apprehended for their violations; police rule bending is often organisationally condoned rather than condemned; police morale is sapped as well as boosted; relationships with colleagues are based on distrust and secrecy rather than honesty and openness; the courts are deceived, defendants misled, and in the end justice is as likely to be undermined rather than promoted.
>
> (Dunningham and Norris, 1996: 407)

In understanding the difficulties and contradictions in generating community trust and embedding community engagement, police culture, especially those aspects highlighted by Skolnick (1966), is a phenomenon which needs to be considered. Skolnick suggests that policing is based culturally on two concepts namely 'danger' and 'authority'. These concepts require officers to protect themselves from the outside world which consequently means at times they must close ranks to protect 'their own' in spite of discomfort with some of the more 'unhelpful' characteristics of their colleagues.

> It is not difficult to occupy the job as long as you do what they want. It is not difficult to occupy the job if you keep your head down. When it becomes difficult to hold the job is when you start questioning their views and their opinions.
>
> Anonymous research respondent (Purwar, 2003)

In this context, it is necessary to consider the impact of diversity on what has traditionally been, according to Waddington (1999: 298) and others, culturally, the domain of 'real men'.

Much has been written about the police 'canteen culture' and the need to break it down in order to ensure a diminution of a macho and ethnocentric 'can do' organisation. The conclusion of the Morris Report (2004), comissioned to investigate the workings of the Metropolitan Police Force, stated that:

> There is no common understanding of diversity within the organisation and it is not embedded in the culture of the Metropolitan Police Service. We fear that it remains, at worse, a source of fear and anxiety and, at best, a process of ticking boxes.

In her research on behalf of the British Association of Police Women, Purwar (2003) notes:

> The cliquey buddy nature of the institutional structures means that senior officers who are made aware of unacceptable behaviour are confronted with dealing with long time colleagues who have become friends. One interviewee who had experienced an officer trying to rip off her stockings in a patrol car described how the Sergeant was reluctant to deal with the perpetrators of a continual litany of sexual harassment because they were his friends. On another occasion she found that the Police Federation representative was a friend of the offending officer.

The modern police service claims to have a more equitable view of minorities within its ranks. However in recent years and this has been challenged by the experiences of Leroy Logan and Ali Dizaei, both senior officers in the Metropolitan Police. Both have found it necessary to defend disciplinary actions taken against them by their police employers as unfounded and racially motivated (Dizaei and Phillips, 2007).

The intermeshed nature of networks within the police makes it difficult for already objectified and marginalized voices to be heard and taken seriously. In addition, the risks of further isolation in a police culture, in which many BME and female staff already feel separate, can cause extreme anguish when taking the decision to complain. Thus the anticipated backlash encourages staff to suffer in silence (Purwar, 2003).

The prevalence of racist language and banter found by studies in the late 1990s, which, like sexism, had not been addressed by senior officers, had significantly declined by 2004, five years after the Stephen Lawrence Enquiry, according to a study by Foster et al. (2005). According to some white officers, however, this was not a response to culture change requirements but more about the atmosphere of 'political correctness'.

> Although the general excision of racist language from the police service is an important and marked change, it raises the question of the extent to which this is indicative of changes in the culture and practices in the police service more broadly.
>
> Foster et al. (2005: 38)

By focusing on what they see as the six strands of diversity most relevant to police work, namely; gender, race, sexual orientation, age, faith and disability, the focus of the police has been to ensure that diversity training targets have been met (HMIC, 2003a). With the advent of National Occupational Standards the development of awareness and understanding has been distilled into a series of performance competences. The work of Foster et al. (2005) suggests that, as long as the police service simply focuses upon visible behaviour without evidence of real understanding there is a danger that there will be a cadre of officers who can 'talk the talk', without the need to 'walk the walk'.

Bond?

The association here is with *James Bond*, the agent who 'saves' the world through a combination of cool personality, high intelligence and physical prowess. Perhaps more apposite would be *Inspector Morse*, the cerebral detective. The picture common to both is of highly professional police activity focused around the crime, the scene of crime and the criminal.

In its 2004 White Paper (Home Office, 2004b: 25), the Government committed itself to a police service:

> freed up from bureaucratic burdens with unnecessary paperwork removed but maintaining a professional, accountable, thorough approach to apprehending offenders; with more officers and police staff being on the front line supported by better IT and scientific improvements.

In 2003 the Home Office, with partners in CENTREX, (from April 2007 the National Policing Improvement Agency (NPIA)) and the Police Standards and Skills Organisation (PSSO, now Skills for Justice) launched its 'PIP' initiative—Professionalising the Investigation Process. This initiative set in motion a process of development and reform through the establishment of transparent standards of best practice. Furthermore, this initiative identified a number of expected outcomes, including; improved public confidence in investigation, increased accountability in investigations, improved attrition rates and improved detection rates. The aim overall was to ensure that the investigative process became, 'more professional, ethical and effective for both officers and support staff involved in investigations' (Home Office, 2003a).

PIP provides a series of training programmes for individuals involved in investigation, and according to CENTREX (NPIA, 2007):

> Our training and development programmes form the career pathway for investigators. They have been designed based on Core Investigative Doctrine and the identified investigative National Occupational Standards.

However research suggests that within the investigation process there may be some disharmony which can negatively impact upon effective outcomes. For example, Williams (2005) identifies the following concerns in relation to one aspect of crime detection work:

> BCU [area] commanders failed to fully understand the potential of scientific support provision . . . Only some forces facilitated meetings which emphasised the co-accountability of divisional investigators and Scientific Support Unit staff . . . On the one hand, emphasis was placed on seeing Scientific Support Unit staff as expert collaborators within the investigative process. On the other, scientific support staff were seen principally as providing technical assistance to investigators . . . When viewed mainly as technical assistants, integration mainly involved placing Crime Scene Examiners within police hierarchies rather than within the investigative process.

Effective police investigation ought to gain momentum from a number of sources. For instance, the National Intelligence Model (NIM) should also make a significant impact on achieving an effective investigatory process. However, John and Maguire (2003) remind us that the big 'if' surrounding the NIM is whether those driving its implementation will be able to overcome familiar obstacles to translating intentions into reality. Not least, they say, is the passive resistance among police middle managers and officers arising from the challenge which the rigorous analytical approach, and even the 'alien' tone and language of the model, represent to traditional police cultures and ways of working.

A further aspect of the challenge was revealed in research commissioned by the Home Office to more fully understand what a police officer actually did on a typical shift. The findings were intended to be utilized as part of the police reform process. The resulting *Diary of a Police Officer* (PA Consulting Group, 2001) indicated that rather than being employed in reassurance policing or in the prevention or investigation of crime, police officers spent almost half of their working time in the police station on 'administration'.

One Officer's Perspective

An internet blog site for police officers records:

> My job is to transfer paper into a box labelled 'detections' whilst at the same time complying with the latest rules set down by crime auditors. . . What possible relevance does an e-mail exhorting me to put criminals behind bars have to do with me, an ordinary policeman?. . . Honestly. Criminals? Behind Bars? They'll be asking me to leave the office next.
>
> (Policeman's Blog, 2006)

In reality, and in spite of the best of intentions and government's desire to profession-alize the service, rather than investigating crime, police officers are still more likely to be seen engaged in office tasks as opposed to applying an understanding of practical investigation techniques (Cavendish, 2007).

Babylon?

The potentially problematic term 'Babylon' (see Barrett, 1977) is used here in a very general sense to represent a state which is viewed by some of its members as oppressive and discriminatory: the state itself perceiving such members as threatening its continuing existence and requiring the strongest forms of defensive action.

That the British police are not armed has been both an 'article of faith' and, internationally, a key distinguishing feature of British policing. While the focused deployment of firearms specialists has been accepted for many years, it is only since 9/11 that armed police have become a common and highly visible presence, re-characterized as providing reassurance to the public rather than fearful and frightening. Babylon—the armed response—is very much with us.

A country facing terrorism often organizes its entire policy framework to combat terror. Further, governments curb civil liberties and some tend to use terror as an excuse to justify authoritarianism. This results in the discounting of the democratic principle and, some argue, underdevelopment and more terrorism. Indeed, in 2004 the then Home Secretary was described by a political commentator (Jenkins, 2004) as the 'judicial equivalent of a football hooligan' for his personal attacks on judges, civil rights campaigners and political figures who opposed his demand for more powers. Coming at a time in history when technological and scientific advances have made surveillance and control easier and more effective, such developments were seen as particularly threatening.

The police, it is argued, require all legal and physical resources possible in order that society at large might be protected. However, the Serious and Organised Crime and Police Act 2005 focuses not simply upon aspects of the terrorist threat but additionally includes five sections that strengthen the existing legislation with respect to Anti-social Behaviour Orders, as introduced by the Crime and Disorder Act 1998. Legislation such as the Regulation of Investigatory Powers Act 2000 (RIPA), which focuses upon directed and intrusive surveillance, and the Terrorism Act 2000 have been perceived by some as in direct conflict with human rights. Some would argue that, when linked to existing powers provided by the Police and Criminal Evidence Act, 1984 (PACE), the inception of which, ironically, was as the result of government's concern to ensure more open communication between police and public, we may be a society potentially at risk from overregulation at the expense of our freedom.

This has been highlighted in more recent questioning of the development of a DNA database in relation to which the Human Genetics Commission, the government's independent DNA watchdog, has set up a public enquiry. Baroness Kennedy of the Shaws QC, chairwoman of the Commission, has said: 'The police in England and Wales have powers, unrivalled internationally, to take a DNA sample from any arrested individual, without their consent'. This inquiry has been set up as a result of what the shadow Home Secretary David Davis has stated is inconceivable:

> that the powers of the police could be extended without a serious and substantive debate in Parliament. They have already encroached on people's privacy without proper debate on this matter and this can go no further.
>
> (Times online, 2007).

According to the government strategy known as 'CONTEST' (Home Office, 2006c), the prime focus of its counter-terrorist initiative is a concentration upon international terrorist threats through the four principle strands of prevent, pursue, protect and prepare. The prevent strand specifically identifies radical Muslims as the main threat to security and has as such made a distinction between the internal and external threats from terror. Thus:

> The principal current terrorist threat is from radicalised individuals who are using a distorted and unrepresentative version of the Islamic faith to justify violence. Such people are referred to in this paper as Islamist terrorists. They are, however, a tiny minority within the Muslim communities here and abroad. Muslim communities themselves do not threaten our security; indeed they make a great contribution to our country.
>
> (Home Office, 2006a: 3)

Animal rights activists and other domestic threats, who may equally resort to direct violence and bombing, are monitored by the National Extremism Tactical Coordination Unit (NETCU). NETCU has a national policing responsibility to provide intelligence and advice on issues of domestic extremism and terror.

Training and culture change

As has been described, criminological knowledge, research and insights do add considerably to the understanding of police practice. If policing is based upon a shifting platform of external events, societal expectations and associated legislative changes, how can a suitable training programme be developed which might meet the requirements of current circumstances and also provide a police officer with a foundation which provides a sound basis for a whole career?

The adoption of the recommendations of the HMIC Report *Training Matters* (2002) and the subsequent closure of police training colleges in the UK have provided an opportunity for the police with, in some areas, their further and higher education partners, to develop and test out new approaches to training. Initial anecdotal evidence suggests that where the police service has decided to work within further and higher education organizations, while there have been some conflicts caused by two radically different cultures coming together, a new more critical and culturally aware and sensitive police professionalism is emerging.

Until the recent changes in police training in the UK, few British researchers appear to have considered the impact of education on aspects of ability and performance in policing. Exceptions are the educationalists, John Elliott and Saville Kushner (2003) and John Davies. For a number of years, they have advocated changes in training which, whilst maintaining a substantial element of the traditional focus on 'learning on the job', would also instil an awareness of society, of ethics and of values, through the development of the so-called 'academic' skills of critical and reflective analysis and an openness to continuing career-long learning. In short, training must produce officers intellectually and practically ready to cope effectively in a rapidly changing social and work environment. Especially, they should have the capacity to deal creatively and safely with incidents the circumstances of which cannot be predicted in advance and which demand responses outside routine and prescribed procedure. This, it is argued, is the nature of the professionalism to which the service needs to aspire.

However, the idea of academic training risks attracting the criticism that officers are not being properly prepared for core frontline work. In this sense, White (2006: 389) has argued that the police service has for many years been 'proceeding down an intellectual cul-de-sac', in that:

> it has failed to engage in a debate over ends having substituted for this simplistic discussion over 'means'. . . . There has been a failure to deliberate over the values of our society and the part the police service is expected to play in it.

Ward and Crisp's (2004) research on the Home Office proposals for change in police training, based on the Initial Police Learning and Development Programme (IPLDP), identified similar tendencies. They argued for a greater concern for, and attention to, the process of learning and for the adoption of modern teaching and learning methods instead of a stultifying 'force-feeding' of factual knowledge and the mechanistic auditing of 'performance competences'. Where the IPLDP has been interpreted and developed by forces in partnership with university course providers, there have been opportunities to incorporate a new learning process, enabling student officers to begin to debate the fundamental issues to which White refers. Such learning is key to the culture change requirements required by the modern police service.

It remains to be seen how far such changes to initial training can be an effective driver for service culture and practice change. Some early anecdotal evidence from the Foundation Degree in Policing at De Montfort University indicates that new student officers are making positive impact in this direction.

Senior officers say that they are already noticing that the new trainees are not only well versed in the practicalities but have a much wider grasp of the social context of policing.

Theory into Practice

It has been the tradition within the police force that newly qualified officers coming through training should update their more experienced area-based colleagues on the latest law. Feedback from shifts has been that the University based trainees are not only up to speed on such knowledge but are presenting this in the wider context of social and community issues. A pertinent example was where a student officer was involved at an incident requiring intervention among a group of young people. Urged by his Tutor Constable to go in assertively it was reported that he commented, drawing from research presented in teaching, that there was evidence that young people's later criminal careers were adversely affected if initial contact with the police was negative. This fashioned the way the incident was handled.

Conclusion

Underlying the Government's agenda for change in policing is recognition that the police can no longer exercise, on society's behalf, the responsibility for social order and control. In line with its communitarian vision outlined earlier 'policing' has to be more widely dispersed throughout the community. At one end of a continuum of crime seriousness it means the community being responsible for resolving minor incidents and low levels of disorder; at the other end, where terrorism is the extreme example, it means having reliable and confident channels of intelligence from the population to assist the effective prevention, detection and control of more serious crime and the maintenance of security from outside threats. Bobby, Bond and Babylon are inextricably interlinked.

The Home Secretary certainly sees it so (Home Office, 2007d: 1):

> It falls to the police service to deliver neighbourhood policing that is accessible and responsive to local people's priorities, while at the same time meeting the threat from serious crime and terrorism. Both are important to the public and are two sides of the same coin. Neither task can or should be downgraded.

Neyourd (2003: 593) argues that the move to public participation in policing, and a police service much more integrated into the community, implies a philosophical shift from leading or controlling to 'enabling', a recognition that good policing entails interdependence with the community and other agencies.

The platform for such an approach is community and neighbourhood policing. In this, as we have seen, the predominant duty of the police is to work in partnership with members of the public and community organizations to promote community responsibility, seeking in the process to gain public confidence and trust so as to facilitate and support the 'harder end' enforcement aspects of the police role.

However, as Neyourd suggests, the circle does not square too easily. It is difficult to see what the right choices would be for controversial areas such as covert surveillance, the use of force, the policing of diverse communities, in which conflicts of 'rights' (suspect, victim, police officer or community) are most clearly exposed (593).

Clearly, as Sir Ian Blair recognized, the challenges facing the police in the 21st century cannot be underestimated. The public has high expectations and, individually, any residual deference to authority is balanced by a consciousness of individual rights and expectations of accountability. As technology advances, forms of crime become ever more complex. In addition, there is the real threat of terrorism, be it 'domestic' or international in conception and strategy. Future developments in police research, practice and training will need to take account of the requirement to balance all these complex issues.

Key arguments

- Whilst historically the focus of the police has been based within the local community over time this focus has become detached, driven by political expediency and performance targets.
- As the nature, expectation and content of society at a macro level and community locally has evolved, the police as an organization caught at the sharp end of the demands of criminal justice have found it difficult to respond. This has become most apparent in the area of diversity awareness, an area which the police service has taken steps to rectify.
- The opportunities provided by police reform (in relation to training in particular) *may* provide newly attested police officers and members of the extended police family with enhanced skills, training and developmental opportunities to better equip them to deal with the dynamic nature of policing in the 21st century.

Further reading

The *Handbook of Policing* (2003) edited by Tim Newburn provides a comprehensive overview of policing issues and links to criminological theory. Peter Joyce's (2006) book, *Criminal Justice*, effectively covers the whole criminal justice system and includes helpful material on policing.

5

PRISONS AND PENAL POLICY

Azrini Wahidin and Jenny Ardley

The ultimate expression of law is not order—it's prison. We have hundreds upon hundreds of prisons, and thousands upon thousands of laws, yet there is no social order, no social peace.

(Jackson, 1972: 52)

The object of penal reformers should be not to reform the prison system, but to abolish it.

Fenner Brockway (1926)

Chapter summary

This chapter:
- Explores the current controversies and problems within our modern prison system.
- Critically appraises key developments in penal history.
- Addresses concerns surrounding the challenges facing the prison system.
- Applies criminological theory, policy and practice to the role of imprisonment.
- Examines abolitionism and argues that the abolitionist approach offers an alternative vision of how we as a society deal with wrongdoing—a vision which contrasts starkly with traditional models of penality.

Introduction

Prisons and imprisonment are key issues in criminal justice and are a highly politicized area of the field. This chapter aims to highlight some of the key issues and challenges in the development of imprisonment and critically appraises the extent to which prison can be considered to work. In doing so the chapter pays particular attention to women prisoners and older prisoners. The chapter also explores the impact of prison conditions on prisoners' experiences of imprisonment by focusing on inspection reports relating to one prison. The chapter concludes by exploring abolitionist perspectives, arguing that we should begin to look beyond alternatives to imprisonment by considering abolition. As such, this chapter considers a question central to criminologists, politicians and policy makers, namely: 'what are prisons for?'

Background

The etymology of the word prison comes from the Latin word meaning to 'seize'. The place itself is defined as a building to which people are legally committed for custody while awaiting trial or punishment. Based on the above definition, prisons have been with us for many centuries. It is important to remember from the outset that if there is no one history of prisons and imprisonment, neither can we claim that there is a linear history of reform. The transition from punishing the body to punishing the soul, known as the 'great transformation' of punishment, was a reflection of enlightenment ideas: a growing sensibility to the excesses of punishment such as; branding, the gallows, transportation, and penal servitude with hard labour. Moreover, the early prisons were characterized by disorder, disease and squalor (*'squalor carceris'*—the squalor of the prison) which led penal reformers such as John Howard to raise the questions, what are prisons for and what is their purpose? When thinking about imprisonment and other institutional responses we should never be complacent about our grounds for punishing. It is often far from self-evident whether prison itself can actually achieve any or all of its aims, and the price to be paid in achieving them remains an unresolved argument (Bottoms, 1995; Sim, 2004).

By the end of the 16th century, transportation to the colonies and penal servitude with hard labour were introduced. Until the 17th century prisons were used to hold people who were in the midst of a legal process. This included waiting to be tried, being held until an amount of money was paid for a debt or a fine, waiting to be sent into exile or until execution. There is a broad agreement among prison historians that before the 17th century the notion of sending offenders to prison as a punishment itself rarely occurred (Fox, 1952), although some commentators have suggested that this did happen, at least from the 13th century for: 'fraud, contempt, disobedience to authority, failure in public duty and petty crime' (McConville, 1998: 2). From the late 16th century in England there was a network of houses of correction, or Bridewells, around the country. Morris and Rothman (1995: 83) state that by the early 17th century there were 170 such institutions. These were used primarily for vagrants and those who were unable to support themselves. Moreover, they were not generally used for ordinary criminals.

The prisons of the 18th century stood in complete contrast to the well-ordered prisons of today. Diseases, such as typhus, were rife. It was seldom easy to distinguish those who belonged in the prison from those who did not. It was only the symbolic tools of the gaolers, i.e. the presence of irons, handcuffs and other symbols of incarceration that differentiated the prisoners from the keepers. Some of the prisoners who could pay the 'keeper' or 'gaoler' lived in ease while others suffered in squalor. Prisons, as Howard (1929, 1977) recorded, were characterized by lack of light, air, sanitation, washing facilities and general cleanliness.

The earliest house of corrections was probably the Bridewell in London, established in 1557. Houses of correction combined the principles of individual reformation and punishment. The usual inmates were able-bodied beggars, vagrants, prostitutes and thieves. However, as the reputation of the institutions became established, more serious offenders, as well as the poor and the needy, were interned. Mannheim (1939) and McConville (1998) both state that houses of correction were the first examples of modern imprisonment: a point underlined by Spierenburg's (1991) preference for calling such institutions 'prison workhouses'. The houses of correction and Bridewells already combined the idea of discipline, work and punishment, in a way which was more readily identified with 19th century reforms. If the houses of correction were a significant area of experimentation into secondary punishments, transportation to the American colonies was just as important. Both initiatives were part of the same search for an alternative intermediate punishment at a time when there was little choice between the scaffold and branding.

The Victorian prison

Following his inspections, John Howard recommended that secure, sanitary and cellular accommodation be provided; that prisoners be separated and classified according to offence: that useful labour be introduced and the sale of alcohol prohibited. In 1816 the first national penitentiary at Millbank was opened. By 1842 Pentonville Prison became the model prison based on a regime of silence and solitude. For a regime that was intended to individualize punishment it did its best to erase any trace of individuality. Prisoners wore hoods when they emerged from their cells. They were issued with standard prison uniforms. Numbers replaced their names. They had separate stalls in chapel as well as separate exercise yards. Pentonville represented the apotheosis of the idea that a totally controlled environment could produce a reformed and autonomous individual. The regime was based on the belief that improvement and reformation could only be achieved through work, harsh physical conditions, education and religious strategies.

The Prison Act of 1898 resulted in what we in terms of today know as the prison. The Prison Act restricted the use of corporal punishment, created three classes of prisoner and introduced remission of sentence for local prisoners. The following year the rule of total silence was abolished. The process of the liberalization of the treatment of prisoners, which was ushered in with the Gladstone Report and embraced by the Liberal Government that came into office in 1908, saw a number of Acts implemented, such as the Probation of Offenders Act of 1907 (the Act provided the legal framework for the probation service). The Gladstone Report introduced two important changes to the prison system. The first was preventive detention, which allowed courts to impose an additional sentence of 5–10 years on habitual offenders. The provision remained on statute until the Criminal Justice Act of 1967. The second was the introduction of a sentence of between one and three years for young men between the ages of 16 and 21 years, with the date of release being dependent on good conduct and response to progress through a series of 'grades'. The first unit for young men under this new sentence was opened in Borstal prison in Rochester. Thereafter, the sentence became known as Borstal training, which remained in existence until 1982.

The Borstal was replaced by a determinate sentence of imprisonment for young people. Euphemisms are ubiquitous—de rigueur—in this field, and the new–old prison hid shyly under the appellation 'Youth Custody'.

By the mid-19th century a number of key shifts had taken place: from arbitrary state involvement in penal practice to a rationalized and centralized state-organized system; from very little differentiation between criminal groups to the classification and categorization of prisons and prisoners into separate groups: men and women, adults and young offenders, remand and convicted, requiring specialized forms of intervention from accredited professionals or experts. Within these processes the prison emerged as the 'dominant instrument for changing undesirable behaviour and became the favoured form of punishment' (Cohen, 1985: 13).

From nothing works to something works

Since its emergence in the late 18th century, the modern prison has been intended to fulfil a number of roles such as **incapacitation**, punishment, **deterrence**, reform and **rehabilitation**.

- **Incapacitation** Punishment which calculates the risk of future crimes and uses a custodial setting to remove the offender from society to protect the public from further harm.
- **Deterrence** Deterrence is the idea that crime can be reduced if people fear the punishment they may receive if they offend: the then Home Secretary, Michael Howard, stated in 1993, 'Prison works . . . it makes many who are tempted to commit crime think twice'.
- **Rehabilitation** Input into the sentence of an offender to re-integrate the offender into society as a law abiding citizen. Punishment reflects society's disapproval of the crime but offers opportunity to reduce re-offending.

These goals have often sat uneasily, and depending on the political pressures of the day, one or more of them has taken precedence over the others. For example, the, 1950s–1960s were characterized by the belief in rehabilitation (see Hudson, 2003). By the 1980s the Thatcher Government 'extolled' the prison as a place to punish. However, at the same time, ministers recognized that for less serious offenders, using prisons was 'expensive and ineffective' (Crow, 2001: 104).

Prisons are complex institutions and the rate of imprisonment is a consequence of overlapping pressures. Some of these pressures are caused by overcrowding, prisoner protests or staff culture. Some are due to law and order campaigns, and tougher sentencing policies. Research has shown that levels of use of imprisonment owe more to public attitudes and political decisions than to rates of crime (Hough and Mayhew, 1985). The increased use of prison has recently been picked up by politicians as a way of responding to modern fears about public safety and the desire to be protected from crime.

On 6 October, 1993 at the Conservative Party conference Michel Howard, the sixth Conservative Home Secretary in 14 years, reasserted the view that prison was the institution for preventing crime through a penal policy based on the punitive combination of; discipline, retribution, deterrence and incapacitation. He outlined his 27-point plan on how to get tough on criminals (in which he set a clear political agenda by declaring 'Let us be clear. Prison works.') by announcing the building of six new prisons and by promising a new era of austerity in prison regimes. Michael Howard in his now notorious speech averred that:

> Prison works . . . it makes many who are tempted to commit crime think twice . . . this may mean that more people will go to prison. I do not flinch from that. We shall no longer judge the success of our system of justice by a fall in the prison population.
>
> (Crow, 2001: 6).

In this pursuit of harsher law and order policies, Howard repealed many of the precepts that had underpinned the 1991 Criminal Justice Act by means of the Criminal Justice Act of 1993. In particular, the ethos of the Criminal Justice Act of 1991 was to reduce the use of custody so that a larger proportion of offenders would be punished in the community. The Criminal Justice Act of 1993 signalled the end to this and public protection became the primary rationale for sentencing, making incapacitation the principal justification for punishment. Like the prisons of the early 19th century, under Howard's lens, the late 20th century descendant was to subject prisoners to regimes based on disciplined austerity (Sparks, 1996).

Prisons today

This section will examine the prison system today. Some could argue that, in reflection on the previous passages, progress to improve the prison system has been extremely slow. Arguably this results not from a lack of desire for change by the professionals within the system, but rather from the rate of increase in the prison population, coupled with a lack of resources, funding and long-term policy initiatives. Indeed some commentators have pointed out that our prisons are the slowest reforming body within our modern society: 'There can be little doubt that John Howard, rising from his grave, would find much more that is familiar to him within the prison than across society as a whole' (Whitfield, 1991: 2).

It must be recognized that our prison system is extremely slow to respond to change, and that a serious result of overcrowding and understaffing has been an increase in deaths in custody, prison disturbances and self harming, to name a few indicators that prison system is failing those in their 'care' (Carlen, 1983) This failure in care is starkly illustrated by the case of Joseph Scholes outlined in Case Study One below.

Case Study One: Joseph Scholes

On 26 February, 2002 Joseph Scholes pleaded guilty to three offences of street robbery. Joseph was sentenced to a two-year detention and training order. During the sentencing hearing on

---

Case Study One: Joseph Scholes—cont'd

15 March, 2002, the Crown Court Judge stated in open court that he wanted the warnings about Joseph's self harming and history of sexual abuse 'most expressly drawn to the attention of the authorities'.

The Youth Justice Board (YJB) was informed of Joseph's vulnerability, his history of anxiety and depression and, importantly, his attempted suicide and self-harming behaviour. A number of people who had worked with Joseph urged the YJB to place him in local authority secure accommodation, where the facilities and staffing levels were more conducive to the provision of the care he needed. Despite this and despite the concerns expressed by those who had the most knowledge and information about Joseph, the YJB placed him in Prison Service accommodation at Stoke Heath's Young Offenders Institution (YOI).

Within days of his arrival, and without consultation with his mother, Joseph was moved to a single cell with no surveillance camera and normal ligature points and was put on reduced observations. He was also deeply anxious about the imminent prospect of being moved onto one of the main wings.

On 24 March, 2002 Joseph retired to his cell where he was later found dead, hanging from a sheet attached to the bars of his cell windows. Joseph died a month after his sixteenth birthday, just nine days into his two-year sentence.

For further details go to: http://inquest.gn.apc.org/joseph_scholes_public_inquiry.html

---

The total figure for deaths in custody from 1993 to 2007 was 2,315 which includes men and women, individuals from Black and minority ethnic groups and those on remand (and therefore unconvicted). For the same period 129 women to date have died in prison (http://inquest.gn.apc.org/data_deaths_in_prison.html). In comparison with other social changes, one can see how the wheels of prison reform turn slowly.

> The most striking aspect of prison reform over the last two centuries is how little of it there has been. . . even the more substantial changes pale against the broad sweep of political, social and economic progress over this period.
>
> (Rutherford cited in Whitfield, 1991: 2)

Women in prison

In a 2007 briefing, the male prison population in England and Wales was 75,966, and 4,396 were female (NOMS, 2007), and by the end of the decade the population is projected to reach 100,000. There are fewer prisons for women than for men (nineteen in England, none in Wales, one in Scotland and one in Northern Ireland). The nineteen prisons used to contain women can be categorized as either closed or open, rather than the four categories for men. Many of the prisons used to accommodate women were formerly used for men or are prisons within a male prison, and thus the facilities are not always appropriate. What is more, there is no separate provision for young female offenders or older women as there is for young and older male offenders.

The female prison population consists of fewer recidivists (repeat offenders) and relatively more foreign nationals and minority ethnic individuals than the male population (Carlen and Worrall, 2004). The culture is explicitly male, especially the attitudes and beliefs of prison staff. Because most prison officers are men (see Table 5.1), it is not surprising that male officers are present in female prisons.

Table 5.1 Gender breakdown of prison staff

	Men		Women	
	Number	**%**	**Number**	**%**
Prison officers	19,455	81	4,470	19
Governor grades	1,044	81	248	19
Other grades	1,528	52	10,502	48
Total	22,027	68	15,220	32

(Source: A. W. had personal communication with the Prison Officers Union)

One of the factors which needs to be considered when looking at women in prison is women's role as parents. Only five prisons have dedicated mother and baby units. Now we shall look in more detail at some specific issues, including female black and minority ethnic (BME) prisoners, young and older prisoners.

When we look at both race/ethnicity and gender, it is noteworthy that 29 per cent of female prisoners were from a minority ethnic group, compared with 22 per cent of male prisoners, and of these 24 per cent were classified as Black compared with 15 per cent of the ethnic minority men. There is over-representation of BME people in the prison population for both sexes, but it is more pronounced for females (Shute et al., 2005; Bowling and Phillips, 2002). Moreover, 20 per cent of women doing time were foreign nationals (the equivalent figure for males is 10 per cent). Why is this figure so high? One reason seems to lie in the fact that 75 per cent of the Black women and (in June 2002) 84 per cent of the foreign nationals in prison had been imprisoned for drug-related offences (Home Office, 2004c). In June, 2005, foreign nationals accounted for 36 per cent of the BME prison population (Home Office, 2006b: 86–7). This is a substantial proportion and suggests that foreign nationals charged or sentenced for importing drugs significantly influence the disproportionate number of BME prisoners. According to Kalunta-Crompton (2004) this is particularly the case for female prisoners. Thus, in June, 1997, Black foreign nationals made up 80 per cent of the UK female foreign nationals serving a prison sentence for drug offences (Kalunta-Crompton, 2004: 13). If foreign nationals are excluded from the equation, 45 per cent of the Black women in jail had been sentenced for drug offences, compared with 26 per cent of the White women. This category of offences also features more heavily than for Black males of whom 18 per cent had committed drug-related crimes.

Case Study Two: Sarah and Pauline Campbell

Pauline Campbell is a former college lecturer in her late 50s, who during 2004 was arrested over ten times as a direct result of her own unique protest aimed at drawing attention to the deaths of women prisoners in British jails. Every time a woman died, Campbell would go to the prison where the death had occurred and stand in the road to prevent any prison van from bringing more women to that jail. The police would be called and Campbell would then be ordered by them to move out of the van's way. She'd refuse and then she'd be arrested. She describes this as her 'one woman, self-funding protest', although it was not something that she had originally been drawn to and Campbell admits, 'I had no idea about the appalling state of women's prisons before Sarah's death.'

<hr>

Case Study Two: Sarah and Pauline Campbell—cont'd

Sarah was Campbell's only child, who died aged 18 in January, 2003 whilst 'in the so-called care of HMP and YOI Styal'. Sarah had spent six months on remand in 2002 and on 17 of January, 2003 was sentenced to a term of imprisonment and returned to Styal. The following day Sarah was taken unconscious to a local hospital and died later that evening without regaining consciousness. Campbell says that she protests to 'demonstrate that prisons are unsafe places which constantly failed to uphold the duty of care that the Prison Service has to all prisoners. People must speak out. It's medieval.'

Women in prison are 40 times more likely to kill themselves than women in the community. From 1996–2007, 119 women have died in prison: indeed in 2004, 23 women—a new record—took their lives in English and Welsh jails. http://inquest.gn.apc.org/data_deaths_of_woman_in_prison.html).

<hr>

Older people in prison

Turning to the issue of older people as the perpetrators of crime, the proportion of older prisoners has been rising over the last two decades. According to Wahidin (2007) the proportion of older prisoners between 1996 and 2007 almost trebled. In 2007, there are just over 6,000 people aged 50 and above in prison (Ware, 2007). In 2007 there were 277 women over the age of 50 and 2,050 men over 60, constituting just over 13 per cent of the total prison population. Many older prisoners have been convicted in later life for sex related offences, including those charged with 'historical offences' (offences committed two/three decades ago) and older female prisoners are mainly charged for violence against the person. Older prisoners present particular challenges for the prison service in terms of providing adequate health care provision, regime and appropriate facilities. For example, in a study by Wahidin(2006) entitled *Managing The Needs Of Older Prison Population*, the Governor at HMP Kingston argues that the closure of the 'Elderly Unit' was led by a policy directive not to make sufficient funds available to sustain the unit. Thus the closure was due to:

> not being able to do what we really wanted to do, with people of this age, and that really was the straw that broke the camel's back. The lows were having to say we would love to do more but we can't because of the lack of resources. At the moment there is no real political imperative to do anything about older prisoners. I did take the prison minister round. He sat on the bed of a dying prisoner. I thought that might make a difference. To be honest—it is *out of sight and out of mind*, because *nobody really wants to know*.

While not all older prisoners are in need of high levels of medical attention, others may suffer from the chronic ill health experienced by many elders in society as a whole: emphysema, arthritis, cardiac problems, hypertensive disorders, osteoporosis, etc. The questions which fuelled the women's fears were; 'What happens when women become infirm? Who looks after them? How do they get about and, finally, is there adequate provision? And if not what are the alternatives?'. These are the issues which confirmed their fears when they saw other women in later life 'making do', with the help of other prisoners but not the prison system (see Wahidin, 2002). In the case study below Wan-Nita, who was 62 at the time of the interview, and had been seriously ill during the first two years of her fourteen year sentence, raises these concerns:

Case Study Three: Wan-Nita

Wan-Nita: I mean what happens when women become infirm, or incontinent? Or, who brings them their food? Who looks after them? How do they get about? What happens if you have got osteoporosis? There just isn't any provision for that kind of thing in prison.

. . . was here, she had osteoporosis. She was very slow at getting up and down the stairs. She used to get other inmates to do things for her. The stairs are also quite narrow. You just have to come down to the boiler and fill a flask full of boiling water and then struggle back up the stairs with it, while other people are pushing past you.

If you are ill, and you don't go to work, you are locked in your cell. So you are punished for being ill. You can't phone home. You lose your association. So even if I'm feeling ill I still make the effort to go to work. Because I know I need to ring home everyday.

The structure of prisons in organization, architecture and training fails to address the diversity of need of those who are other than able-bodied. The kinds of problems women in later life may, and do, experience in the prison system largely result from the fact the prison is geared for the able-bodied young male. Prisons have not previously been designed with the disabled or elderly person in mind. It is the discourse of the essential woman, the malingerer, which informs health care practices discriminating against women throughout the life-course, and the sentence for older women becomes harder to bear (Sim, 1990). In some of the prisons visited, ground-floor accommodation was either not available or lacked washing facilities, which then necessitated the use of stairs to get from one floor to another, and in some cases the stairs were extremely narrow. Many women, regardless of age, would have found the stairs a problem when contending with people pushing past, crutches to negotiate and a flask to struggle with. Elders who were convalescing depended on other women to assist them in their survival, instilling a sense of rolelessness and helplessness.

This can create a tense atmosphere, impinging on the rights of others and positing the elder in a potentially very vulnerable position. In these circumstances the needs of elders must be taken into account to fulfil the mission statement and avoid accusations of injustice and lack of care. For particular prisons, it is the absence of basic facilities, such as having a medical centre on site, and ground-floor rooms, which emphasise how women throughout the life course are discriminated against within the penal system. This is how discrimination manifests itself upon elders and how they feel constrained by the triple bind based on their age, having offended the nature of their sex, and the actual offence. A further effect of being ill in prison is that the person is paid at the basic rate and therefore has little chance to buy phone cards to maintain contact with the outside, thus compounding the sense of dislocation and isolation with the feeling of rolelessness in society. Even when women showed exemplary behaviour and were placed on an enhanced regime they could be excluded from the privilege because of their age-related illness and the lack of adequate facilities in prison to cater for their needs. Thus, many felt they were punished further because they were excluded from earning a higher wage and from moving to better parts of the prison even though they were entitled to.

Prison conditions

In the summer of 2006 the prison system of England and Wales reached a critical level of overcrowding. This was a situation that had been building up over several years, despite a prison building scheme and more places being created. More offenders are still being sentenced to longer periods of incarceration. It came as no surprise to experts within the field or to overstretched, under-resourced prison officers that our prison system has reached its critical mass (see Bennett et al., 2007).

The statistics demonstrate how stretched the prison service now is:

- In 2005 England and Wales had the highest prison population in Western Europe: 144 per 100,000 of the national population (Home Office, 2004c: 118).

- The average prison population had quadrupled from 17,440 in 1990 to 75,966 in 2007 (NOMS, 2007).

- There was a 31 per cent increase in the prison population between October 2005 and October 2006 (Carter, 2003; Home Office, 2004c).

The overcrowding crisis is leading to a breakdown in ideals that the prison service has been attempting to inculcate and maintain over the years. The prison service's own statement of purpose states that it has a duty to look after prisoners with humanity (see text box below). It is much more likely that situations of unrest will occur in conditions that are very overcrowded. 'A total of 53 out of 60 boards of visitors were "very troubled" by the overcrowding and there are genuine fears that prison riots could break out as a result' (Bromley Briefings Prison Fact File, 2006: 6). In a state of severe overcrowding there is much less opportunity for rehabilitation which in turn calls into question the statement of purpose of: 'lead[ing] law abiding and useful lives in custody and after release'. Studies have shown that conditions such as the ones outlined, including whether prisoners are treated humanely and with dignity, can have a significant impact on prisoners' well-being. Mental health disorders may be created and such conditions will intensify existing disorders, thus increasing the rates of suicide, self-harm and self-mutilation among the prisoners (Dell and Robertson, 1988).

Since the 'enlightenment' period it has been recognized that to enable rehabilitation there must be time and resources invested in the reform of prisoners. In today's terms this means constructive regimes, education and skills training. It should also entail positive environments where suicide, self-harm and bullying are minimised.

> Any realistic attempt to improve prison conditions must take all account of two pivotal aspects of the prison system, namely population and capacity. Indeed, the inter-connections of this penal trinity of population, capacity and condition forms the heart of the reform quagmire.
>
> (Rutherford cited in Whitfield, 1991: 4)

The prison service in its own statement of purpose sets out three objectives which are vital to the protection of the public:

> • Holding prisoners securely.
> • Reducing the risk of prisoners re-offending.
> • Providing safe and well-ordered establishments in which we treat prisoners humanely, decently and lawfully.
> (HM Prison Service http://www.hmprisonservice.gov.uk/abouttheservice/statementofpurpose)

It can be argued most strongly that these objectives are difficult to achieve in the everyday running of a modern prison. However with the current level of overcrowding, the task is made near impossible.

Although the media recognizes that the prison service is in crisis, this never diminishes the public's desire, fuelled by sometimes unhelpful and biased reporting, to see criminals 'behind bars' rather than accepting the need for greater use of community penalties. The standard media reaction to any politician promoting the use of alternative sentencing ideas is usually to suggest that anything less than a prison sentence is not within the ideals of punishment. The public debate surrounding offenders is limited to the desire to 'keeping them off the streets'. It is therefore difficult to impress upon the public the realities and the necessity for prison reform. This creates difficulty in forming an adequate public debate. As Stern argues:

> The mystery that shrouds even the most mundane parts of the operation of prison system is not easy to explain. . . one is the public's wish not to know, not to even have to think about people who it is felt have, by their own actions, put themselves beyond the reach of legitimate concern. There is an urge to be able to forget them, and reassurance comes from knowing they have been 'put away' for a long time.
> (Stern, 1987: 2)

It is not surprising, therefore, that this limited public debate merely puts pressure on the Government to be seen to be doing something about the perceived problem of crime and disorder. Over recent years legislation has been enacted that has given tougher, longer penalties for more crimes, and has led to the current state of crisis in our prison system. However, in reality prison is not providing an effective protection from crime, either in the short term or the long term. The high recidivism rate illustrates that in terms of reducing offending, prison is a failure.

> The majority of people released from prison commit further offences whereas community sentences can reduce re-offending by 14 per cent. Offending by prisoners will increase as prisons are unable to cope with sheer numbers of people.
> (Howard League for Penal Reform press release November, 2006)

If the public was made more aware of these failures and the potential successes of community sentences, more progress might become possible. There is a need for recognition that victims and offenders mostly live in the same communities and geographical areas, and that for longer-term community and public safety, criminals need to be punished in a way that is effective for reduction of crime and recidivism.

A case study in overcrowding

By using as an example the inspectors' report on an unannounced visit to HMP Leicester, we can illustrate that the effect of overcrowding is the biggest current concern of any aspect of penology. Sadly the conditions found in HMP Leicester are not unique and many recent reports have expressed grave concern over the effects of overcrowding.

> At the time of the inspection it was operating under the acute pressures caused by a record national prison population. . . It is clear from this report that the strains were showing.
>
> (Owers, 2006: 5)

HMP Leicester, like many other local prisons, is housed in a building dating back to Victorian times. Built in 1825 it now finds itself in the centre of a busy city; it is unable to expand and conditions are cramped. It typifies old-fashioned prison design that is perhaps now outdated and is in dire need of modernization. CCTV is now the main method of prisoner surveillance. This takes Bentham's panoptical ideas for prison design, with emphasis on control, one step further. This reliance on technology, however, does cause concern over the safety and security of prisoners.

Staff shortages due to underfunding, high levels of stress-related staff sickness and constantly increasing prison numbers result in prisoners not being monitored as closely as they should be.

The Inspectorate's report found that in the 28 months preceding the report there had been nine deaths, of which seven had been self-inflicted. It also found that there was a high level of self-harm. Suicide is recognised nationally as a problem closely connected to overcrowding and the lack of high staff–prisoner ratios. This contradicts the Prison Service's own objective to provide a safe environment for those in its care. Towl and Crighton have illustrated that a safe environment has to be part of the balance (with care and control) of any effective suicide prevention programme (Towl and Crighton, 2000: 25). This is another aspect that will be diminished if sheer numbers of prisoners result in staff being overstretched and unable to perform their pastoral roles effectively (see Case Studies One and Two).

There are certain times in a prisoner's sentence where intense supervision may be needed. For example the first 24 hours of a new sentence may be a vital time for staff to impart information to a prisoner. As research has shown 'The tendency to commit suicide is greater during the first week of imprisonment than at any subsequent period' (Hobhouse and Broadway cited in Towl and Crighton, 2000: 24). More action is needed than simply reducing numbers, but there is no doubt that overcrowding exacerbates all existing problems within the institutional environment, simply by increasing the number of people who need individualized care.

> Leicester shows, in a microcosm, some of the problems faced by an over-crowded and stretched prison system. It is not essentially a prison with a negative culture. Nevertheless some of the deficits, particularly in safety are unacceptable and need urgently to be remedied.
>
> (Owers, 2006: 6)
>
> Government research into prisoner-on-prisoner homicide has also highlighted the danger of overcrowding inmates who are vulnerable or susceptible to violence.
>
> The rise (of the prison population) coupled with insufficient accommodation to house such large numbers of prisoners has led to overcrowding being a more acute problem. This is creating a potentially dangerous situation as the negative consequences of overcrowding include violence.
>
> (Satter, 2004: 4)

The overcrowding situation is not unfamiliar to professionals, government ministers and most members of the public. The details of the effects of this situation need greater exploration by most people if they are to gain a better understanding of the whole system. Most members of the public can only imagine the horrors of the realities of an overcrowded, under-resourced prison with all the surrounding issues of violence, bullying, suicides, drug abuse and self-harm. As Stern says 'Prison must be one of the least known aspects of British life' (Stern, 1987: 2). This would be less harmful if the public were not to have such influence on the policy debate surrounding modern penology.

If the prison system is to develop and adhere to its own statement of purpose, overcrowding must be brought under control. There is little point in trying to maintain constructive regimes and employ imaginative methods for rehabilitation and recidivism reduction, if the day-to-day running of a prison is reduced to crowd control and achieving the basic minimum of care with overstretched, under-resourced and demotivated staff. In times of overcrowding many ideals fall by the wayside, and we have seen deaths in custody, self-harm, violence in prison and drugs increase in the male and female prison estate. This is not acceptable in a modern day institution. What makes it unacceptable is the simple fact that it fails to reduce recidivism and the prison population rises. In such circumstances, prisons revert to simply being the warehouses for prisoners that were familiar 200 years ago.

Does prison work?

Prison is not working

61 per cent of all prisoners released in 2001 were reconvicted within two years.
73 per cent of young male offenders released in 2001 were reconvicted within two years.

Prison is a brutalising and damaging experience

During 2004, 95 people killed themselves in prison service care. This included 50 people on remand and 13 women.
   In addition, a 14-year-old boy took his own life in a Secure Training Centre in 2004.
   Data shows that in 2003, 30 per cent of women, 65 per cent of females under 21 and 6 per cent of men in prison harmed themselves.

Prison is expensive

During 2003–2004, it cost an average of £27,320 per year to keep someone in prison.
   To build a new prison costs the equivalent of two district hospitals or 60 primary schools.
   Source: http://www.howardleague.org/index.php?id=fact2.

In 2003, more than 8.75 million people were confined in 205 countries, about half of them in the USA (1.96 million), China (1.43 million) and Russia (0.92) million. The UK has the highest rate of imprisonment in the European Union (Table 5.2) (Walmsley, 2003: 1). Globally, with the dramatic rise in the prison population and the rapid development of private prisons, the prison system has become a growth industry which employs thousands of workers, from those managing and building institutions to those providing high-tech security equipment and contracted-out health care, education and catering. The 'prison industrial complex' is now one of the fastest growing industries in the USA.

Table 5.2 Imprisonment in Europe in 2006: rates per 100,000 population (selected countries)

Country	Prisoners per 100,000 population
Norway	66
Ireland	72
Finland	75
Sweden	82
France	85
Germany	94
Italy	104
Austria	105
Portugal	120
Netherlands	128
Scotland	141
Spain	145
England and Wales	147

(Source: World Prison Brief, International Centre for Prison Studies, King's College London.)

All historical and comparative studies concur to demonstrate that the level of incarceration of a given society bears no relation to its crime rate: it is at bottom an expression of cultural and political choices (Christie, 1998b). The overdevelopment of the penal sector over the past three decades is indeed a reflection of the shrivelling of the welfare state, and the criminalization of the poor. Just as in other societies, the discourses that seek to connect crime and punishment on both sides of the Atlantic 'have no value other than ideological' (Wacquant, 2005: 7). We will argue that it is only by exploring alternative possibilities to prisons that we can begin to move beyond our over-reliance on imprisonment. At one level it can be argued that it is only through well funded alternatives to custody, changes in sentencing and a concerted effort to divert offenders from custody that this can be achieved. The reason for caution is that research has shown that programmes that have been introduced into the women's prison have been appropriated by the prison system. Hannah-Moffat (2002) used the concept of *encroachment* to describe how pre-existing organizational norms frequently encroached upon and undermined the rationale of these programmes. Secondly, the reliance on alternatives to custody fails to critically address social divisions such as class, age, gender and ethnicity.

Abolitionism: an alternative vision

By turning our attention to the abolitionist debate we can see how this perspective can take the penal policy debate beyond alternatives to custody by creating an alternative vision of justice. The term 'abolitionism' stands for a social movement, a theoretical perspective and a political strategy. As a social movement, it is committed to the abolition of the prison or even the entire penal system. Abolitionism originated in campaigns for prisoners' rights and penal reform and, as Sim has pointed out:

> [the abolitionist debate is] increasingly connected with the emerging discourses and debates around human rights and social justice which [abolitionists] see as mechanisms for developing negative reforms, thereby promoting a response to social harm that is very different from the destructive prison and punishment systems that currently exist.
>
> (Sim, 1994)

Subsequently, abolitionism developed into a critical theory and praxis concerning crime, punishment and penal reform (see Sim, 2002). As a theoretical perspective, abolitionism takes on the twofold task of providing a radical critique of the criminal justice system while showing that there are other, more rational ways of dealing with crime. Abolitionism emerged as an anti-prison movement when at the end of the 1960s a distinctive impulse took hold of thinking about the social control of deviance and crime among other areas (Cohen, 1985). In Western Europe, anti-prison groups aiming at prison abolition were founded in Sweden and Denmark (1967), Finland and Norway (1968), Great Britain (1970), France (1970) and the Netherlands (1971).

This movement demanded change in general thinking concerning punishment, humanization of the various forms of imprisonment in the short run, and in the long run the replacement of the prison system.

Abolitionists argue that punishment cannot be justified at all: they challenge the conventional assumption that punishment is a necessary feature of any modern society and that we should aim not simply to refer or limit our penal practices and institutions, but to abolish them (Mathiesen, 1974, 1986; Christie, 1981; Bianchi and van Swaaningen, 1986; de Haan, 1990; Duff and Garland, 1994). From the abolitionist point of view, the criminal justice system's claim to protect people from being victimized by preventing and controlling crime is grossly exaggerated. In the words of the Dutch abolitionist William de Haan, prison 'is counter productive, difficult to control and [is] itself a major social problem' (de Haan, 1991: 206–7). Punishment is seen as a self-reproducing form of violence. The penal practice of blaming people for their supposed intentions (for being bad and then punishing and degrading them accordingly) is dangerous because the social conditions for recidivism are thus reproduced. Morally degrading and segregating people is especially risky when the logic of exclusion is reinforced along the lines of difference in sex, race age, class, culture and religion. As abolitionists like Mathiesen have maintained, the prison has to be understood both as a material place of confinement and as an ideological signifier. Not only does the institution reinforce powerlessness and stigmatization, but it also establishes 'a structure which places members of one class in such a situation that the attention we might pay to the members of another is diverted' (Mathiesen, 1990: 138).

As Mathiesen (2004) points out, a theoretically refined abolitionism can offer a new way of thinking about the world and a vision of the future which contrasts sharply with traditional methods of penality based on incapacitation, deterrence, punishment and rehabilitation. It directly confronts the 'cynicism and anomie' of postmodernism, it reaffirms the argument that prisons don't work 'either as punishment or as a means of ensuring the safety and stability of the commonwealth' and it recognizes that predatory behaviour needs to be responded to and dealt with within the structural and interpersonal contexts of power and politics (Thomas and Boehlefeld, 1991: 246–9). This vision can be compared with the present situation here and elsewhere, which is evoked in the quotation with which the chapter begins. In thinking about abolition we should examine how important it is to abandon the very concept of crime as signifying wrongdoing to which the community should respond with condemnation.

Conclusion

Our view is that prisons cannot plausibly claim to rehabilitate when their primary custodial role requires regimes which debilitate, degrade and deprive offenders in their 'care' of liberty. In these circumstances all that can be hoped for is humane containment. It is only by thinking about alternatives to imprisonment that we can begin an imaginative re-thinking of the whole penal policy debate.

Our own position is that while prisons are likely to be with us for the foreseeable future, the abolitionist perspective is necessary to make us question some of the taken-for-granted assumptions about the inevitability of imprisonment as a standard response to crime. This search for alternatives to custody reflects growing disillusionment with the efficiency of prison for reforming the criminal, as well as alarm at the soaring costs of mass imprisonment. On average it costs the British taxpayer over £35,000 per year to keep a person in prison. The questions that we need to ask when thinking about prisons and prisoners as prison numbers spiral out of control are these:

> • How do penal policies intersect with other spheres of culture, politics or economic structures of the social formations from which they arise (see Sparks, 2003: 105).
> • Can we develop informal modes of justice—procedures which would be participatory but which would not themselves become oppressive?
> • What are prisons for?
> • What purpose do they serve?
> • What conditions should prisoners be held in?
> • Should prisons be abolished?

Although the prison in various guises has survived for over 200 years and has been a dominant institution in society, we must become more imaginative in finding an alternative to our over-reliance on this institution. Moreover, as the prison system is at crisis point and as the revolving door spins out of control, the question the reader must ask is how best to break the cycle of crime which brings the same people back, year in, year out, to repeated terms of imprisonment—disenfranchising whole sectors of community. We need to have a critical review of what we mean and understand the role of prison to be, and we as a society must find a different and more humane strategy for responding to phenomena as socially complex and controversial as crime and punishment. As Garland comments:

> The punishment of offenders is a peculiarly unsettling and dismaying aspect of social life. As a social policy it is a continual disappointment, seeming always to fail in its ambitions and to be undercut by crises and contradictions of one sort or another. As a moral or political issue it provokes intemperate emotions, deeply conflicting interests, and intractable disagreements.
>
> (Garland, 1990: 1)

Key arguments

• There are various theories concerning the purpose of punishment ranging from retribution, through prevention, deterrence, retribution, prison reform and abolitionism.
• The themes running throughout penological theory is the nature of and the power of imprisonment and the purpose it serves in relation to discursive rationales of punishment.
• It is by examining why the prison in England and Wales is in crisis can we begin to explore alternative visions of justice.

Further reading

Morris, N. and Rothman, D. J. (eds) (1995) *The Oxford History of the Prison*, Oxford, Oxford University Press traces the history of punishment and incarceration from ancient times to the present, setting the extraordinary transformation of the ideology and practice of imprisonment into the larger context of social and political change. Wahidin, A. and Cain, M. (eds) (2006), *Ageing, Crime and Society*, Cullumpton, Willan provides an excellent source of material around ageing issues in relation to crime and the criminal justice system, focusing on areas such as elder abuse, older prisoners and older people and fear of crime. Bowling, B and Phillips, C. (2002) *Racism, Crime and Justice*, Harlow, Longman focuses on 'race' issues in relation to criminal justice, highlighting many key areas of research and policy.

6

ACCOUNTABILITY, LEGITIMACY AND DISCRETION: APPLYING CRIMINOLOGY IN PROFESSIONAL PRACTICE

Rob Canton and Tina Eadie

Good reasons must individuate. They must be based on the circumstances of the case, and a decision can be impugned as unfair if either it is based on some factor that is not relevant or it fails to take into account some factor that is.

(Lucas, 1980: 13)

Are individuals . . . accountable first and foremost to the Government that sets the agenda, to the management that is responsible for their careers, to the customers who create the need for this service, or to the taxpayer who foots the bill?

(John Mackinson, quoted in Faulkner, 2006: 81)

People who regard legal authorities as legitimate are found to comply with the law more frequently.

(Tyler, 1990: 64)

We're governed by rules, and there is a saying that exceptions prove the rule. The most important thing is to know when that exception should be used.

(Sparks et al., 1996: 155)

Chapter summary

This chapter examines:
- The 'how' and the 'what' of criminal justice decision making in relation to ensuring a fair and just process.
- Tensions between following rules and respecting relevant differences.
- Relevance for decision making in police, courts, probation and prison settings.
- Implications for professionalism.

A conventional approach to understanding the criminal justice process is to see it as a sequence of decisions (Bottomley, 1973). However, little is known about precisely how these decisions are taken; statute and regulation are among the parameters, but a range of other considerations is involved besides. How then can it be ensured that decision making by key players[1] throughout the criminal justice process is undertaken on fair and proper grounds? The concepts of accountability, legitimacy and discretion are plainly central to this and give rise to further questions:

- How and by whom should practitioners be held to account for decisions they take?
- What contributes towards a legitimate—or just—decision?
- How much discretion should individual workers be allowed to hold?

This chapter will argue that accountability has often been understood in narrow, managerial terms, and that the concept should be widened; practitioners must be able to give account to their managers, but should also be accountable to others—not least to those most affected by their decisions. This is a critical component of legitimacy— itself an indispensable precondition of just and effective criminal justice practice. To do justice, moreover, practitioners should be empowered to use their professional judgement, or discretion. The right decision is that which is the most appropriate in all the circumstances of the case, with the safeguard against arbitrariness or unfairness in the process being the requirement and willingness of the decision maker(s) to give account to anyone with an interest in the decision, as opposed to the simple application of a practice rule or standard.

In its exploration of the concepts of accountability, legitimacy and discretion, the chapter draws on literature that points to different pathways into and out of crime, all of which vary with a range of factors including race, social class, age and gender. It takes issue with an uncritical dependence on actuarial tools and the 'value-neutral' managerialism which currently pervades criminal justice agencies, arguing that these constrain professional discretion and reduce effectiveness, not least by undermining the relationship between officer and offender which has been shown to be central in effecting positive change (Bailey, 1994; Rex, 1999). In identifying with criminology as a 'contested, contradictory and interdisciplinary discourse' (McLaughlin and Muncie, 2006: xiii), the authors acknowledge the contribution of sociological thought to the criminological debates entered into here and the challenge it poses for 'New Public Management'. Linking these debates to literature from agencies including the police, courts, prison and probation services, the chapter proposes that the criminal justice system will become a more effective arena for accomplishing fair and legitimate practice, including effective rehabilitation, if the informed use of discretion by its many professional agents is both acknowledged and positively encouraged alongside full accountability for their decision making.

Setting the context

Textbooks often represent the process through various criminal justice agencies as a flowchart, a sequence of decisions. Sometimes the decisions are dictated by statute, but more commonly law is supplemented by rules, standards or codes. Yet however

---

[1]Commonly regarded as Police; Crown Prosecution Service; Courts; National Probation Service; Prison Service.

tightly these rules are framed, there is still a judgement to be made—a case has to be recognized (or more accurately *constructed*) as falling under the relevant rule.

> Revised *National Standards for the Supervision of Offenders in the Community* (Home Office, 2000) require probation staff to instigate breach action when a second appointment is missed without reasonable explanation, but a judgement remains about which explanations are reasonable or indeed what accounts for a missed appointment—for example, when does late become unacceptably late? Is missing the bus acceptable? Does the fact that the bus was delayed in heavy traffic contribute to lateness being deemed to be acceptable rather than unacceptable?

Organizations set their own priorities and have to decide on an efficient disposition of resources. Performance targets set priorities and shape practice decisions, as can resource constraints—for example, a particular prison regime may be appropriate for an offender but there may be no place available. Again, despite the promulgation of national codes and standards in many agencies, local differences still obtain. Sometimes these may have no rational basis and simply reflect local habits; at other times, variances may constitute a very appropriate recognition of the distinctiveness of local circumstances.

> If an area has a particularly high incidence of a certain type of offence, this could be argued to be a good reason to prosecute rather than caution, or to impose weightier penalties for this offence.

Professional associations commonly adopt their own codes of practice and commend these to their memberships. These will represent each profession's best conception of how it should practise, but associations also serve the interests of their membership and this can influence their statements of preferred practice. Professions may also devise an unwritten set of pragmatic tactics to respond to the challenges they most commonly encounter. Policy may be elegantly constructed, but the real world is full of dilemmas and uncertainties.

> The police 'canteen culture' (Reiner, 2000) is sometimes criticized for its obduracy and conservatism, but at its best, staff room culture can consolidate a great deal of practice wisdom grounded in the experiences of principled people having to deal with the realities of the job.

Nor should personal values be overlooked. Decisions can be tainted by personal preferences—and perhaps prejudices. Unbounded discretion in some situations can lead to inconsistency and injustice. At the same time, people are not the same and circumstances differ in all kinds of ways; relevant differences should therefore be respected in order to prevent unfair outcomes, and a responsible professional should be willing *and able* to depart from the customary practice to ensure justice. Finally— though perhaps most importantly—comes professional knowledge and expertise, acquired and developed in training and practice, informed by criminological insight and other theoretical disciplines, and responsive to experience.

Figure 6.1 below (adapted from Canton, 2005) sets out some of the parameters that influence decisions.

Figure 6-1 What influences criminal justice decision making?

These influences are applied to the facts of the case. It is important to recognize, however, that these are not self-evident: there are any number of ways of constructing or describing a state of affairs and the identification of factors as relevant is shaped by all these influences. Once a decision is taken, its implementation is again mediated by these influences.

The recognition of the range of influences that shapes a decision reasonably evokes concern about consistency and fairness. The managerialist response has been to prescribe practice ever more tightly through regulation. Often these regulations flout the experience of practitioners and ignore legitimate (as opposed to idiosyncratic) local difference. Even more seriously, regulations assume a standard case—a suspect, a defendant, an offender, a prisoner—but as Hudson states 'Once the subject of justice is given back his/her social context and flesh and blood reality, it is clear that difference is the standard case, and that differences are routinely irreducible.' (Hudson, 2001: 166). Preoccupation with regulation suppresses individualization and disregards the many factors that contribute to a wise decision.

Accountability in the context of 'New Public Management'

A powerful influence in the oversimplification of decision making has been 'New Public Management' (NPM). The history of this process of change and reform in the criminal justice context, and the impact of managerialist ideas on practice, has been well told (see Raine and Willson, 1993; James and Raine, 1998; Brownlee, 1998). As the 20th century closed, the whole of the public sector—criminal justice included—was adjusting to increasing direction from central government and the requirement to demonstrate value for money and accountability for resource allocation. Described as a period of 'rapid and confusing change, and sometimes difficult adjustment' (Faulkner, 2006: 11), professional, managerial and even judicial judgement began to be taken by the centre.

Among the precepts of NPM set out by Hood (in Raine and Willson, 1993: 68) are three that have most relevance for our discussion here:

- Hands-on professional management.
- Explicit standards and measures of performance.
- Greater emphasis on output controls.

Hands-on professional management is the first 'villain of the piece'. This entails an active, controlling and we suggest intrusive style of management, which confuses management with control (see Vanstone, 1995). Clear lines of accountability assign responsibility for decision making, but managerialist accountability is about power— which rests with managers; workers are told what to do and, increasingly, how to do it. With this comes the inherent danger that boundaries become blurred between those tasks of management that are legitimate and those that properly belong to practitioners.

The second 'villain' is a style of management that is target driven and requires explicit standards and measures of performance. Crucially, the targets chosen are those which are most readily auditable, so indicators of success are most often expressed in quantitative terms of 'how much?' and 'how many?'. Data collection becomes paramount and the meeting of targets is presented as a key indicator of success—what cannot be counted does not count—risking the marginalization of qualitative factors. Numerical targets encourage a 'creative' presentation and also begin to distort practice and subvert more important considerations. For example, having been set an (arbitrary) target for the number of completions of accredited programmes, probation areas have sometimes been under pressure to include offenders who would not otherwise be suitable (nor indeed for whom there is evidence that the programmes will 'work')—with predictable consequences for drop-out rates and the viability of programmes and their integrity (Kemshall and Canton, 2002).

Third numerical targets tend to favour output rather than outcome measures and as the following quotation puts well:

> [there is] a tendency in courts and other social agencies towards decoupling performance evaluation from external social objectives . . . such technocratic rationalization tends to insulate institutions from the messy, hard-to-control demands of the social world. By limiting their exposure to indicators that they can control, managers ensure that their problems will have solutions'.
>
> (Feeley and Simon cited in Raynor and Vanstone, 2002: 65)

The associated concept of actuarialism (statistical risk calculation) has had a strong influence on criminal justice. Originating, perhaps, in well-founded misgivings about the ability of practitioners to make sound judgements case-by-case, actuarial instruments have been developed that claim to make reliable assessments. In the prison and probation services, the Offender Group Reconviction Scale (OGRS) has been developed to gauge the likelihood of reconviction within two years. *On aggregate*, decisions taken in this way will mostly be sound, so that the temptation—against which all commentators warn—of drawing inferences from the aggregate behaviour of a large group to an individual member of that population can prove irresistible to managers. Agencies, accordingly, are able to inform their stakeholders that they met their target, irrespective of the number of social casualties or how much better they might have done by other means. This approach too, as we shall see, critically undermines legitimacy, taking away people's individuality and reducing them to carriers of risks and needs.

A further critique of managerialism is that it tries to deny the moral significance of practice by concentrating on ostensibly value-neutral objectives and giving priority to efficiency, economy and effectiveness. However, it is meaningless to talk about effectiveness without an idea of objective, and to choose some objectives rather than others involves judgement about respective worth. It is in this context that the idea of accountability has come to prominence. Whilst the insistence on accountable practice made a positive contribution towards the credibility of criminal justice agencies, the narrow frame in which this took place has been much less helpful. Accountability to managers—and, in the case of public sector organizations, ultimately to government and to parliament—is a critical part of the discipline of working in an organization. But it is important not to lose sight of the principle that criminal justice practice and the institutions of punishment may need to give account to and engage with many other important constituencies besides—including local courts, communities, victims and indeed offenders. Wood and Kemshall (this volume) instructively explore this principle in relation to the supervision of high-risk offenders in the community. They note that unless agencies make themselves accountable to offenders (as well as, of course, to others), compliance is less likely. Accountability here is achieved through the explanation and justification of decisions; where this is not accomplished, where people feel that they have been dealt with unfairly or capriciously, there is likely to be resentment and avoidance. The legitimacy achieved through open accountability accordingly brings strong support to a risk management strategy.

Political debate, by contrast, has worked with an impoverished concept of accountability, as observed by Faulkner (2006: 63):

> When accountability is discussed in government, it is not usually democratic accountability that is at issue, but internal accountability brought about by the processes of inspection, audit and performance management.'

Gelsthorpe (2001) too has emphasized the ethical significance of accountability and its importance in respecting diversity. Accountability in its fullest sense is not just a managerial requirement, but involves a preparedness to explain decisions to colleagues, courts, the community and indeed to all with an interest in the decision, and especially to those most affected by it. This requires dialogue about the manner in which decisions are taken, and, through the process of debate, negotiation and explanation, understanding is achieved.

Discretion in the context of NPM

Insisting on high levels of accountability—rightly, albeit with an attenuated sense of the term *accountability*—NPM wrongly infers that this entails narrow discretion (Eadie and Canton, 2002). We argue that narrow discretion is neither just nor effective; nor is it a necessary consequence of accountability. A preliminary distinction should be made between authorized discretion (*de jure*) and the discretion that practitioners take for themselves (*de facto*).

> With the exception of a few mandatory sentences, the Courts have a very wide discretion to decide sentences as they think fit. By contrast, police constables have relatively much less authorized discretion, but the nature of their work restores a great deal of discretion in practice.

Arguably, discretion cannot be removed. It can be concealed—by staff constructing a case in a manner that accords it with their own preferred decision. It can be moved around within the organization—National Standards, in classic civil service style, move discretion up the organization so that middle and senior managers make judgements that used to be made by front-line staff. Or it can be moved between organizations—mandatory sentences move discretion from Courts to prosecuting authorities whose decision about which offence is to be charged becomes correspondingly much more significant.

Are these pathological or deviant manoeuvres? Or are they appropriate? Or indeed inevitable? Criminology reminds us of the sheer diversity of human circumstances and the many different reasons why people might commit crime, and the range of responses to being a victim. A just implementation of punishment cannot ignore the real impact of penalties that weigh differently on people. Desistance studies (see, for example, Burnett, 2000; Maruna, 2001; Farrall, 2002) suggest that there are different pathways into and out of crime and that these vary with race, social class, age and gender. This poses a challenge to managerialism as any imposition to treat people as units loses the nuances, the subtleties and all the 'evidence led-ness' that ought to be enriching practice. Government's professed commitment to evidence-based policy and practice has been a strong feature of the New Labour time in office (although Tonry (2003) calls into question the extent to which this claim is warranted). If, however, science and technology are assumed to be able to provide all the answers, there is a danger that the use of judgement by practitioners becomes redundant, or at best is not valued, generating, in Faulkner's words (2006: 45), 'a form of pseudo-science, with its own language and patterns of thought, which will come to gain an air of spurious authenticity'.

Practitioners then need to be equipped to provide an *appropriate* response, individualized to each person's unique situation. That is, they need to be given the authority to exercise intelligent judgements and in doing so restore the latitude that managerialism has removed. Taking the role of the probation officer as an example, Fellowes (1992: 93) has suggested it is about '. . . working *with* offenders, rather than *on* them'. Dowden and Andrews emphasize the importance of 'open, warm and enthusiastic communication' and 'mutual respect and liking' between offender and officer (2004: 205). Without this, the words of the supervising officer risk sounding hollow and disaffected individuals, struggling with the very difficulties for which they were placed on a community order, might choose not to comply. The centrality of the relationship is a feature of Bailey's research—in this instance between young adult offenders and their supervisors:

> • I realised he [her probation officer] was the first person I could really open up to about my home, job worries, being in Care, people that I mixed with, drug abuse and things like that. I trusted him, which is really unusual for me: I don't trust anyone. (LILY in Bailey, 1995: 129).
> • He's like a Dad to me, the way he talks. Nobody's ever talked to me like the way he has. He talks straight to me. He's not like *my* Dad, not at all, but he's like a Dad. (TOM in Bailey, 1995: 135).

By the end of the 20th century the government was demanding harder and more quantitative evidence of output measures that would justify expenditure on a range of services across the whole of the public sector. As New Labour strove to appear as tough on law and order as the Conservatives (see Downes and Morgan, 2002) the lack of evidence that orders were enforced appropriately (that is, sufficiently strictly) led to criticisms that supervisors were siding with offenders rather than working in the public interest (Hedderman, 2003: 182).

Respect for individuality means entering into a discussion about reasons for a person's absence and negotiating a response. Although the explanation given might be rejected, the individual concerned will at least feel heard, encouraging the maintenance of the relationship. Without this form of exchange, and with reference to a standardized response (currently more than one unacceptable absence requires breach action to be instigated), it is more difficult for the officer to demonstrate the understanding, tolerance, even fairness which make the relationship real. It pulls away from legitimacy and the normative claims which are known to be linked with compliance and desistance (Rex, 1999; Bottoms, 2001).

It might also be suggested that 'following the rules' and failing to make wise differentiation among offenders goes against the three central tenets of effective practice:

- The 'risk principle' implies varying intensity of supervision.
- The principle of criminogenic need insists that priority should be given to those factors most closely associated with offending.
- Responsivity recognizes diversity and the need to work with it rather than trying to suppress it through assumptions of uniformity.

Nor must one overlook the racial effects of these developments. Kemshall, Canton and Bailey (2004) are among the more recent writers to commend the idea that any new policy proposal should be 'disparity proofed'—that is, required to consider its impact on particular groups. Are there, for example, higher rates of non-compliance by offenders from minority ethnic groups? Her Majesty's Inspectorate of Probation has commented on this (HMIP, 2004), but the information is not reliably available. Other things that we know about probation performance would not make it unlikely.

Enforcement here is a special case of a general principle: sound decision making involves attention to all relevant circumstances and this cannot be achieved by an abstractly-framed rule designed for 'the offender' in all circumstances. This inescapably entails wide practitioner discretion which should be properly authorized and supported through the processes of management across the range of criminal justice agencies.

Accountability in the context of NPM

Our discussion so far has tried to argue for reversing trends of NPM, trusting professionals (while holding them fully accountable) and restoring their wide discretion. But this conclusion exposes a central problem for the administration of justice. Justice, after all, insists that like cases should be treated alike; citizens must know where they stand in relation to the law and what formal consequences will result from their behaviour. People must be dealt with in a consistent and sufficiently predictable manner. This surely implies less discretion and more regulation.

Yet while justice may require that like cases should be treated alike, it no less requires that relevant differences must be respected. Cases may differ one from another in many ways and the tighter the specification of the rules, the less opportunity there will be to accommodate relevant difference. This too may be a source of unfair discrimination. The difficulty for those taking the decision, then, is to determine which differences are relevant, but this difficulty is not resolved by ignoring one horn of the dilemma and assuming that treating everyone the same is a guarantee of justice.

In her recent research, Rex found the offenders she interviewed gave strong endorsement to the statement that 'all offenders are different and should receive different punishments' (Rex, 2005: 142). Similarly, in the prison context, Liebling and Price (2001: 143) found that prisoners recognize that equality of treatment can lead to an unfairness of outcome and their ideal is said to be 'flexible consistency'. This amounts to a strong prima facie case for wide discretion but, as Gelsthorpe and Padfield note (2003: 1), discretion is one of the most contentious concepts in criminal justice, and how broad discretion can be prevented from deteriorating into arbitrariness or unfairness is the central dilemma in this debate. The use of discretion is not necessarily benign; as Davis claimed 'the exercise of discretion may mean either beneficence or tyranny, either justice or injustice, either reasonableness or arbitrariness' (1969: 3). Davis argues for openness to guard against unfair or capricious decisions and Canton and Eadie (2004) therefore urge high levels of accountability.

Davis recognised that 'The goal is not the maximum degree of confining, structuring, and checking: the goal is to find the optimum degree for each power in each set of circumstances' (1969: 3). This promising formulation implies that there can be no a priori determination of the appropriate balance between the demands of consistency and predictability and the principle, also required by justice, that there must be enough flexibility to respect difference: it will depend on the context and the nature of the decision to be taken.

Criminal justice decision making takes place in a myriad of different settings and arenas: police practice in relation to stop and search; crown prosecution lawyers in respect of the public interest; sentencing in open court; the decision of a probation officer to instigate breach proceedings for failure to report; action taken by a prison officer to place a prisoner on report. The professional nature of this decision making, and the extent to which practitioner discretion should be circumscribed (plus how and by whom) requires further exploration and is our focus here.

Narrow discretion is not required by the principle of accountability (Eadie and Canton, 2002), and certainly does not guarantee it. However, it is no doubt true that that unfettered discretion can lead to unfairness and to discrimination (Davis, 1969; Fitzgerald, 1993). Codes and National Standards therefore try to circumscribe or at least to structure discretion, but attempting this sometimes achieves a superficially satisfying bureaucratic sameness at the cost of ignoring relevant differences. Justice requires that relevant difference be respected no less than that like cases should be treated alike. This consideration has important implications for appreciating diversity.

Players in all criminal justice agencies use discretion in their day-to-day decision making and it is this that is the 'stuff of justice' (Gelsthorpe and Padfield, 2003: 1) and—most importantly—which can make for justice or injustice. Taking key criminal justice agencies, the exercise of discretion in each one is explored and the dangers of standardized practice highlighted. It will be argued that rules can be constructed out of a 'case law' based on an accumulation of fair and transparent decisions emerging from the predicaments of practice. Diversity can be respected within a framework of consistency but not sameness.

Police

As individual officers and as an institution, the legal power of the police is considerable and, it is argued, needs to be constrained (Miller and Blackler, 2005). There are a number of ways to achieve this including, as in the UK, to devolve police authority to local government oversight and control. This includes holding both the institution and individuals within it to account. Enforcing the law necessarily requires decision making and the use of discretion (Finnegan, 1978: 64) in a myriad of situations and circumstances: which reported crimes are followed up?; in which localities are police resources going to be most heavily deployed?; which laws will be enforced most rigorously? (Finnegan refers to an unspoken agreement amongst police officers that 'certain offences will be winked at' (1978: 65)); which suspects will be granted bail? and so forth. Discretionary powers are therefore inevitable, but what is the proper extent of police discretion?

Powers of stop and search, and of arrest and detention, represent considerable legal power. Maintaining proper accountability whilst also enabling police officers to make appropriate decisions in relation to the diverse incidents with which they deal is a complex task and Miller and Blackler (2005: 42) outline instances of this. The use of discretion within the police is finely balanced; the law has to be interpreted and applied in concrete circumstances and it is legally permissible for the police not to enforce a law in particular circumstances—which is not the same as saying that they are ignoring the law. The law does not and cannot exhaustively prescribe and often it grants discretionary powers, or has recourse to open-ended notions such as that of 'reasonable suspicion'. On the basis of these powers, two different decisions by two different officers can both be legally 'right'. Opportunities for inconsistent and discriminatory practice abound in these circumstances unless police professionals are made fully accountable for their decision making in all circumstances.

> Using discretionary powers for these aims might include the decision whether or not to shoot a suspect who is believed to be armed and is refusing to respond to instructions, or the decision whether or not to arrest a known trouble-maker at a public event while his or her behaviour is still relatively low-key.

Further, upholding and enforcing the law is only one of the ends of policing. Other aims include the maintenance of public order, the preservation of life and securing convictions.

There is often a hard choice to make in relation to using specific means to achieve the ends of policing, for example in the routine use of coercion when questioning suspects under arrest. At what point might the use of discretion as to which methods to employ cross the line and become both unacceptable and illegal—such as the use of torture?

The discretion not to prosecute young offenders has been a long-standing feature of police decision making. There has been a massive shift from informal measures (the infamous 'clip round the ear') to increasingly formalized policies and procedures regarding pre-court decision making. The conclusions of a study into this process in one county fit our discussion well. Kemp and Gelsthorpe state (2003: 45):

> Managerialist interventions . . . have focused on the need to drive through national policy without necessarily recognising difficulties and consequences on the ground. In this regard then, we cannot assume that increased managerial control means better justice. It may be that we should look at more and better training, supervision and accountability at a local level.

> Three young men are sitting in a bus shelter smoking. As Karin, a newly qualified police officer, passes them she thinks she can smell cannabis. She wonders whether to stop and search the men for controlled drugs. As she hesitates, two of them extinguish what they are smoking and the third places it behind his back. The fact that the third young man appears to be trying to hide something would justify the search. In her deliberations Karin considers a number of factors including: the age of the young men (she has more discretion if they are over 17 years of age); whether the bus stop is near a school or likely in some other way to influence younger children; the extent to which the illegal use of cannabis been highlighted as a problem in the area; and whether there is any indication of intent to supply a controlled drug (did one of the young men appear to be 'dealing'?).

Courts

Sentencing guidelines are being promulgated in the interests of justice and consistency. While UK versions are careful to insist on the court's discretion case-by-case, there is a continuing debate about who 'owns' sentencing—the courts or the government. In some parts of USA, sentencing grids or tables have been developed which effectively eradicate sentencer discretion and leave courts with only the sentencing options that the legislature has permitted them. Tracing down one axis of the table to find the index offence and across the other axis to track the previous record, the judge finds the cell which contains the prescribed penalty and reads it out. As Nils Christie has said, 'In these circumstances, Lady Justice does not need to be blindfolded. She has nothing to look at, except a Table.' (Christie, 2000: 169). This approach to sentencing was intended to capture the essence of retributive justice—nothing is relevant except the index offence and the record, so everything else is written out of the sentencing formula. Not surprisingly, this approach has done nothing to address the racial over-representations in US prisons.

Does strict uniformity entail uniform strictness? There is no necessary connection between retributive justice and heavier sentences. On the contrary, retributivism allows the protest that a sentence is too severe and is a safeguard against the limitless inflationary push of protective sentencing. Yet the sentencing grid's indifference to mitigation and to circumstance is an example of how prescription can completely fetter discretion and lead to injustice and cruelty. The following (quoted in Doob, 1995: 229) illustrates this perfectly:

> One day last week I had to sentence a peasant woman from West Africa to 46 months in a drug case. The result for her young children will undoubtedly be, as she suggested, devastating. On the same day, I sentenced a man to 30 years as a second drug offender... These two cases confirm my sense of depression about much of the cruelty I have been party to in connection with the 'war on drugs'.... At the moment . . . I simply cannot sentence another impoverished person whose destruction has no discernible effect on the drug trade . . . I am just a tired old judge who has temporarily filled his quota of remorselessness.

> Kevin and Wayne are being sentenced for a house burglary they undertook together. Kevin has previous convictions, is excluded from school and has limited support at home from his (lone parent) father. It is Wayne's first offence. He is doing quite well at school; his parents are very upset and offering their son firm support while undertaking to the Court that they will make sure that this won't happen again. Wayne insists that he was not 'led astray' and in fact seems to be the stronger personality. The Magistrates discuss whether they should be sentenced in the same way.

Probation service

Many in government believe that 'strict adherence to National Standards is in the interests of the general public, of offenders, and of the service itself' (Hopley, 2002: 297) and towards the end of the 1990s the performance of areas in relation to the enforcement of these standards was a key measure of effectiveness. Hopley suggests—wrongly in our view—that opposition to the imposition of Standards was in some instances because staff do not like to be told what to do, and in others because there was distrust of anything that tried to impose consistency (2002: 298). Hopley confuses the argument that 'clients' are all different with one stating that they need to be helped; whether or not they need help is a different point from one stating that they have different needs.

> Barbara has been released from prison on licence. She committed a very serious offence, but she has no record to speak of and her risk of reoffending is assessed as relatively low. On balance, she seems to be doing well: factors linked with the chances of reoffending are improving. But she resents having to report, saying that it feels like another punishment on top of prison. She says that having to see the probation officer is a reminder of the past and she wants to build her future. She has missed appointments without giving an adequate explanation. Having been told that this could not continue, she misses again. The officer's duty is clear: but should people like Barbara be sent back to prison?

Probation officers must also recognize the importance of a responsible use of power; some of the decisions that they take regarding enforcement could lead a person back to court, and from there into custody. A failure to comply with the requirements of an order might follow from an officer's lack of engagement with that person as an individual—through time pressures, through lack of training or through other factors. Accountability is pertinent here because if important decisions are being taken about people, there is an ethical and prudential responsibility to explain the reason(s) for this—and to be prepared to listen to their rejoinders and satisfy both yourself and them that the action is justified—not in an adversarial way, but to explain one's case.

Prison service

The point has been made (Sparks et al., 1996: 155) that a good prison officer will bend the rules for the right reasons. Knowing what *are* the right reasons and when they should be used requires sound judgement and contributes substantially towards prison officer professionalism. The flexible interpretation of rules can demonstrate the best and the worst of prison work (Liebling and Price, 2003). The suspension of rules can be traded for both short and longer-term compliance and this very possibility opens up the possibility of abuse and corruption; while rule suspension can be used as a bargaining tool and as a reward for good behaviour, rule enforcement can be used to punish and discriminate between prisoners.

Relationships are seen as more important to the success of prison officers in maintaining good order and discipline than the use of physical force or the power of their position. Liebling and Price refer to this as a sort of 'quiet power' (81), making the point that power is fundamentally *relational*. Different terms have been used for the ways in which prison officers seek to use rules and personal relationships to maintain good discipline; Liebling and Price state that they and others have used the term 'peacekeeping' (Liebling, Elliott and Price, 1999) whereas Sykes (1958) used the term 'corruptions' and Sparks et al. (1996) called them 'accommodations'. There are no doubt some practices that are properly described as corrupt—for example, where officers take decisions in their own interests, perhaps for personal gain—but more commonly the 'corruption' involves the setting aside of a rule because it is recognized as inapplicable or unfair in the specific circumstance. In terms of an earlier distinction, staff would not have to take discretion illegally were they not compelled into it by excessive regulation.

> Paul, a serving prisoner, has been in a very bad mood on the wing. He is not usually like this, but today he seems to be looking for a row. He has just sworn and shouted at an officer in front of other prisoners. Everybody knows that he had a letter yesterday from his former partner saying that their young daughter wouldn't be coming to visit next weekend as planned, because there was no-one who could bring her—and contact in the future also now seems unlikely. Paul has committed a clear disciplinary offence. What should the officer do?

Accountability, discretion and legitimacy

Legitimacy is becoming recognized as a central concept in criminal justice. It is crucial to government, public and participants' trust in the system and the authority of its key players. Cavadino and Dignan (2002) see the 'prison crisis' as essentially a crisis of legitimacy and it is also regarded as critical to the success of community supervision (Bottoms, 2001). Halliday (Home Office, 2001b: 1.3) states:

> At its roots, sentencing contributes to good order in society. It does so by visibly upholding society's norms and standards; dealing appropriately with those who breach them; and enabling the public to have confidence in its outcomes. The public, as a result, can legitimately be expected to uphold and observe the law, and not to take it into their own hands. To achieve this, there must be confidence in the justice of the outcomes, as well as in their effectiveness. Achieving a satisfactory level of public confidence is therefore an important goal of sentencing, and the framework for sentencing needs to support that goal.

This public confidence—which applies not just to sentencing but to all aspects of criminal justice—includes recognition that the system is fair, which is the basis on which it can make claims for citizens' respect and compliance. The police too must command legitimacy to achieve policing with consent, without which policing will be both coercive and ineffective. Along with *structure* and *function* Mawby (2003) sees legitimacy as one of the main concepts to be used to analyse systems of policing.

Of what does this legitimacy consist? Appreciation of and respect for diversity is a critical component, as is accountability in its widest sense (Gelsthorpe, 2001). Unless people believe that their individual needs and predicaments are understood and have decisions explained to them, they will not feel that they are being fairly dealt with. As we have seen, this attention to people's needs implies a high degree of individualization and, correspondingly, a high degree of practitioner discretion in working with them (Canton and Eadie, 2004). Rex found that the offenders in her research study generally believed that sentencing failed to take sufficient account of their backgrounds and of the real impact that the punishment might have upon them. She continues:

> One might speculate that offenders' perceptions that their circumstances were not being adequately considered may account for some resistance on their part to receiving, or simply an inability to comprehend, what was being conveyed to them.
>
> (Rex, 2005: 106)

If communication forms at least part of the purpose of punishment, this perceived neglect of individual diversity has the most serious implications.

Individualization is required by justice, since just punishment must take account of its real impact. It is also required by the principles of effective practice, since risk and criminogenic need, as we have seen, may not be assumed to be the same for different groups. Appreciation of diversity makes it no longer tenable to limit discretion for the sake of a contrived consistency: fairness is not treating everyone the same, but acknowledging and acting on relevant differences.

Discussion: accountability, legitimacy and discretion in the arena of professional practice (the proper boundaries of discretion?)

A key point arising from our discussion so far is that NPM does not actually call people to account at all most of the time—despite the fact that it trumpets precisely that as its rationale. It does not *grant* enough discretion, but in practice is (inevitably) incapable of preventing the taking of discretion—it forces practitioners into dishonest practices. Among the most important reasons to limit discretion is to ensure accountability. However, as we have attempted to demonstrate in the previous section, it does nothing of the kind because individual practitioners across all settings will always have a range of options open to them and much of their day-to-day work will not be monitored; the prison officer in sole charge of a landing has the capacity to manage his or her charges as he or she sees fit. If a situation arises which is outside of the more routine or 'technical' aspects of the job, specialist knowledge and judgement must be drawn on to manage these more 'indeterminate' or uncertain circumstances.

It has been proposed (Jamous and Peloille, 1970) that the balancing of 'technicality' with 'indeterminacy' is a key feature of professional practice and an indicator of the professional status of an organization. That is, the greater degree of indeterminacy permissible, the higher the professional status of practitioners and the organization as a whole. Likewise, if technicality takes over from previously indeterminate roles, a reduction in professional status results. Whether practice is predominately technical or indeterminate in nature however, it is of course important that accountability is retained for all interactions. It is equally important that these are of the highest quality. Focusing on meeting a strict deadline, for example, might lead to a loss of quality—a box can be ticked by a probation officer confirming that the person has reported, but if no time was given to undertaking any meaningful work with that person quality standards have not been met. This is not just unprofessional but dangerous practice when a key role for probation staff is being vigilant about and managing risk throughout the order. The technical act is ticking the attendance box, while the more indeterminate function is the amount and type of interaction that takes place between officer and offender. The fully accountable officer will work within the rules and his or her own judgement about what will work best for each offender under supervision.

Criteria for good practice should therefore focus on good judgement as well as standards for practice, and officers should be praised for records which reflect a depth of work—work which not only 'follows the rules' but also sets out the full range of issues arising throughout the order and explains why, for example, it was necessary to depart from National Standards in some instances. This is not the same as videoing groupwork sessions to make sure officers are following the script and thereby maintaining the integrity of the programme, which we would view as 'managerialist accountability'.

Professional practice should of course incorporate the requirements of both account-ability and discretion whether or not practitioners are being monitored or inspected. This relates to Schön's (1991) concept of 'reflection-in-action'—the ability to reflect on the need for and to make subtle adjustments in the moment—for example, in an interview when there is a sense of it not going as planned. This might include notic-ing a shift in body language, picking up signs that something that has been said has upset the person and needs to be addressed before he or she walks out of the door or—in some cases—becomes violent. It is at this point that the skilled practitioner can change direction and get the interview back on track.

Schön illustrates this ability to reflect on how something is being done at the same time as doing it with the example of jazz musicians improvising as they play together and manifest a 'feel for' their material (1991: 55). Schön's concept of reflection-on-action—thinking through something once it has taken place—is equally important. This requires practitioners to ask themselves 'What was happening there?; what worked?; did I get out of it what I meant to?', incorporating a level of self-supervision which contributes to their accountability.

Professional practice and the use of judgement then goes beyond technical competence (which might ensure that rules are followed, but will not make necessary adjustments in the light of individual circumstances). The argument is not that discretion must be maximized to promote the professionalism of the practitioner; rather that the nature of the work calls for a high degree of responsible and intelligent discretion that can only be accomplished by trained and experienced practitioners, supported by a management structure and system that authorizes this practice while ensuring accountability throughout.

Conclusion

Can this account help to resolve the dilemma of discretion—the need for both the impartiality and predictability of rules, and the flexibility to take account of the very many ways in which circumstances and individuals may differ? One possibility is that rules might emerge from practice rather than being imposed upon it. By this is meant that rules would be constructed as principled practitioners tried to manage the predicaments of practice in a wise and fair-minded manner. Rules are never final, in the sense that a new set of circumstances might call for their enhancement. A 'case law', as it were, could develop with the possibility of departure from the rules only in those circumstances in which a relevant distinction could be made between the present case and earlier ones. This *ratio decidendi* would then come to inform and enhance the rules. The defence against capriciousness and unfairness would be, as Davis (1969) proposed, openness and accountability in the widest sense, as explained earlier. Criminology challenges managerialist standardization by stating that *diversity* is the norm; people are very different from one another and if we pretend that they are not we are going to get it wrong as often as we get it right, and we are going to block practitioners from doing the things that they need to be able to do.

This chapter has asked how the criminal justice process can ensure that proper account is given to people whose lives are most affected by the decisions taken—specifically offenders, but also victims and the general public. It has applied criminological and philosophical insights to criminal justice practice in a range of professional settings, demonstrating their utility to practitioners as they go about applying their discretion and power. How they do this, and what outcomes result should be a key concern of policy makers.

Key arguments

The chapter is designed to interrogate questions of justice and fairness in relation to criminal justice decision making and the extent to which practitioners should be held to account for the decisions they make and, most importantly, to whom. NPM imposes accountability through rules and standard setting, whereas it is suggested here that accountability is best seen as a process or dialogue with relevant individuals involved in each case, with rules and procedures emerging from good practice rather than being imposed from above.

Further reading

Eadie and Canton's (2002) *Practising in a Context of Ambivalence: the challenge for youth justice workers* argues that best practice with young offenders (and, we would suggest, with all offenders) requires *both* high accountability *and* wide discretion. Gelsthorpe and Padfield's (2003) edited collection, *Exercising Discretion. Decision making in the criminal justice system and beyond* continues the theme of discretion as a highly contentious and yet fundamental concept in criminal justice decision making. Nicola Padfield's (2007) edited collection, *Who to Release? Parole, fairness and criminal justice*, offers a more specialist analysis of the decision- making processes which result in the release of serious offenders back into 'the community'. See especially Alison Liebling's Chapter 5, 'Why fairness matters in criminal justice'. Finally, Chapter 3 'Rules are Rules' of Fineman, S., Gabriel, Y. and Sims, D. (2002) *Organizing and Organizations*, pp.22–37, explores similar debates but within a much broader organizational context than that of criminal justice.

7

YOUTH JUSTICE POLICY AND PRACTICE: RECLAIMING
APPLIED CRIMINOLOGY AS CRITICAL INTERVENTION

Barry Goldson and Joe Yates

It is my view that the model outlined . . . is probably more appropriate than ever for dealing with contemporary delinquents. Despite its demonstrated success, however, it has not grown or developed as a philosophy of correctional treatment and practice. This is hardly surprising in an era when we must hide any intention of treating young offenders with compassion or understanding . . . In the final analysis, however, the survival of any model in this politicized field will not be based on results. It will . . . be a matter of chance, of happenstance, of politics and mood. The same can be said of the current destructive juvenile justice system.

(Jerome G. Miller, 1998: xiv)

A few sociologists may be sufficiently biased in favor of youth to grant credibility to their account of how the adult world treats them. But why do we not accuse other sociologists who study youth of being biased in favor of adults? Most research on youth, after all, is clearly designed to find out why youth are so troublesome for adults, rather than asking the equally interesting sociological question: 'Why do adults make so much trouble for youth?'

(Howard S. Becker, 1967: 242)

Chapter summary

This chapter:
- Examines the means by which criminological knowledge was applied to positive effect in the youth justice system in England and Wales throughout the 1980s and up to the early 1990s.
- Analyses the political conditions that emerged in 1993 that severed the youth justice research–policy–practice relation and considers the extent to which the application of criminological knowledge to policy formation is 'a matter of chance, of happenstance, of politics and mood'.
- Critically assesses recent constructions of 'evidenced-based' policy formation and their application within youth justice in England and Wales since 1997.
- Reviews illustrative examples of the means by which qualitative research—that 'grants credibility to [young people's] accounts of how the adult world treats them'—together with research-based campaigning, can be applied to youth justice as forms of critical intervention.
- Assesses the challenges that confront applied criminology and the development of progressive youth justice.

Background

Throughout the 1980s and into the 1990s, youth justice in England and Wales was informed by the symbiotic intersection of academic investigation, practitioner experience and responsive policy. Indeed, the relation between researchers, practitioners and policy makers sustained a progressive consensus that articulated itself through three key objectives: *diversion, decriminalisation* and *decarceration*. The received wisdom was that transitory delinquent episodes were a relatively 'normal' part of adolescent transition, most young offenders 'grow out of crime' and formal criminal justice interventions were best avoided whenever possible (Rutherford, 1992).

> • **Diversion** refers to the policy and practice of systematically diverting children and young people away from formal criminal justice interventions. Diversion is underpinned by research evidence and practice experience showing that premature intervention and formal criminalization is potentially damaging and counterproductive; it is likely to confirm 'delinquent identities' and entrench young people in 'criminal pathways'. Diversionary practices—including cautioning and informal action—provide alternatives to prosecution and court-based intervention.
> • **Decriminalization** derives from diversion. It is a process whereby deviance and minor offending are primarily conceptualized and understood as 'normal' features of adolescent development that young people ultimately 'grow out of'. As such, it is argued that the principal agents of social control should avoid criminalizing such behaviours (rather they should be decriminalized).
> • **Decarceration** refers to the policy and practice of keeping children and young people out of custodial institutions and replacing penal detention with forms of intensive community-based intervention. It is informed by a robust international evidence base confirming the damaging and counterproductive tendencies of custodial establishments.

In the early 1990s, however, a series of events combined to fracture the consensus that had formed and developed throughout the previous decade. Moreover, since the election of the first New Labour government in 1997, youth justice policy has effectively taken a U-turn. Diversion and decriminalization have been displaced by an increasing emphasis on early intervention on the one hand, whilst on the other hand the expansion of custodial disposals signals the abandonment of decarceration. Furthermore, not only youth crime, but civil transgressions, youth disorder and anti-social behaviour are now routinely conceptualized as major social problems, as distinct from relatively 'normal' and short-lived episodes of adolescent deviance. Accordingly, the youth justice system has expanded on an industrial scale and increasing numbers of children and young people are being swept up in its wake and exposed to correctional 'programmes'.

This major shift in youth justice policy raises fundamental questions concerning applied criminology. On what basis were the policy priorities of diversion, decriminalisation and decarceration superseded by their polar opposites—early intervention, criminalizing system expansion and incarceration? Why should a consensually effective approach to youth crime and youth justice (such as that which prevailed in the 1980s and early 1990s) be replaced by an alternative system that consistently attracts widespread criticism (such as the current youth justice system in England and Wales)?

What political circumstances have served to distort research-informed policy and practice? Can applied criminology be reclaimed in the youth justice sphere as a mode of critical intervention that takes account of young people's perspectives and circumstances and seeks to develop progressive approaches to policy and practice? This chapter will examine such questions in exploring the application of criminological knowledge to contemporary youth justice law, policy and practice.

Applied criminology and rational policy

It is a curious paradox of the 1980s and early 1990s—a time when 'Thatcherite' Conservatism was at its most commanding period that witnessed the most determined assault upon social justice—that criminal statute provided the space within which a progressive, effective and humane youth justice developed (Goldson, 1997a, 1997b). The principles of diversion, decriminalization and decarceration, to which we have referred, comprised the cornerstones of policy responses to children and young people in trouble and informed dynamic practices constructed around: minimum necessary intervention; systematic diversionary approaches; supervision in the community and direct alternatives to custody (Pitts, 1990; Rutherford, 1992).

Moreover, the formulation of policy was underpinned by a coalescence of academic research, lessons drawn from 'juvenile justice' practice experience and specific political imperatives of successive Conservative administrations. It was a delicately balanced consensus forged around an improbable coincidence of interests, but it was sufficiently robust to steer a progressive line for youth justice policy and practice for the best part of a decade.

Academic research and practice experience combined to affirm that for the majority of young offenders their criminal transgressions were petty, opportunistic and transitory. Pitts (1988: 133) described juvenile crime as 'usually episodic and unplanned and often a complete shambles' and Dunkel (1991: 23) referred to its 'relative insignificance', later adding that it is little more than a 'ubiquitous and passing phenomenon linked to age' (1996: 37). Research evidence and practice experience moved beyond simply asserting the relative 'normality' of much youth crime, however, it also combined to demonstrate that criminalizing children and young people by means of formal intervention and 'labelling' tended to produce counterproductive outcomes. Such reasoning was derived from the work of the American sociologist and criminologist Edwin Lemert (1951). Lemert distinguished between what he called 'primary' and 'secondary' deviance, arguing that the former was often little more than temporary transgression with the perpetrators having little or no conception of themselves as 'offenders'. 'Secondary deviance', according to Lemert, is *created* through negative *social reaction* and processes of formal *labelling* and *criminalization* that serve to establish and confirm 'criminal' identities. Lemert's principal conclusion—that social control *causes* deviancy, inadvertently or otherwise—comprised a significant advance in understanding the potentially problematic nature of criminal justice interventions in general and youth justice processes in particular. His ideas were later developed by John Kitsuse (1962),

Howard Becker (1963) and Kai Erikson (1966) who argued that the key to understanding deviance lay in the *reactions* from agencies of social control rather than in the original deviant act. They contended that formal intervention, labelling, criminalization and negative social reaction created, or at least compounded, the very problems that youth justice systems aim to resolve. Such ideas were very influential and, in their applied form, they underpinned the philosophy and practice of diversion within the youth justice system in England and Wales throughout the 1980s and early 1990s.

The theoretical claims and empirical insights provided by Lemert, Kitsuse, Becker and Erikson expressed themselves most clearly through the practices of informal warnings and cautions, as alternatives to formal prosecution. Such practice effectively served to *divert* children and young people from court—thus avoiding the inherent problems of formal criminalization—and this was fully facilitated by developments in policy. Indeed, two particularly important Home Office Circulars—14/1985 and 59/1990—actively promoted the use of such *diversionary* measures (Home Office, 1985, 1990). Home Office Circular 59/90 explicitly stated that the purpose of cautioning was to deal quickly and simply with less serious offenders, to divert such offenders from the criminal court and to reduce the likelihood of reoffending. In some cases cautions were administered within hours of the commission of an offence. In others, the police would determine that further information was required necessitating a visit to the child's home and consultation with other agencies. In certain areas quite sophisticated diversionary partnerships and inter-agency arrangements were developed such as the Northamptonshire Juvenile Liaison Bureau (Bell, Hodgson and Pragnell, 1999).

The Northamptonshire Juvenile Liaison Bureau

This was a multi-agency diversion scheme based in Northamptonshire, England. Decision making was operationalized through a panel comprising senior representatives from local agencies (including the Police, the Probation Service, the Education Authority, the Youth Service and the Social Services Department). The panel met weekly to consider all the case files relating to children and young people arrested and who admitted their guilt. The panel decided whether the young person should be cautioned (diverted) or prosecuted (criminalized). The Bureau aimed:
• To divert young people wherever possible from penal and welfare intervention systems into informal networks of control, support and care.
• To avoid the imposition of those forms of penalties and welfare intervention that tend to aggravate the very problem they seek to reduce.
• To enable agencies to respond to delinquent behaviour in ways that may reduce offending and enable young people to become more responsible adults, and to encourage 'normal' institutions of society to respond constructively to adolescent behaviour.

The effect of the Home Office Circulars, together with the development of strategic diversionary practice—in Northamptonshire and elsewhere—was not insignificant. Gibson and Cavadino (1995: 56) note that the number of 'young offenders' cautioned doubled between 1985 and 1995, and Gelsthorpe and Morris (1999: 210) observed that 'most children who offended over this period were diverted by the police: 90 per cent of boys and 97 per cent of girls in 1993'. Furthermore, cautioning was widely held to be a success by professional, academic and government sources (Newburn and Souhami, 2006). Many local schemes, such as the Northamptonshire Bureau, were identified as models of 'good practice' allowing for expeditious and economical *diversion* and *decriminalization* (Jones, 2001) and providing an 'effective means of preventing re-offending by young people' (Reid, 1997: 4).

If criminological theorising and empirical research was being applied to positive effect at the 'shallow end' of the youth justice system via diversionary and decriminalizing practice, it also informed *decarceration* strategies at the 'deep end'. John Pitts observed that:

> In as much as social scientific research can ever 'prove' anything it has proved that locking up children and young people in an attempt to change their delinquent behaviour has been an expensive failure . . . more and more studies have demonstrated the tendency of these institutions to increase the reconviction rates of their ex-inmates, to evoke violence from previously non-violent people, to render ex-inmates virtually unemployable, to destroy family relationships and to put a potentially victimised citizenry at greater risk'.
>
> (Pitts, 1990: 8)

Furthermore, as stated, the positive interrelation between research and practice during this period was bolstered by its paradoxical compatibility with discrete government policy objectives. Throughout the 1980s successive Conservative administrations were determined to relieve the Treasury of public spending commitments and, as Pratt (1987: 429) noted, 'to reduce the custodial population on the grounds of cost effectiveness . . . led to general support for alternatives to custody initiatives'. The combination of research evidence and political imperative to reduce public sector spending provided the basis for *decarceration*. In this way, the 1988 Green Paper contained an explicit policy commitment drawing heavily on the very language of academic research (the 'growing out of crime' thesis and 'labelling' perspectives):

> Most young offenders grow out of crime as they become more mature and responsible. They need encouragement and help to become law-abiding. Even a short period of custody is quite likely to confirm them as criminals, particularly as they acquire new criminal skills from more sophisticated offenders. They see themselves labelled as criminals and behave accordingly.
>
> (Home Office, 1988: paras. 2.17–2.19)

David Faulkner, the Head of the Home Office Crime Department between 1982 and 1990 (who worked particularly closely with Douglas Hurd, Home Secretary from 1985 to 1989), later reflected that:

> The guiding principle of much of the policy in relation to juvenile offenders was one of the *minimum use of custody* and that policy was considered . . . to have been *successful* in the *visible reduction in known juvenile offending* during that period.
>
> (Panorama, BBC Television, 01.11.93, emphases added)

Indeed, the number of 'juveniles' sentenced to custody between 1981 and 1990 fell from 7,900 to 1,700 (Home Office, 1991). Most compelling, however, was the apparent success of policy and practice, with the increased emphasis on diversion, decriminalization and decarceration producing a corresponding decrease in the incidence of juvenile crime. The Children's Society Advisory Committee noted that:

> Home Office statistics suggest that there has been a 37 per cent decline in the number of known juvenile offenders since 1985. This is partly attributable to demographic changes—the juvenile population has fallen by 25 per cent. However, the number of known juvenile offenders per 100,000 of the population has also fallen, from 3,130 in 1980 to 2,616 in 1990, a drop of 16 per cent. It remains true that juveniles commit a high proportion of all detected offences but this also appears to be declining. In 1980 juvenile crime represented 32 per cent of all crime; in 1991 that figure has dropped to 20 per cent.
>
> (Children's Society Advisory Committee on Juvenile Custody and
> its Alternatives, 1993: 21)

It would be misleading to describe the developments in policy and practice during this period in terms of unqualified success, not least because the 'justice' that prevailed was permeated with institutionalized injustices particularly in respect of 'race' and gender (Goldson, 1999). Despite this, significant progress was made in applying criminological knowledge towards the development of rational, humane and effective youth justice policy and practice. The significance of political support for such developments was crucial however. If political imperatives were to shift, as they did in the 1990s, the limitations of applied criminology in forging rational policy making would be exposed. Herein lies a familiar theme within the political history of youth justice policy in which government can be seen 'imputing credibility to those (policies and practices) that fit current ideology and disregarding those that don't' (Miller, 1991: 240).

Politicization and irrational punitiveness

The sociologist and criminologist Stan Cohen (1972: 9–11) famously noted:

> Societies appear to be subject, every now and then, to periods of moral panic. A condition, episode, person or group of persons emerges to become defined as a threat to societal values and interests; its nature is presented in a stylized and stereotypical fashion by the mass media . . . [it can have] serious and long-lasting repercussions and might produce such changes as those in *legal* and *social policy* . . . public concern about a particular condition is generated, a '*symbolic crusade*' mounted.
>
> (Emphases added)

The key significance of Cohen's observations for our purposes here rests on two levels: the *symbolic* ('symbolic crusade') and the *institutional* ('legal and social policy').

In 1993, sustained media coverage of car crime, outbreaks of civil unrest within which children and young people appeared to be prominent players, and the construction of the 'bail bandit' and 'persistent young offender' (children apparently beyond the reach of the law) fuelled 'moral panic' and the 'folk devilling of children and young people' (Carlen, 1996: 48). Such 'folk devilling' (a 'symbolic crusade') conjoined with 'institutional' responses (law and policy) and ultimately led to a repudiation of the policy and practice of diversion, decriminalization and decarceration.

Furthermore, Bottoms and Stevenson (1992: 23–4) have observed that:

> It is a fact well known to students of social policy that reforms of the system often take place not so much because of *careful routine analysis* by ministers and civil servants in the relevant Department of State . . . but because one or more *individual incident(s)* occurs, drawing public attention to . . . policy in a dramatic way which seems to demand change . . . the reforms would not have taken place without the public attention created by the original incident'.
>
> (Emphases added)

The death of two-year-old James Bulger in February, 1993, and the subsequent arrest and conviction of two ten-year-old boys for his murder, became one such 'individual incident'. Within a context of 'moral panic' and 'folk devilling', the 'incident' was taken as the defining expression of 'childhood in crisis' (Scraton, 1997). Young offenders were portrayed as the new 'enemy within', the language of punishment and retribution echoed through populist discourse and youth justice soon became highly-charged and politicized. If the political conditions in the 1980s and early 1990s had opened up spaces for criminological knowledge to be applied to youth justice policy to positive effect, the exact opposite was the case in the post-1993 period when political posturing gave rise to a wave of irrational punitiveness.

By 1993, various opinion polls indicated that the political fortunes and popularity of the Conservative Party—that had been in government since 1979—were finally beginning to wane, and many influential Tories felt that the time had arrived for re-stating traditional values and ideological convictions. The Conservative Party had conventionally been associated with a 'tough' line on law and order and it soon re-engaged with established practice, with specific emphasis placed on youth crime and justice. Just days after James Bulger's death, the Prime Minister, John Major, proclaimed that 'society needs to condemn a little more and understand a little less' and the Home Secretary, Kenneth Clarke, referred to 'really persistent nasty little juveniles' (*Daily Mail* 22 February, 1993). Three months later, and after a Cabinet re-shuffle, Michael Howard made his first public pronouncement as the new Home Secretary, referring to what he called a 'self-centred arrogant group of young hoodlums . . . who are adult in everything except years [and who] will no longer be able to use age as an excuse for immunity from effective punishment . . . they will find themselves behind bars' (*Daily Mail* 3 June, 1993). At the Conservative Party Conference in October, 1993, Howard declared that he was 'speaking for the nation . . . we are all sick and tired of young hooligans who terrorise communities'. He promised a 'clamp down' and claimed that 'prison works' (Goldson, 1997a). Moreover, the Conservatives' 'symbolic crusade' (to recall Cohen's phrase) was translated into law and policy, marking a reactionary new direction for youth justice. Rutherford (1995: 58) notes:

> Rapidly drafted legislation during 1993 shot great holes in the Criminal Justice Act 1991, which was shortly followed by the Criminal Justice and Public Order Act 1994. Where the 1991 Act had removed 14-year-olds from the prison system, the 1994 Act seeks to create a new generation of child prisons for 12–14-year-olds. This is not a return to the 1970s but to the period preceding the Children Act 1908.

For its part, the re-styled New Labour project—emerging under the steadily increasing influence of Tony Blair—broke with its conventionally moderate position on questions of criminal justice policy. Instead, it competed with the Conservatives on punitive terms. In January 1993, Tony Blair—as Opposition Home Secretary—coined what was to become a key New Labour motif in declaring his intention to be 'tough on crime, tough on the causes of crime'. Furthermore, throughout the period 1993 to 1997, New Labour policy makers published a wide range of briefing documents focusing on youth justice and related matters, within which a creeping punitivity was increasingly evident (Jones, 2002).

Michael Tonry (1996: 179) explains that:

> It is easy to seize the low ground in political debates about crime policy. When one candidate campaigns with pictures of clanging prison gates . . . and disingenuous promises that newer, tougher policies will work, it is difficult for an opponent to explain that crime is a complicated problem, that real solutions must be long term, and that simplistic toughness does not reduce crime rates. This is why, as a result, candidates often compete to establish which is tougher in his views about crime.

The period from 1993 to 1997 exemplified this. The two main political parties competed on the 'low ground' each purveying 'simplistic toughness' in debates around youth crime and justice. The same period also revealed the limitations of applied criminology in mediating irrational punitivity. Despite the fact that Michael Howard's and Tony Blair's policy pronouncements were criticized from almost all quarters including: child welfare organisations; penal reform groups; the probation service; academia; Home Office officials; the Judiciary; the House of Lords; the United Nations Committee on the Rights of the Child (Goldson, 1997a: 138–43), they bulldozed their way into law and policy. Ultimately, the application of criminological knowledge and the development of rational policy is contingent and, in many respects, such contingency is defined by political context. To recall our introductory quotations, this is what Jerome Miller (1998) means when he argues that: 'in the final analysis . . . the survival of any model [of youth justice] in this politicized field will not be based on results, it will . . . be a matter of chance, of happenstance, of politics and mood'. In this way, as Howard Becker (1967) observes, 'adults make so much trouble for youth'.

The 'new youth justice': selectively applied criminology

In May 1997, a landslide general election victory returned the first New Labour government and youth justice policy formation took another crucial turn. David Smith (2006) notes that the 1999 *Modernising Government* White Paper proposed that policy should be informed routinely by evidence and subject to regular evaluative scrutiny and audit. It appeared to many that the government had committed itself to 'professional' policy making soundly based on evidence of 'what works' with offenders (Cabinet Office, 1999). In turn, this appeared to re-open the door to applied criminology and to signal a rational shift from *opinion-based* to *evidence-based* policy; from ideological conviction and/or pure speculation to 'scientific realism' and the 'pragmatic solution' (Muncie, 2002).

Indeed, the *rhetoric* of 'evidenced-based' policy and 'what works' rationales have gained prominence within modern youth justice discourse. At their simplest, they imply a mechanistic formulation whereby youth justice policy is no longer 'hampered' by any adherence to competing philosophical principles and/or ideological convictions. Rather, policy makers simply need to translate 'hard evidence' into policy by means of technical scientific transfer. The *reality*, however, is that both the social world and the processes of youth justice policy formation are far more complex and there are multiple problems and controversies associated with 'evidence-based' policy and 'what works' rationales as they are currently formulated within contemporary youth justice. It is not practical to engage with the detail of this here (for a fuller discussion see Goldson and Muncie, 2006), although it is particularly important to highlight the processes of selective filtering that are applied. This occurs where some 'evidence' is privileged and emphasized, whilst other 'evidence' is marginalized or 'forgotten'. Such *subjective* and *selective*, as distinct from *objective* and *scientifically comprehensive* processes, are clearly problematic and they seriously compromise the notion of a 'pure' applied criminology.

The key to understanding this is the continuing *political* significance of youth crime and youth justice. On the one hand politicians and policy makers are ostensibly keen to adhere to the 'evidence base', yet on the other hand they are even more determined to maintain a 'tough' line that is immune to 'excuses' (Home Office, 1997). In other words, a new language of rationality, modernization and evidence has come in, but it has failed to eclipse the old language of populist toughness. According to Garland (2001: 172) this is symptomatic of:

> A new relationship between politicians, the public and penal experts . . . [whereby] politicians are more directive, penal experts are less influential, and public opinion becomes a key reference point . . . [Youth] justice is now more vulnerable to shifts of public mood and political reaction . . . and expert control of the policy agenda has been considerably reduced.

This creates complex tensions between what is regarded as legitimate and/or politically acceptable 'evidence' and what is not—what is to be applied and what is not. It also raises questions about the scientific and/or methodological rigour of the preferred 'evidence' and/or the means by which research findings are interpreted (Goldson, 2001; Wilcox, 2003; Yates, 2004a; Bottoms, 2005). As Muncie (2004) has argued, the selective interpretation and application of 'evidence' means that certain youth justice policies continue to be driven as much by *political* motivation as by theoretical purity, empirical integrity or 'what works' effectiveness. The prime exemplar of this phenomenon is the government's stubborn attachment to youth imprisonment, despite the extraordinary weight of evidence pointing to the spectacular failures, corrosive damage and enormous expense of incarcerative interventions (Goldson, 2006a, 2006b).

Reclaiming applied criminology as critical intervention

Despite the *new* rhetoric of evidence-based policy, *old* political imperatives have continued to undermine the application of criminological knowledge and distort youth justice policy formation. Paradoxically, and to paraphrase Howard Becker's opening words, the youth justice system in England and Wales continues to 'make trouble for youth'. Just under 4,000 Anti-social Behaviour Orders were imposed on children and young people between April 1999 and December 2005, with an average 47 per cent breach rate and as many as 500 children a year being imprisoned as a consequence (Bateman, 2007). The abolition of cautioning and the introduction of reprimands, final warnings and referral orders further extended net-widening and institutionalized child criminalization (Kemp et al., 2002; Pragnell, 2005). Intensive Supervision and Surveillance Programmes (ISSPs)—including electronic monitoring—have been widely applied, but have failed to reduce the numbers of children and young people being sent to penal custody. In 2005 to 2006 alone, 2,738 children were breached for failing to comply with such programmes and 825 were imprisoned as a consequence of breach proceedings (Youth Justice Board, 2007a), implying that ISSPs are serving to increase rather reduce custodial sanctions. England and Wales makes proportionately greater use of penal custody for children than most other industrialized democracies in the world and the crises that beset the institutions within which children and young people are detained continue, including: overcrowding; children held at great distance from home; endemic bullying; strip-searching; solitary confinement; physical restraint; self-harm and, ultimately, child deaths in custody (Goldson, 2006b). The problems that confront the community when children and young people are released from custody also endure, via exceptionally high reconviction rates (House of Commons Committee of Public Accounts, 2004).

There is no rational criminological justification for such harmful and counter-productive policies and practices. There is, therefore, a pressing need to reclaim applied criminology as a form of critical intervention into youth justice policy and practice debates. By briefly drawing upon some of our own work, we move towards concluding this chapter by considering three illustrative examples of how this might be achieved. First, by 'listening to youth' (Brown, S., 2005) in both communities and custodial institutions and, to recall the words of Becker again, 'granting credibility to their accounts of how the adult world treats them'; second, by applying principles informed by research and practice to campaigning activity.

Case Study One: Listening to Youth in Communities

The children and young people who are most heavily exposed to the youth justice system in England and Wales are routinely drawn from some of the most disadvantaged families, neighbourhoods and communities. Young people for whom the fabric of life invariably stretches across poverty; state welfare neglect; poor housing and/or homelessness; loneliness and isolation; severely circumscribed educational and employment opportunities; 'hollowed-out' communities and the most pressing sense of structural exclusion, are the very young people targeted by the youth justice apparatus. This is a population of young people growing up in 'concentrated poverty areas' (Child Poverty Action Group, 1997: 17), who typically experience the official adult relation as an antagonistic, coercive and/or authoritarian presence. The unique perspectives and experiences of such young people are normally shut out, silenced and thus disqualified within mainstream youth justice discourse (Yates, 2004).

It is only by actively and deliberately engaging the participation of such young people through the research process, either by ethnographic methods (Yates, 2004, 2006a, 2006b) or by qualitative in-depth interviews and focus groups (Goldson, 2003), that their experiential expertise and understanding can be 'given voice' and applied to the policy and practice debates. Such research reveals complex and seemingly contradictory messages. Place-attachment and territorial identities are often strong in multiply disadvantaged communities given that 'residents of poor neighbourhoods spend more time in their local areas than do residents of wealthier neighbourhoods' (Kearns and Forrest, 1998: 13). Yet there is a paradoxical sense in which the community offers least to those for whom it has greatest significance, and this is particularly true for young people in the modern age (Yates, 2006a). The remarkable message to emerge from our research with young people in such neighbourhoods is that their conceptualizations of community, together with their expectations and aspirations, are singularly unremarkable. They are very grounded and 'ordinary'. Young people want to be listened to and taken seriously; they want to be able to form meaningful relationships with adults providing that such engagements are underpinned by *mutual* respect and recognition; they want to see real, maintained and sustainable improvement in their communities; they want to see the development of appropriate resources; they want to be able to look forward to futures in which employment is a key element. The very ordinariness of such aspirations goes some way to 'de-demonize' the young, to profile their normative and pro-social energies, and to recognize their strengths and resistances as well as their inherent and structural vulnerabilities.

Case Study Two: Listening to Youth in Custodial Institutions

If the youth justice system is a means of controlling and regulating the young poor, it is particularly so in its custodial application. It is now widely acknowledged that the biographies of young prisoners are normally scarred by multiple disadvantage and intersecting forms of social exclusion (Challen and Walton, 2004; Children's Rights Alliance for England, 2002; Commission for Social Care Inspectorate et al., 2005; Goldson and Coles, 2005; Worsley, 2007). For the overwhelming majority of child prisoners the combination of: their removal from all that is familiar to them; their daily experience of bullying; the officially approved practices of 'restraint', strip searching and segregation; and the limits that are imposed upon exercise and access to fresh air perpetuate insecurity, fear, damage and harm (Goldson, 2006b). For some such prisoners the cumulative pressures are too much to bear. In a single year, there were 1,324 reported incidents of self-harm by children in Young Offender Institutions in England and Wales (Her Majesty's Chief Inspector of Prisons, 2006: 16). Ultimately, the pain of confinement is relieved only on release. For other child prisoners 'release' takes a fatal form. Between July 1990 and November 2007, 30 children died in penal custody in England and Wales, 28 in state prisons and 2 in private jails (Goldson and Coles, 2005).

Continued

Case Study Two: Listening to Youth in Custodial Institutions—cont'd

Not unlike our community-based research it is only by interviewing young prisoners in situ that the researcher can gain a rounded insight into their experiences of confinement. This might also be supplemented by in-depth interviews with prison staff and other professionals located in custodial institutions. In this way, a twelve-month intensive study involving: 111 in-depth interviews; detailed institutional observations; professional consultations with representatives of key 'stake-holding' agencies; extensive documentary analysis; a national questionnaire survey and an audit of assessment documentation served to reveal the daily miseries of youth imprisonment (Goldson, 2002). When the narratives of young prisoners are combined with those of experienced prison service personnel, a powerful critique of the dehumanizing and corrosive realities of life inside is constructed. When this is placed alongside the statistical evidence with regard to patterns of post-custodial reconviction, the youth prison is stripped of any remaining remnants of criminological rationality and legitimacy.

Case Study Three: Research and Practice as a Basis for Campaigning

Many non-governmental organizations seeking to influence the policy making process base their campaigning activities upon the messages from research and practice experience. The National Association for Youth Justice (NAYJ) was established in Britain in 1994 following the merger between the National Intermediate Treatment Federation (NITFed) and the Association for Youth Justice (AYJ). It is a membership organization managed by an elected national committee and both its membership and its committee comprises of a broad range of youth justice practitioners, managers, researchers and academics. The NAYJ holds an annual conference and organizes regular regional workshops/seminars, it supports a learned journal (*Youth Justice: An International Journal*), it regularly responds to government consultation exercises on matters of child/youth policy and it campaigns for justice for children in trouble. The NAYJ 'philosophical base' informs all of its activities. It is underpinned by applied criminological knowledge (drawn from research findings and practice experience) and it takes explicit account of international human rights imperatives. In this sense, the NAYJ is truly 'evidence based' and independent of any party-political interests. The core elements of the NAYJ 'philosophical base' include the following statements:

• Children are entitled to equality of opportunity and access to relevant services. They are particularly vulnerable to, and must be protected from, discrimination. (Discriminatory youth justice interventions apply particularly through gendered and racialized contexts and, as discussed, disadvantaged children are disproportionately exposed to early intervention, criminalization, labelling and, ultimately, incarceration).

• The establishment, application and protection of children's rights within national and international law and convention is essential. (This takes account of the United Nations Convention on the Rights of the Child and other international human rights instruments that have been formally ratified by the UK government).

• Children are best looked after within their family or community, however these may be constituted. (This is derived from a wealth of research evidence and practice experience that serves to illuminate the counterproductive tendencies of institutional care and custody).

• Children and young people are less likely to offend if their physical, emotional, educational and social needs are met throughout childhood, with protection from all forms of neglect, abuse, exploitation or poverty and opportunity for development of full potential and achievement. (This also derives from a body of evidence confirming that the best form of youth crime prevention is the provision of universal services that meet young people's needs and safeguard them from social harm).

• Locking up children is inherently damaging and contrary to the promotion of healthy development. Children should not be locked up and services should be developed and provided with a view to achieving that aim. (This is informed by the research evidence discussed earlier in the chapter and centres on the provision of 'alternatives to custody' services).

> ## Case Study Three: Research and Practice as a
> ## Basis for Campaigning—cont'd
>
> • Children should be helped to take responsibility for their decisions and actions in accordance with their stage of development and understanding. (This is particularly significant with regard to the age of criminal responsibility. In England and Wales children are held to be fully responsible for any criminal transgression once they reach the age of 10. The NAYJ believes that the age of criminal responsibility should be significantly higher, as it is in many other European countries).
> • Most children and young people offend and will mature into responsible, law-abiding adults. The labelling of children's behaviour as criminal is likely to be injurious to their normal development. (This is a re-statement of the 'normality', 'growing out of crime' and 'labelling' theses that we considered earlier in the chapter.)
> For a full version of the NAYJ 'philosophical base' see: http://www.nayj.org.uk/website/

Seeking out, and granting credibility to, the perspectives of children and young people in communities and institutions, and building campaigns based upon research and practice experience, offers some prospect for reclaiming applied criminology as a form of critical intervention. The directions that contemporary youth justice policy and practice have taken in England and Wales are irrational. They have no valid claim to criminological legitimacy. Academics and practitioners with integrity have a responsibility to challenge such harmful irrationality, to make critical interventions and, ultimately, to 'speak truth to power' (Said, 1994). Within the limits of a single chapter we have attempted to illustrate why this is important and to signal some ways in which it might be achieved.

—— Applied criminology and progressive youth justice: limits and potential ——

Reece Walters (2003: 160) argues that historically, mainstream criminological research has been 'dominated by a spirit or legacy of pragmatism, which has promoted a scientific and administrative criminology to aid the immediate policy needs of government'. This follows Wright Mills's (1959: 193) observation that the relationship between academic social science and the state is limited to what 'they [state officials] find useful, which is to say that we [social scientists] become technicians accepting their problems and aims, or ideologists promoting their prestige and authority'. In this way, mainstream criminology has largely focused on the concerns of the state and it has allowed its *raison d'etre* to be narrowly defined in terms of providing knowledge-based insights on how to manage and regulate individuals and groups who are deemed to be problematic. Hudson (1997: 452) reflects that: 'criminology is itself part of the apparatus of social control'. Furthermore, Brown (Brown, S., 2005: 119) suggests that 'youth criminology perhaps remains the field most trapped by its past and most confounded by uncritical supposition', leading to a preoccupation with governmental agendas focusing upon identifiable constituencies of young people (for example working class, ethnic minorities) and their construction as archetypal 'folk devils'. This represents a stultifyingly limited 'applied criminology'.

In contrast, more critically oriented sociological criminology seeks to resist such slavish 'incorporation' and to stand outside of the 'mainstream'; to interrogate contradictions in the social order, to explore the intersecting nature of social (in)justice and criminal (in)justice and to analyse the complex relations between individual agency and socio-economic and political structures. Here the conceptualization of 'applied' hinges less in terms of doing the state's 'dirty work' and more in terms of exposing and critiquing it. This is an approach, within the context of youth justice, that sets out to engage the 'view from below' and 'grants credibility to [young people's] accounts of how the adult world treats them'. It is an orientation that articulates the voices of young people, values partnerships and builds alliances with practitioner groups and non-governmental campaigning agencies. It is a perspective that both recognizes and challenges the fact that the research–policy relation is 'a matter of chance, of happenstance, of politics and mood'. It is a theoretically informed, empirically grounded, experience related, policy relevant form of critical intervention that, to paraphrase Wright Mills (1959: 193), may not 'save the world' but sees 'nothing at all wrong with trying'. This offers the promise and potential of a dynamic 'applied criminology'.

The prospect of progressive youth justice in England and Wales currently seems remote, however. The seemingly entrenched politicization of youth 'disorder', 'anti-social behaviour' and 'crime' has served to demonize identifiable constituencies of the young, to legitimize 'ill-considered but attention grabbing tough-on-crime proposals' (Tonry, 2004: 2) and to 'institutionalise intolerance' (Muncie, 1999). Moreover, as we have discussed, 'zero tolerance', 'tough on crime' and 'no more excuses' sentiments have claimed significant material purchase with regard to policy formation, system expansion and practical intervention. Senior politicians repeatedly refer to an increasingly anxious, risk-averse and fearful public and selective constructions of 'public opinion' are mobilized and presented as primary legitimizing rationales for the 'tough on crime' agenda. Perhaps the ultimate irony here is the repeated claim that youth justice policy is 'evidence-based'.

A genuinely evidence-based approach to youth crime and justice must first transgress crude politicization and the perpetuation of 'populist punitiveness' (Bottoms, 1995) and engage instead with more sophisticated, measured and dignified approaches. Ultimately, this requires the depoliticization of youth crime and justice and the development of more progressively tolerant, human rights compliant, non-criminalizing, inclusionary and participative strategies. It is to this that 'applied criminology' must strive.

Key arguments

- Criminological knowledge was applied to positive effect in the youth justice system in England and Wales throughout the 1980s and up to the early 1990s.
- However, post-1993 research evidence and criminological knowledge have been selectively applied in youth justice.
- Mainstream criminology has largely focused on the concerns of the state and it has allowed its raison d'etre to be narrowly defined in terms of providing knowledge-based insights on how to manage and regulate individuals and groups who are deemed to be problematic. This represents a stultifyingly limited 'applied criminology'.
- Constructing applied criminology as critical intervention both recognizes and challenges the fact that the research–policy relation is 'a matter of chance, of happenstance, of politics and mood'.

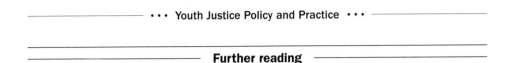

Further reading

Goldson, B. (ed.) (2008) *Dictionary of Youth Justice*, Cullompton: Willan. This text is the only specialist dictionary available comprising alphabetically arranged entries that cover all aspects of contemporary youth justice. Each entry starts with a short definition, followed by discussion and analysis and concluding with a concise listing of key texts and sources including, where relevant, website references.

Goldson, B. and Muncie, J. (eds) (2006) *Youth Crime and Justice: Critical Issues*, London: Sage. This volume comprises essays from leading national and international experts in youth justice. It provides a systematic critical analysis of evidenced-based policy formation and a vision of a 'principled youth justice'. Muncie, J. and Goldson, B. (eds) (2006) *Comparative Youth Justice: Critical Issues* London: Sage. This book provides the most up-to-date analysis of convergence and diversity across international youth justice systems.

Muncie, J. (2008) *Youth and Crime*, 3rd edn, London: Sage. This is the key textbook on contemporary youth justice and it provides an excellent overview of historical, theoretical and modern policy and practice contexts.

National Association for Youth Justice—http://www.nayj.org.uk/website/ This website sets out the philosophical base of the National Association for Youth Justice. It also provides topical analysis and comment on developments and current issues in youth justice. The website provides an excellent resource for students and practitioners.

Youth Justice: An International Journal—http://yjj.sagepub.com/ This is an international, peer-reviewed journal that engages with the analyses of juvenile/youth justice systems, law, policy and practice around the world. It contains articles that are theoretically informed and/or grounded in the latest empirical research. It is the leading journal in the field and it is supported by an editorial board comprising some of the world's leading youth justice scholars.

8

INTERVENTIONS: RESPONSIBILITY, RIGHTS OR RECONCILIATION?

Roger Smith

[W]ho are all those busy people and what might they be doing? Therapists, correctional counsellors, group workers, social workers, psychologists, testers, psychiatrists, systems analysts, trackers, probation officers, arbitrators and dispute-mediation experts? And the para-professionals, semi-professionals, volunteers and co-counsellors? And clinical supervisors, field-work supervisors, researchers, consultants, liaison staff, diagnostic staff, screening staff and evaluation staff? And what are these parents, teachers, friends, professors, graduate students and neighbours doing in the system and why are they called 'community crime control resources'?

(Cohen, 1985: 41)

The question mark after What Works is now usually omitted, but many of the answers remain to be investigated. While there is now a rapid accumulation of understanding and knowledge in this field, choosing and implementing interventions in a changing social and political landscape will have to be the subject of continual enquiry.

(Burnett and Roberts, 2004: 11)

Chapter summary

- This chapter provides an overview of the history and development of community interventions, especially in youth justice.
- This is a complex and changing story because the uses and justifications for community sentences have constantly shifted over the years. In fact, it is suggested here that current provision can be seen to reflect a variety of different purposes, although some, such as correctionalism, risk management and crime control, have come to dominate.
- The range of possible interventions is discussed here, and there is some discussion of their impact, which has been mixed, often due to the emergence of 'unintended consequences', such as the intensification of community punishment rather than the replacement of custody.
- The chapter concludes that there is still a place for meaningful community interventions in youth justice, but only if we apply some of the lessons offered by criminological study and research.

Community sentences: aims and meanings

The history of non-custodial forms of intervention to respond to the problems associated with offending can be traced back at least as far as the Probation of Offenders Act 1907, although court-based welfare services had been provided informally prior to that legislation, too. Community disposals have come to play a very significant part in the justice system, amounting to some 181,844 (13 per cent of all sentences at magistrates' courts) by 2005, for example (Solomon and Rutherford, 2007: 11).

For young offenders (aged 10 to 17), the comparable figure in 2005–2006 was 36,778 (17 per cent), according to the Youth Justice Board (2007a). In strictly numerical terms then, this range of sentences plays a significant part in the overall profile of disposals; but it is also important because of its relationship to criminological ideas and sentencing principles. Community-based measures for dealing with crime are not only practically distinct from other disposals such as custody, but they represent distinctive ideological currents drawing on wider debates about the appropriate purposes and outcomes of sentencing practices in general. In other words, their distinctive characteristics reflect continuing arguments about where and on what basis to draw the line between unequivocally punitive measures of incarceration, and those which appear to espouse a wider range of objectives. The position of these 'alternatives' to custody has always been, and will remain, anomalous *because* they are located and, indeed, conceptualized within a broader penal landscape. As a result, they are conventionally understood and evaluated 'in the shadow' of ideas and practices which are shaped by the logic of punishment.

Definition: Community Interventions

By community interventions we mean those means of dealing with reported (and admitted) criminal offences which do not result in the offender being detained in a secure setting. Some of these interventions, such as the reprimand and final warning, are administered by the police and do not go any further, whilst others are made as a result of court proceedings, such as the Referral Order, Action Plan Order and Supervision Order. Some interventions, such as the ISSP are not free-standing interventions but incorporated as a requirement of a court order.

As we will see, this is heavily contested terrain, with a wide variety of justifications and practices incorporated under the broad umbrella of community sentences, and it will be important here to try to disentangle these, in order to illuminate wider criminal justice debates as well as the challenges for those engaged in direct practice. Confusion and uncertainty of purpose are widespread, and this is not surprising given the underlying tensions and conflicts. This should not, however, lead one to the conclusion that these problems cannot be addressed or resolved satisfactorily.

Indeed, as we shall see, focusing particularly on developments in youth justice, some approaches to community sentencing are more plausible than others, and may point the way towards more positive practice developments in the future.

Confused purposes?

Part of the problem for those involved in administering community sentences is to make sense of the array of different aims and objectives articulated by different constituencies within and outside the justice system. Muncie (2002) has suggested that the youth justice system, in particular, has witnessed a kind of augmentation process, whereby new ideas and practices have continually been overlaid on what preceded them, with the result that there has emerged an array of competing and sometimes contradictory interventions, each with rather different underlying justifications. According to this account:

> Youth justice is now an amalgam of:
> 1 Just deserts
> 2 Risk assessment
> 3 Managerialism
> 4 Community responsibilisation
> 5 Authoritarian populism
> 6 Restorative justice.
>   (Muncie, 2002: 156)

This particular combination of purposes is shaped, in Muncie's view, by the wider political context, which is characterized primarily by 'fear of an undisciplined underclass'. As a result, these priorities have helped to shape a prevailing approach to crime control which is predominantly punitive and exclusionary, rather than being directed towards social integration or tackling inequality.

However, it may also be argued that the portfolio of community sentences and the practices they represent are informed by a much wider set of influences. For instance, practitioners in the youth justice system retain an obvious commitment to meeting the 'welfare' needs of young people for whom they are responsible; they are not exclusively driven by 'managerial' (see Canton and Eadie, this volume) imperatives, or the dictates of containment and control. Contradictions are evident, as indeed Muncie suggests, with the result that there is a complex relationship between different aspects of intervention, and different orders of the court, which criminology has to address, in theory and in practice.

Community disposals: purposes and rationale

It can be argued that over time at least seven distinct positions have developed which inform the construction and content of community interventions. Some of these can be more or less closely identified with specific disposals, such as the Referral Order, whilst others are reflected in uneasy tension *within* sentencing options, such as the Action Plan Order.

Welfare

Since the early 20th century, there has been an explicit recognition that 'welfare' is a legitimate objective for disposals administered by the justice system. Notably, during the 1960s this was associated in England and Wales with a detailed legislative programme which sought to remove sentencing powers from the courts and to allow social services agencies to take lead responsibility for determining how to intervene with children who offend. At the same time, in a parallel development, the Children's Hearings system was established in Scotland, which created a rather different model for negotiating interventions for young offenders. 'Welfarism' was probably at its peak as both rationale and practice in the early 1970s, but was quickly discredited because on the one hand it was felt to be a 'soft option', and on the other, because it spawned a massive expansion of institutional responses to children's offending ('net-widening') which were of little benefit to them, and in some cases appeared to be harmful. Despite this, there is still a residual commitment to addressing the 'needs' of children who offend, expressed implicitly through the holistic frameworks of policy developments such as *Every Child Matters* (DfES, 2003), and explicitly in the distinctive strategy for youth justice now adopted in Wales.

Diversion

Partly as a reaction to the net-widening effects of the welfare model, and partly in opposition to excessively punitive approaches to sentencing, the principle of 'minimum intervention' became a significant feature of the youth justice system by the mid-1980s, with areas such as Northamptonshire becoming recognized as primary exponents of informal means of dealing with youth crime (see the chapter in this volume by Goldson and Yates for a further discussion). This approach was based on the view that offences could be dealt with satisfactorily outside the formal processes of the courts, and that this would also ensure that the damaging consequences for young people of being 'labelled' or institutionalized could be avoided. This approach to youth offending, supported by an active 'systems management' strategy, became increasingly influential up to the early 1990s, with a number of areas of the country (notably Hampshire) able to claim that they had established 'custody-free zones'. Despite its apparent success, the diversionary philosophy was unable to withstand the influence of the 'punitive turn' of the early 1990s (see Goldson and Yates, this volume). The Crime and Disorder Act 1998 appeared to offer limited endorsement of the principle of 'diverting' offenders with its provisions for reprimands and final warnings, but the net effect was to reduce the discretion of the police and the influence of other stakeholders, drawing more young people into the formal system as a result.

Justice

Probably the most well-established and in many ways uncontentious sentencing philosophy is offered by the 'justice model', which holds that offences should be dealt with strictly according to agreed criteria of seriousness and persistence, and punitive sentences applied accordingly. The influence of the 'tariff' has always pervaded the thinking behind sentencing models, and this is reflected in the location of community sentences at the mid-point of the overall portfolio of disposals. The 'justice' approach also reflects a view that all sentences must contain a punitive element, whether that is the duration of specific requirements and conditions, or the content of the intervention programme. The increasingly punitive climate of the 1990s and beyond has led to a greater emphasis on punishment as a result, and thus disposals such as the ISSP stipulate mandatory and substantial attendance requirements, with a heavy associated emphasis on the use of powers of breach, and more punitive sanctions for non-compliance. It is also significant that this disposal sits (apparently) at the threshold to custody and thus seeks to mirror certain of its characteristics, such as containment and enforced activities.

Control

Sharing many of the characteristics of the justice approach, but also diverging from it to an extent, are those interventions which are supported by a rationale of 'crime control'. Here, the emphasis is not so much on holding individuals to account for their behaviour, but on developing the most effective means for identifying threats of a criminal nature, predicting future risks and working to eliminate them. Some such interventions are situational rather than directed toward potential offenders, so the development of CCTV (closed circuit television) and other 'target hardening' methods reflects this philosophy. However, to the extent that 'actuarial', risk-based (Smith, 2006) techniques can be applied to known or potential offenders, interventions may be tailored to limit their capacity to reoffend. Thus, surveillance techniques, the use of specific conditions and attendance requirements, tracking and tagging, are all features of community sentences which are future oriented and seek primarily to prevent further crime. The emergence of these forms of intervention is also associated with more systematic forms of assessment (such as ONSET and ASSET), which are utilized to predict the risk of further offences and so that methods of 'control' can be tailored accordingly.

Definition: ONSET and ASSET

ONSET and ASSET are assessment frameworks for young people 'at risk' of offending, or already involved in the justice system respectively. Both frameworks seek to use predictive instruments to calculate the likelihood of the young person concerned offending in the future, and they are intended to provide the basis for planned and focused preventive intervention.

These are now associated with the 'scaled approach', introduced explicitly by the Youth Justice Board in 2007 as a 'risk-based approach to interventions', which relate the 'intensity' of intervention to the level of risk associated with the offender concerned. (See www.yjb.gov.uk for further details.)

This kind of rationale can also be used to justify behavioural interventions (such as Drug Treatment and Testing Orders) which may be specifically focused on removing identifiable 'triggers' to the commission of offences.

Correctionalism

In similar vein, the correctional approach focuses on the offender and her/his behaviour. The aim of community interventions adopting this strategy is, as might be expected, to remove those factors or characteristics which might predispose the individual concerned to commit further offences. Although similar to the 'control' perspective, correctional practices attempt to tackle beliefs, motivations or psychological problems which might underlie anti-social or criminal behaviour. Community interventions such as Supervision Orders may thus incorporate requirements to attend 'anger management' or 'offending behaviour' programmes whose aim is to equip offenders with the insight and personal control mechanisms to resist impulses to commit offences. Interventions based on this perspective are thus capable of being justified in terms of the positive gains promised, both to the community and the individual. There may be potential risks in terms of disproportionate or oppressive treatment as a consequence of this kind of logic.

Developmentalism

In a similar vein, some initiatives (Intensive Intermediate Treatment during the 1980s, for example) have sought to adopt a strengths-based approach, based in the belief that developing young people's abilities and promoting opportunities will be beneficial to them whilst also reducing the likelihood of further offending. Like the welfare approach, this form of intervention is highly offender focused, but by contrast it focuses on potential and positive attributes rather than needs or disadvantages. The developmental aims of youth justice interventions can still be identified in the educational and vocational elements of a range of disposals, including Action Plan Orders, Supervision Orders and the ISSPs.

Reparation

Increasingly influential, with its origins in the diversion movement of the 1980s and the early community service schemes prior to that, is the principle that offenders should make amends for their wrongdoing, either to the community in general, or directly to the victim of the offence. Either in the form of stand-alone disposals, such as Reparation Orders, or as conditions of other orders (Action Plan Orders, for example), offenders may be required to pay compensation, to offer apologies, or to carry out work on behalf of the community (see Stout and Goodman Chong in this volume). The idea of paying back victims or communities for the offence is attractive and seems to carry an essential quality of fairness about it, and the principle has gained increasing prominence in debates about the proper objectives of court disposals. However, it is deceptively simple, not least because it inserts another stakeholder, the victim, at the heart of the process. This raises a variety of concerns, for example about whether the 'justice' meted out to the offender is fair and equitable at the same time as it meets the needs of victims, whose expectations may not all be consistent.

Reintegration

The emergence of 'restorative' ideals as a distinctive rationale for the justice system has begun to have a direct influence on the kind of interventions available within the sentencing framework. Thus, significantly, the development of the Referral Order as a specific (and mandatory in certain circumstances) disposal following the Youth Justice and Criminal Evidence Act 1999 seems to represent a substantial modification of prior assumptions and practices. This order is based on the principle that offenders should be expected to take responsibility for their actions and, in consultation with others including victims, agree a programme of actions to put right the harm done, and also to promote their own 'reintegration' into the community. Successful completion of the order should ensure that the offence does not count against the offender in future. Despite the constraints under which it was introduced (it is only available on the offender's first court appearance, notably), the Referral Order offers the hope of an ideological breakthrough in that reconciliation and solving the problems surrounding an offence take precedence over calls for 'just deserts' or containment and control. Interestingly, the development of models of community justice in Northern Ireland seems to have taken these principles much further, and to have placed them much more firmly at the heart of the justice system.

Given that these approaches to intervention can all be identified to a greater or lesser extent in contemporary youth and criminal justice systems, it will be important also to try to make sense of their interrelationships and the changing nature of debates between apparently competing perspectives.

Understanding complexity: the challenge for applied criminology

In light of apparent inconsistencies and contradictions, the task for criminology is to try to articulate a considered analysis of the unfolding dynamics evident in practice, as different positions appear to become dominant or alternatively diminish in significance at different points in time. It is clear, for example, that the influence of 'welfarism' on thinking and practice in youth justice reached its peak in the late 1970s, and has since been subject to sustained criticism and marginalization. Critics, in this instance, condemned the welfare perspective for both being 'soft' on crime, on one side, and encouraging excessive and damaging intervention, on the other. Welfare has always struggled to gain legitimacy as a rationale for intervention in criminal matters because it smacks of excuse making and going easy on offenders; but it has also been seen as inadequate more recently in that it has failed to deliver the beneficial outcomes and improved well-being that it has claimed in its favour.

By 1997, the incoming New Labour government was able to claim that the 'welfare' needs of young people could be met purely by holding them to account for their offences, as if the two outcomes were interchangeable. Although this is inherently implausible, it serves to demonstrate the rapid weakening of the welfare movement in youth justice. It is, of course, part of a wider project of establishing the 'hegemony' (Gramsci, 1971) of a particular ideology of criminal justice that different perspectives are subsumed under common arguments and practice initiatives.

Definition: Hegemony

Hegemony is a useful shorthand term to describe a complex process whereby powerful interests utilize a variety of means, including legal structures, media and public institutions, to try and create a sense of inevitability and 'naturalness' about the way in which the social order is constructed and society operates (in their interests).

Apparent differences and possible sources of conflict are absorbed into a broad sense of consensus and common purpose, so as not to disturb the status quo.

However, we also know from the construction of different interventions that their individual elements can and do come into conflict, and this is a reflection of theoretical and ideological inconsistencies, and unresolved tensions.

Making sense of different perspectives

There are a number of dimensions against which we can evaluate the perspectives identified in order to elaborate and make sense of their competing assumptions or belief systems.

Individualization

To a greater or lesser extent the various approaches can be seen to take an 'individualistic' view of crime and criminality. Thus, for example, those which are based on justice or correctionalist models locate responsibility entirely with the offender. The response therefore must be directed exclusively at her/him, with the aim of deterring further crime or achieving behavioural change. It is interesting to note, however, that these approaches would differ on other dimensions, such as the degree of 'rationality' to be ascribed to the offender. The justice model would draw on the language of blame and personal responsibility, whilst a correctional model would explain criminality more in terms of inadequate socialization or maladjustment.

For other perspectives, however, including those taking a welfarist position, or proponents of restorative measures, responding to the offence would not simply be a matter of dealing with the perpetrator in isolation. It would be necessary to understand the social origins of the criminal act in order to develop an inclusive response (welfare), or to consider its meaning to the victim and the wider community as well as to the offender (restorative).

Offender focus

In similar vein, it can also be observed that different strategies are concerned to a greater or lesser extent with the specific offender and her/his characteristics. Thus, the 'crime control' model is primarily concerned with taking action to reduce the likelihood of further offences, irrespective of the perpetrator. This lends itself to a calculative model (Muncie, 2002; Smith, 2006) which applies generalized predictive techniques and intervenes accordingly, on the basis of estimated probabilities of future harm.

Case Example: A Predictive Approach to Crime Control

Youth Justice: the scaled approach seeks to introduce a new way of working that allows youth justice services to appropriately direct time and resources to young people in accordance with their risk assessment.

> There are currently four Youth Offending Teams (YOTs) who are working with the YJB in piloting a risk-based approach to interventions . . . All are using ASSET to make an assessment of re-offending, alongside other factors such as risk of serious harm (using the ASSET— Risk of Serious Harm tool) or risk of vulnerability, to identify the risk factors and deliver interventions accordingly.
> ... High risk offenders would receive more intensive interventions and greater supervision, thus increasing public protection, and low risk offenders would receive less intensive supervision. This will better enable YOTs to balance demands on their resources, while providing a good quality service.

(Youth Justice Board, 2007b)

Reintegrative measures, by contrast, seek to tailor interventions to the highly specific circumstances of the offender in order to generate a personalized programme to promote social inclusion. Both approaches are concerned to prevent further offending, but their views on the best means to achieve this are diametrically opposed.

Crime prevention

It is significant that the overarching aim of the youth justice system has been identified as 'preventing youth crime' according to Section 37 of the Crime and Disorder Act 1998. This clearly skews the emphasis of interventions with young people who offend in a particular direction. However, it is also clear that the range of disposals falling under the umbrella of the youth justice system is broader than this in intent and function. Whereas 'crime control' and 'correctionalist' measures might be said to be unequivocally about preventing further crime, this is not so clearly the case for other perspectives. Thus, the justice model and the associated notion of 'just deserts' emphasises the importance of appropriate punishments, irrespective of the impact they might have on reoffending. This is pertinent, of course, in light of what we know about the very high levels of reoffending associated with custodial sentences. Equally, a pure reparative approach is concerned only with putting the wrong caused by the current offence to rights, and is indifferent to whether or not this is also preventive.

The 'causes of crime'

Notwithstanding sound bites about being tough on crime and tough on its causes, the various perspectives on intervention identified reveal no common understanding of just what the causes of crime are. Assumptions are clearly made, however, revealing fundamental conflicts. Thus, the welfare model assumes that the causes of crime can be found in the social circumstances of offenders, and they are based in inequality, disadvantage and damaging personal experiences. On the other hand, 'correctional' interventions locate causal factors with the individual, attributing offending to faulty socialization. Other models ('crime control', justice) might take the view that crime is a rational activity based on perceived opportunity and judgements of the likely rate of return as against the risk of being caught. Restorative interventions may share the welfarist view that offending is rooted in social divisions, although their emphasis would be more on the failure of social networks and breakdown of established institutions (such as the family) rather than on poverty, inequality or discrimination.

Offender 'engagement'

Different ideological positions hold divergent views about whether or not there is anything to be gained from entering the process of engaging young offenders in determining the shape and content of interventions. Some, such as the justice, reparation and crime control perspectives would take the view that the issue is simply a matter of responding to the criminal behaviour in the most suitable way, and that the perpetrator's views or attitudes are irrelevant. Other approaches, notably those concerned with integration (restorative justice) or social inclusion (welfare, developmentalism), would argue that it is only possible to provide a holistic and effective response by taking account of and responding to the views of the offender.

We have thus been able to identify a number of dimensions according to which alternative perspectives on appropriate intervention strategies share common ground or diverge significantly. They are all to be found to a greater or lesser extent embedded in contemporary community interventions. Because their relationship is complex and unstable, we are likely to find evidence of continuing tension and fluctuation in the realization of criminal justice in the community.

Current trends: dominant perspectives and 'hegemony'

In light of these observations, it will be helpful to consider the current position in more detail in order to draw out some conclusions about the changing relationship between differing perspectives and what this means for community interventions now and in the future. As we saw earlier, Muncie (2002), for example, has argued explicitly that a particular viewpoint is dominant, which appears to favour proponents of a 'crime control' strategy for dealing with youth crime. Thus, a particular narrow interpretation of 'prevention' comes to the fore, and shapes all aspects of policy and practice in consequence:

> Because of their ill-defined and kaleidoscopic nature, preventative strategies are readily co-opted and added into existing youth justice discourse. New Labour's 'modernization' of youth justice and crime prevention holds authoritarian, responsibilization and remoralization discourses firmly in place. Pragmatism, efficiency and the continual requirement to 'get results' by any means necessary

take precedence over any commitment to due process, justice and democratic accountability.

(Muncie, 2002: 158)

As I have argued elsewhere (Smith, 2006), this limited preoccupation with anticipating and controlling risks of crime can be equated to an 'actuarial' view of youth justice, whose primary concern is to assess the likelihood of future offending and then act to eradicate identified risks. Interventions based on this model therefore rely increasingly on predictive tools such as ASSET, and subjugate other considerations (whether welfare oriented or restorative) to the primary task of preventing offending. Interventions are thus targeted on 'at risk' communities or individuals, and seek to 'divert' them into non-offending activities, or to ensure that their time is accounted for, and they are denied opportunities to offend. Not all such activities will be perceived or experienced negatively by young people engaged in them, and, indeed, this may be one of their selling points. However, they are likely to be judged not in terms of the quality of experience offered, but primarily in terms of their efficacy in preventing crime (Smith, 2006: 103).

Definition: Actuarialism

The notion of 'actuarialism' in criminal justice was probably first theorized by Feeley and Simon (1994), and it has been characterized as a risk-based approach grounded in:

> the attempt to perfect *scientific* means of quantifying the potential for the commission of offences, and second, the application of *managerial* techniques to control the threat to the community thus identified.

(Smith, 2006: 93)

Whilst it seems clear that the contemporary emphasis on controlling and reducing the risk of crime offers little room for welfare, diversionary or restorative (despite much current rhetoric) agendas, it is also interesting to note how this prevailing approach interacts with other perspectives, such as those concerned with 'justice' or 'corrections'. On the face of it, it may seem that these positions have much in common. They are all concerned, for example, with offending behaviour in isolation from broader social or contextual influences. They also share a commitment to forms of calculative assessment which determine levels of risk and accountability, and they all seek to determine the appropriate interventions on the basis of these. Thus, in a sense the dominant (authoritarian) approach to dealing with youth crime is based on a coalition of perspectives which share certain presumptions about causes and effective responses. However, it is of interest to note that this coalition also necessitates certain questions going unasked, or at least unanswered. Assessment tools, for example, are known to be relatively inaccurate, with the result that 'correctional' interventions will, in effect, be applied to a significant number of individuals who are unlikely to reoffend. Equally, we know that disposals based on the 'justice' model are more likely to be influenced by the idea of a sentencing tariff than they are by their potential impact on future offending.

The consensus around punitive measures of crime control thus seems to be based at least partly on a readiness to ignore unsettling or inconsistent evidence which might throw one or more of its justifications into question. As community penalties increasingly become assimilated into this discourse of punishment and control, their characteristics can be seen to change, whilst 'awkward' issues recede into the background.

The Intensive Supervision and Surveillance Programme— a hegemonic compromise?

To illustrate the above discussion, it will be useful to consider the emerging status of the ISSP as a significant community intervention. Its characteristics are noteworthy because they reflect the different preoccupations of the distinctive positions we have identified. It is thus clearly tariff-based (justice oriented), to the extent that it is intended to operate at the threshold, and essentially as an alternative to custody. It is correctional in that its various components include programmes designed to challenge attitudes and behaviours associated with offending; and it is focused on crime control in its use of stringent attendance requirements, as well as the machinery of tracking and tagging to monitor young people's movements and activities. Associated with this is a strong emphasis on the use of breach procedures for failure to comply. The place of the ISSP in the justice system was clearly mapped out in its initial formulation and identified aims, which were primarily concerned with reducing reoffending directly, as well as reducing the 'risk factors' associated with criminal behaviour (Moore et al., 2004: 38), including the 'underlying problems' of young people on the programme. It was also intended to take its place in the sentencing tariff by offering an alternative option to custody which would reduce the numbers of young people incarcerated.

Definition: The Intensive Supervision and Surveillance Programme

According to the Youth Justice Board:
ISSP is the most rigorous non-custodial intervention available for young offenders. As its name suggests, it combines unprecedented levels of community-based surveillance with a comprehensive and sustained focus on tackling the factors that contribute to the young person's offending behaviour.
ISSP targets the most active repeat young offenders, and those who commit the most serious crimes.

The programme aims to:
• reduce the frequency and seriousness of offending in the target groups
• tackle the underlying needs of offenders which give rise to offending, with a particular emphasis on education and training
• provide reassurance to communities through close surveillance backed up by rigorous enforcement . . .
Most young people will spend six months on ISSP. The most intensive supervision (25 hours a week) lasts for the first three months of the programme.
Following this, the supervision continues at a reduced intensity (a minimum of five hours a week, and weekend support) for a further three months.
(Youth Justice Board, 2007c)

The construction of the ISSP programme pursued the (custodial) logic of containment and control, with a strong emphasis on attendance, and 'structured' activities, especially in the early stages (Moore et al., 2004: 43). Thus, the first three months of a programme should incorporate participation for at least five hours a day in specified activities. These might include restorative elements, or even family support, although the primary goal would remain the reduction of offending. Equally strongly emphasised in the original formulation of ISSP was its commitment to 'community surveillance' (Moore et al., 2006: 44), so much so that to many young people, ISSP became known simply as 'the tag' (Moore et al., 2006: 129):

> The objective is to ensure that the young people themselves are aware that their behaviour is being monitored and to provide reassurance to the community that their whereabouts are being checked.
>
> (Moore et al., 2004: 44)

Clearly, the 'crime control' element of the programme has taken a prominent position according to this observation.

Despite this, other discourses are evident in the construction of the ISSP programme. It might, for example, be argued that 'developmentalism' is prominent in at least one of the 'core modules' which is required to focus on 'education and training', as well as secondary elements such as encouraging 'constructive leisure/recreation'. The 'multi-modal' nature of ISSP might allow its proponents to claim that it is healthily eclectic, being geared as a flexible and effective response 'to the variety of problems that offenders present' (Moore et al., 2004: 44). However, a more cynical reading of this initiative might be that there is a process of cooption taking place, whereby certain perspectives (such as developmentalism, restoration, welfare and even reparation and diversion) may be incorporated in service of other dominant aims (justice, crime control, correctionalism). Certainly, as we have seen, from the point of view of young people themselves, the prevailing ethos of ISSP has become one of 'control', and this appears to have superseded other purposes.

Of course, it is important to attempt to understand not only the ethos of interventions, but also their impact. These cannot be separated, in the end, not least because the question of 'effectiveness' depends on what it is we are trying to achieve and what we believe we should be achieving. This is particularly the case for the ISSP, because the early findings from its evaluation suggest that in its own terms it has been singularly *ineffective*. Completion rates were low, high levels of breach were recorded, and ISSP had manifestly failed to provide a credible alternative to custody (Moore et al., 2006). Indeed, the emphasis on compliance may itself have been counterproductive, to the extent that high breach rates undermine 'credibility' with sentencers (189), and demonstrate clearly that community disposals can only offer limited reassurances in terms of 'crime control'. Indeed, political considerations seem to require a particular construction of success and failure, whereas other criteria could be utilized, such as: 'tackling underlying problems and the reintegration of offenders into the community' (Moore et al., 2006: 215).In the specific case of ISSP, this may be a form of post hoc reasoning, seeking to introduce alternative justifications in the light of its limited impact on offenders' behaviour and compliance. However, it also helps to open up broader questions of what is either feasible or desirable (or both) for community programmes with young offenders to achieve?

Normative and practical challenges

As we have seen, there are a number of conceptual difficulties in bringing a diverse range of justifications or rationales into the service of any particular intervention. In the case of ISSP, this appears to result in anomalous practices, problematic outcomes, and distorted perceptions of the programme on the part of participants. Is it the case, then, that any given intervention will be shaped by certain dominant discourses and (normative) beliefs about what is desirable, which may either obscure or compromise alternative perspectives? More problematically, these dominant assumptions and value judgements may be seen to pervade the entire range of community responses, with inevitable consequences for the way in which they are delivered and experienced, and how and to what extent their 'success' or 'failure' is judged. Thus, the Referral Order, ostensibly rooted in a philosophy of restorative justice, is significantly circumscribed by a number of limiting factors. It is, for example, only at present available to the courts at a certain point in the young person's offending career (a 'justice' principle), and is also imbued with expectations about the 'correctional' focus of interventions and the importance of securing compliance (Haines and O'Mahony, 2006: 121).

McNeill (2006) also takes the view that a narrow approach to community interventions is likely to have unproductive consequences. Importantly, and sometimes overlooked, the perceptions and responses of young people themselves are influenced by the way in which interventions are constructed and presented to them. Like Muncie, McNeill is concerned that 'managerialism' is not just a matter of seeking technical efficiency, but it also affects the fundamental quality of the programme itself, as it is experienced by participants (see also Canton and Eadie, this volume, who make similar points about the impact of the NPM on professional behaviour).

McNeill argues that it is 'a recurring finding that no method of intervention is, in and of itself, any more "effective" than any other; rather, there are common features . . . that are most likely to bring about positive change' (McNeill, 2006: 130), by which he means both personal and social development *and* desistance from crime. These features include: empathy, person-centredness and collaborative approaches. These are far more likely to be realized through forms of intervention that are not highly structured, prescriptive or coercive, in his view, tending more towards the kind of welfare models which have generally been discredited in recent times.

It seems to be the case that community programmes driven by ideas of compliance, correctionalism and just deserts may share a common logic, but they are ill-suited to either the community setting or the realities of young peoples' lives:

> With regard to the policy and practice of community supervision, [the] 'scientific' evidence seems to counter the prevailing tendency of narrowing the gaze to

responsibilising correctionalism and to challenge its more authoritarian and coercive imperatives.

(McNeill, 2006: 130)

Even when considered in the restricted terms of 'desistance' from offending, coercive interventions are shown to be of limited value, and it is relationships and social networks which provide the support young people need to make alternative (non-offending) choices. It might seem, then, that the question of what is achievable in community interventions may come into line with the issue of what is practical and desirable.

It is self-evident that community interventions are not well equipped to offer guarantees about compliance or crime control, since these depend largely on the choices young people make. At the same time, correctional programmes are of limited value if they rely on compulsion to secure attendance, and do not engage with young people on their own terms. It thus follows, in the case of youth justice disposals which are community based, that certain forms of rationale actually coincide more closely with the context and structure of interventions than others. Those which emphasize engagement with the young person, a problem-solving ethos, and which are concerned with wider measures of well-being are both easier to deliver, and, it seems, more likely to achieve beneficial outcomes. McNeill (2006: 135) concludes that interventions must focus on creating effective 'relationships', attending to 'social contexts' and pursuing 'social advocacy' with and on behalf of young people who become involved in offending. He concludes that the reasons for resisting what he identifies as 'correctionalism' are both 'ethical and empirical'; in other words, coercive measures of community control are ineffective and, at the same time, unjustified.

Meaningful community interventions: applying criminology effectively

The purpose of this discussion has been to generate some ideas about the ways in which community interventions draw on a range of ideological justifications, asking questions both about their rationale and the practical consequences. A considerable repertoire of available rationales has been considered, and we have seen some of the continuities and disparities between them. Whilst different themes have tended to come to the fore over time, none has been able to lay exclusive claim to credibility or effectiveness. Thus, interventions almost inevitably reflect a process of assimilation and compromise. Whereas in the 1980s, for example, diversion, restorative principles, developmental and even justice models appeared to coexist comfortably and profitably, at other times, both before and since, more problematic alliances can be identified. The juxtaposition of welfare and justice in the 1970s led to a massive spiralling in institutional forms of intervention with children, whilst in the current era, the convergence of crime control, corrections and justice models has resulted in the pervasion of all aspects of youth justice with a 'punitive' ethos, including those which claim rather different justifications, such as reparation or restorative principles (Haines and O'Mahony, 2006).

Whilst this raises serious ethical questions, it would be a less problematic position if the prevailing approach could at least claim to be 'effective' in its own terms.

However, both specific measures such as ISSP (Moore et al., 2006), and the generality of community interventions (Smith, 2007) have failed to demonstrate their ability to achieve their stated objectives, notably the 'principal' aim of reducing offending.

It is at this point that criminology has a responsibility to offer a critical perspective, both in terms of honest and accurate evaluations of effectiveness, but also in terms of making normative judgements about the desirability and value of interventions.

For example, questions about rights and participation cannot be overlooked, simply because the 'target' population is made up of officially-recorded offenders. This again brings us back to the question of how (and in whose terms) we define concepts such as 'effectiveness'. For those involved in theorizing and researching these difficult topics, the boundaries are not set simply by dominant assumptions about the purposes and 'outputs' of the justice process.

Models of justice can be developed based on principles of 'rights' and 'reconciliation' for example, which draw on but go beyond the ideas incorporated in welfare and restorative models, leading to ideas and practices which give a quite different feel to the idea of 'community intervention'. Such models can be found in action in a number of settings, for instance in the forms of 'community justice' being developed in Northern Ireland (see Stout and Goodman Chong, this volume), although not without difficulty (Eriksson, nd), and in peer-led decision-making processes in Canada (Hogeveen, 2006). The language of these initiatives is not that of 'programmes' and 'targets', but of problem solving, mutuality and social justice. This lens is at least as appropriate (and arguably more so) as a focal point for the criminological gaze as that of control, crime reduction and offender management.

Key arguments

- There is a long history of community interventions in youth justice rooted in traditions of rehabilitation and welfare.
- As they have developed, community interventions have begun to incorporate a greater number of aims and purposes deriving from differing ideological perspectives.
- As a result, the challenge of making sense of community interventions, their objectives and impacts for criminologists and practitioners is complex and often contradictory.
- Despite the inherent tensions identified, it is also clear that at specific points in time, certain perspectives have become dominant; at present, this appears to be reflected in an emphasis on the justice, control and correctional aspects of community interventions.
- However, critical criminology would question this preoccupation, identifying both conceptual flaws and practical failings in the prevailing approach to community interventions. Alternative community intervention strategies, based on problem solving, reconciliation, children's rights and social justice appear to offer significantly greater hope of achieving positive outcomes in youth justice, it is concluded.

Further reading

Although over 20 years old, Cohen's (1985) *Visions of Social Control* is an excellent, and prescient critical analysis of the use of techniques of control in community settings.

Further critical discussion of recent developments and present day policy and its application to practice can be found in Smith's (2007) *Youth Justice: Ideas, Policy and Practice*. By contrast, attempts (not always uncritical) to defend and promote current practice as reflecting an 'evidence-based' approach can be found in Burnett and Roberts' (2004) overview *What Works in Probation and Youth Justice*, Moore et al.'s (2006) *Managing Persistent and Serious Offenders in the Community*, and Crawford and Newburn's (2003) *Youth Offending and Restorative Justice*.

As noted elsewhere, the Youth Justice Board (www.yjb.gov.uk) remains an important source for practice guidance and evaluation reports, although these should always be read carefully and with a pinch of salt at the ready.

9

RISK MANAGEMENT, ACCOUNTABILITY AND PARTNERSHIPS IN CRIMINAL JUSTICE: THE CASE OF MULTI-AGENCY PUBLIC PROTECTION ARRANGEMENTS (MAPPA)

Jason Wood and Hazel Kemshall

It is important to end the cyclical process by which popular fears give rise to populist public policies which reinforce public fears. Responsible risk management requires government policy to shape as well as be shaped by public opinion.

(Matravers and Hughes, 2003: 76)

Chapter summary

- Multi-agency Public Protection Arrangements (MAPPA) are an example of statutory partnership arrangements that bring together agencies from across criminal justice and social welfare.
- MAPPA developed out of an increasing concern with high risk offenders, particularly sex offenders and a growing preoccupation with assessing and managing risk.
- Being accountable in partnership arrangements is inherently complex, and needs to take into account the needs of different 'stakeholders' including other agencies, the public, victims and offenders.

Introduction

Partnerships as a mode of governance began to gain ground throughout the 1980s and 1990s building on a historical tradition of attempts to create joined-up government (Newman, 2001). The distinction between these newer arrangements and the former is that partnerships came to be emerging form(s) of governance associated with increasing fragmentation and complexity in the public realm (Newman, 2001). New models of partnership working took different forms, across different spheres of government. These ranged from private/public partnerships across central and local public service delivery, to local community-based partnerships often led by the voluntary sector with the goal of addressing local problems.

In addition, the 1980s and 1990s saw the rise of local collaborative developments around tackling crime and other community issues (Newman, 2001). These arrangements heralded a greater community involvement in crime prevention initiatives (Garland, 2001) though the empirical reality of this claim is somewhat disputed (see Hughes, 2007).

Many criminal justice partnerships are characterized less by localized co-operative working based on incentives, and more by central statutory requirements. For example, the establishment of YOTs was underpinned by legislation, and brought together key agencies in partnership with new roles designed to manage the arrangements. Similarly, several key crime and justice legislative developments led to a duty of partnership characterized by central government prescription and control (Newman, 2001). Here, agencies were compelled to contribute to partnerships that may not immediately be within their traditional scope of work. Some commentators have rightly signalled this as a widening net of criminal justice (Yates and Goldson, this volume), a point that we shall return to later.

The perceived benefits of increased co-operation included:

- **Overcoming departmental barriers and the problems of silo management**
  In line with the developments in Social Inclusion policy (e.g. see Social Exclusion Unit, 1999), there was an increasing recognition that joined-up problems required joined-up solutions. Thus, in child protection it was becoming increasingly common for social workers to link up formally with education welfare officers, through structured partnership arrangements.
- **To deliver better policy outcomes by using multiple players at different levels** Of particular importance here was the growing link between centralized government aspirations, targets and guidance with localized partnership arrangements. In regeneration, the government established a link between poor housing, neighbourhood renewal and the incidence of anti-social behaviour. Thus, local arrangements would be established that would include housing agencies, residents, youth and community workers and community police representatives.
- **To improve coordination and integration of service delivery among providers** An attempt here to increase the likelihood of effective interventions that, as we discuss later, is prone to difficulty. Whilst agencies undoubtedly work more closely together, their accountability to one another is not clear. Thus coordination is increased but integration and delivery not necessarily so.
- **To develop new approaches to policy development or service provision by bringing together expertise** A recurring theme is that agencies bring to partnerships a tradition of expertise that others can benefit from. For example, in public protection partnerships the role of the social worker in considering child protection issues, the victim liaison officer in considering the needs of victims and the housing officer in understanding specific housing issues are all beneficial to a more comprehensive risk assessment and management plan (Wood and Kemshall, 2007).

(Adapted from Newman, 2001: 109)

Multi-agency public protection arrangements

Multi-agency responses to managing sexual and violent offenders offer an interesting exemplar of the development of statutory partnership arrangements, and their consequent benefits and problems.

In the 1990s, the USA began to develop monitoring systems for sexual offenders released from custody. These commenced with tracking systems requiring sex offenders to register their address with local police, culminating in federal legislation around community notification, known as 'Megan's Law'[1]. Community notification in these cases is justified where it is necessary and relevant for public protection (Maguire and Kemshall, 2004). The extent to which this legislation has actually had an impact upon child sex offending is disputed (see for example Fitch, 2006).

The UK adopted some of these measures with the introduction of the Sex Offenders Act (1997) which directed offenders to register their name and address with local police within 14 days of caution or conviction and within 14 days of moving residency. The duration of reporting requirements varied extensively, depending on the offence and length of sentence, with some offenders on the register for life. As a consequence, the number of offenders on the register will inevitably increase year on year (Kemshall et al., 2005).

In the late 1990s, it became clear that registration requirements were both clearly understood and largely adhered to, but there was no clarity or consistency provided by the legislation as to what police responsibilities were in relation to those who were registered (Maguire et al., 2001) given that 'registration in itself could not deliver child protection' (Kemshall, 2001: 5). It was therefore the emerging local practice, underpinned by Home Office guidance, that led to a range of risk assessment and management responses, notably:

- Police-led, formal risk assessment in consultation with the local probation service for every offender who registers.
- Where the level of risk is high enough, local plans should be drawn up to manage the risk, including sharing information with other agencies where appropriate.
- Case-by-case decisions made by the police as to whether information about the offender should be disclosed to other organisations, individuals or the community as a whole.

(Maguire et al., 2001: 3)

As a consequence, the risk assessment and management partnerships that emerged were characterized by inconsistency and diversity (Maguire et al., 2001). Of note:

- This included differences in names, representation on panels, chairing arrangements, referral procedures and case management responses. This resulted in a lack of national consistency, particularly in structural differences across areas and whether a one-tier or two-tier panel system was adopted.
- Partnership arrangements between police and probation also differed, with well-developed inter-agency partnerships in some areas. There were also examples of more 'one-sided' arrangements (usually police dominated) and with other agencies playing a more marginal role.
- Difficulties with information exchange and disclosure were also noted. Information exchange was largely limited to offenders on the sex offender register although panels covering other categories of offender were exchanging information between police and probation and making routine child protection checks with social services. Respondents identified the systematic recording of actions and risk management plans as an area for development.

- Risk management varied and there was inconsistency in the use of risk categorizations (low, medium, high and very high) to allocate risk management resources.
- Systems of accountability and oversight also varied, with a lack of genuine multi-agency structures. The management and accountability of the system 'tended to depend too much upon informal processes and informal networks' (Maguire et al., 2001: 50).
- The work was seen as an 'add-on' to existing workloads and was not subject to appropriate financial planning and review. Dedicated clerical resources and a central co-ordinator were recommended as best practice developments.

In response to Maguire et al.'s research, the partnership arrangements were given new statutory force and clarity with the implementation of the Criminal Justice and Court Services (CJCS) Act (2000) that placed a responsibility on police and probation to:

> Establish arrangements for the purpose of assessing and managing risks posed in that area by:

(a) relevant sexual and violent offenders, and

(b) other persons, who, by reason of offences committed by them (wherever committed), are considered by the responsible authority to be persons who may cause serious harm to the public.

(CJCS, 2000: s. 67(2))

The MAPPA commenced, with each responsible authority establishing consistent approaches to the identification, assessment and management of high-risk offenders. More prescriptive statutory guidance followed (e.g. Home Office, 2004d, 2007d) that attempted to ensure areas were adopting similar practices and standards for risk assessment decision making and risk management planning.

In 2005, an evaluation of the effectiveness of these legislative developments in strengthening MAPPA was conducted (Kemshall et al., 2005). The research noted that MAPPA had become more consistent, adopting a tiered approach to risk management and allocating offenders across three levels of risk management as enshrined in the guidance(see box). A range of agencies made contributions to risk assessment and risk management as active partners.

Risk Management: The Tiered Approach

- **Level 1—ordinary risk management** Where the agency responsible for the offender can manage risk without the significant involvement of other agencies. This level of management is only appropriate for category 1 and 2 offenders who are assessed as presenting a low or medium risk.
- **Level 2—local inter-agency risk management** Where there is active involvement of more than one agency in risk management plans, either because of a higher level or risk or because of the complexity of managing the offender. It is common for Level 3 cases to be 'referred down' to Level 2 when risk of harm deflates. The permanent membership of Level 2 should comprise those agencies that have an involvement in risk management. Responsible Authorities should decide the frequency of meetings and also the representation, taking an active role in the convening of meetings and quality assurance of risk management.

> ## Risk Management: The Tiered Approach—cont'd
>
> - **Level 3—Multi-agency Public Protection Panel (MAPPP)** For those defined as the 'critical few', the MAPPP is responsible for risk management, drawing together key active partners who will take joint responsibility for the community management of the offender. An offender who should be referred to this level of management is defined as someone who:
>   (i)   is assessed under OASys as being a high or very high risk of causing serious harm; **AND**
>   (ii) presents risks that can only be managed by a plan which requires close co-operation at a senior level due to the complexity of the case and/or because of the unusual resource commitments it requires; **OR**
>   (iii) although not assessed as a high or very high risk, the case is exceptional because the likelihood of media scrutiny and/or public interest in the management of the case is very high and there is a need to ensure that public confidence in the criminal justice system is sustained.
> (Home Office, 2004d: para. 116)

The wider context

Parallel to the governance developments outlined in the first section of this chapter, a qualitative shift was occurring in relation to the management of sexual and violent offenders. Public protection had become a key aim of the probation service, with its manifestation most acute in the management of high risk offenders (Kemshall and Wood, 2007a). Two key strands to this are worth reviewing here: firstly a growing concern with child sexual abuse, and secondly the broader risk context.

The legislative and policy developments of the 1990s illustrated a growing concern with child abuse and in particular the 'discovery' of the predatory paedophile. Studies revealed the extent of the problem (e.g. Cawson et al., 2000) but in doing so found high levels of under-reporting (Fisher and Beech, 2004) and poor conviction rates (Prior et al., 1997). Thus the true extent of the problem was somewhat unknown and criminal justice agencies had faced extensive criticism for not adequately dealing with sex crimes. There followed a growing penal preoccupation with sex offending against children (Kemshall, 2003) in response to high-profile cases, a growing familiarity with the concept of the paedophile and a media-constructed moral panic (Kitzinger, 1999a, 1999b; Kemshall, 2003). This media interest was perhaps most pronounced in 2000 when a campaign was launched to 'name and shame' paedophiles in response to the murder of Sarah Payne. The calls for community notification similar to that found in the USA were resisted on the grounds that it would drive offenders underground (Maguire and Kemshall, 2004) a position still held by probation, police, social workers and other professionals in more recent research (Wood and Kemshall, 2007).

The second and interrelated contextual shift was the rise of the 'new penology' of risk and actuarial justice (Feeley and Simon, 1992, 1994; Kemshall, 2003). A marked decline in confidence in liberal crime management strategies, together with economic pressures on crime management and concern with how to manage the most dangerous and habitual offenders, led to a focus on risk management over and above rehabilitation (see, for example, Garland, 2001). In relation to the management of sex offenders, this manifested itself in increasing convictions, new post-custody licence conditions that imposed restrictions, curfews and the community management of sex offenders *in place* (Kemshall and Wood, 2007a). In addition, the emphasis on risk assessment came to the fore with increasing measures to calculate likelihood, imminence and seriousness of reoffending. Technical and actuarial methods were promoted as consistent tools to facilitate this process.

This new penology, enacted through MAPPA in this case, represents what Connelly and Williamson (2000) have called the 'community protection model' which prioritizes public protection and the management of offenders through restriction, conditions, sanctions and enforcement. Within this approach, public protection is seen as the preserve of the experts, with public involvement in the processes limited and often at one remove (Kemshall and Wood, 2007b). The construction of the offender is understood as a rational choice actor, who with the right restrictions in place will desist from offending behaviour and ultimately, reduce the risk of reoffending.

The process and content of community management

The process by which offenders become subject to community management is reasonably straightforward. There are a number of stages that are characteristic of MAPPA. These are illustrated in Figure 9.1.

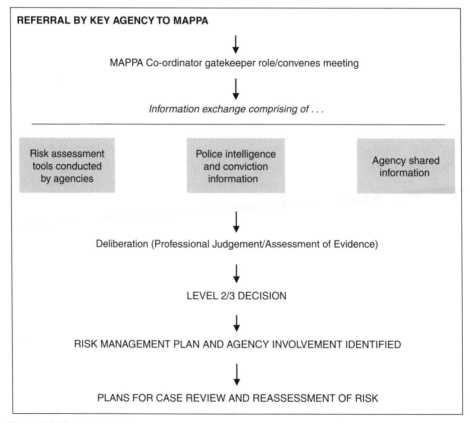

REFERRAL BY KEY AGENCY TO MAPPA

↓

MAPPA Co-ordinator gatekeeper role/convenes meeting

↓

Information exchange comprising of . . .

| Risk assessment tools conducted by agencies | Police intelligence and conviction information | Agency shared information |

↓

Deliberation (Professional Judgement/Assessment of Evidence)

↓

LEVEL 2/3 DECISION

↓

RISK MANAGEMENT PLAN AND AGENCY INVOLVEMENT IDENTIFIED

↓

PLANS FOR CASE REVIEW AND REASSESSMENT OF RISK

Figure 9-1 The MAPPA process

Assuming that the offender who has been referred to MAPPA is appropriate, the process of risk assessment commences. This draws upon three significant strands: the risk assessment tools conducted by agencies, the intelligence from police and the inter-agency information-sharing exercise at the MAPPA meeting.

Risk assessments draw on static and dynamic factors. These are relatively self-explanatory, with static defined as those factors that may never change—they are constants. Dynamic factors are perhaps more complex, interchangeable and subject to greater degrees of review. They depend very much on assessing the inter-related, criminogenic needs of an offender. Typically, dynamic risk factors may include:

- **Relationships** with other offenders, with victims and with potential victims.
- **Accommodation** particularly in relation to post-custody supervised accommodation and the stability of subsequent housing arrangements.
- **Access to sites of risk** for example, schools, swimming pools or other access points where children are.

Risk assessments most commonly comprise the use of actuarial and clinical methods to determine these static and dynamic factors. Actuarial approaches select, from a large number of cases, the common factors that statistically relate to risk. These factors are referred to as static risk factors—deemed to remain unchangeable. Actuarial assessment can be used to:

- Establish those risk predictors which have a proven track record
- Establish the relevant base rates for a clinical assessment
- Increase the accuracy of risk assessments; and
- Increase levels of consistency and reliability.

(Kemshall, 2001: 16)

Clinical methods derive from diagnostic assessment work most commonly found in medical and mental health fields. Based upon detailed interviewing, the process collects information on the social, behavioural and personality factors that have resulted in previous offending (Kemshall, 2001). Flaws can be numerous, not least with the impact of subjective bias on the collection of information, but the exercise can build a much more holistic and fuller picture of risk factors than simple statistics alone.

Maguire et al. (2001) and Kemshall (2001) uncovered a variety of risk assessment tools in use across the different police and probation areas. This has changed somewhat with MAPPA guidance indicating a move towards the consistent use of one tool— the electronic Offender Assessment System (e-OASys) (see box).

E-OASys

E-OASys combines both reconviction indicators with criminogenic needs and is designed to:
- assess how likely an offender is to be re-convicted
- identify and classify offending related needs, including basic personality

---

Continued

E-OASys—cont'd

- characteristics and cognitive–behavioural problems
- assess risk of serious harm, risks to the individual and other risks
- assist with the management of the risk of harm
- link the assessment to the supervision or sentence plan
- indicate the need for further specialist assessments; and
- measure change during the period of supervision/sentence.

(Home Office, 2004d: para. 97)

Further, in combining a thorough assessment of needs (ranging from pre-convictions through to educational attainment) with an offender's self- assessment, the tool acts as a useful basis for both assessing risk factors and planning a risk management response. E-OASys has been used as a standard tool in probation and prisons since 2003, and is now the centrally recommended tool for MAPPA.

Taking into account the information based upon the various tools, and the police intelligence, the next key component of a risk assessment most relevant to MAPPA is the information-sharing exchange. Here agencies are encouraged to contribute to risk assessments by sharing information from their own specialist domains. For example, social workers may provide information on contact with family members and psychiatrists on the offender's involvement with mental health services. Other agencies outside of the criminal justice system therefore have an increasingly important role to play in risk assessment, though this is not without difficulties and some of these are explored below.

A comprehensive risk assessment should inform an effective risk management strategy. In this context risk management is defined as the processes designed to be responsive to identified risk factors in order to minimalize the likelihood of negative outcomes. Again, the inter-agency component is particularly important here since a risk management plan may depend on various inputs offered by several key organizations. An example of a typical risk management plan is offered in Table 9.1.

Table 9.1 Typical risk management plan for a paedophile subject to MAPPA

Agency	Responsibility
Police	Home visits at set times according to risk, 'lifestyle' monitoring including surveillance.
Probation	Supervision, hostel supervision, cognitive behavioural therapy and monitoring of group treatment programme.
Community Psychiatric Nurse	Treatment for associated mental health problems.
Local housing authority representative	Arranging post-hostel accommodation that is appropriate.
Social worker	Regulate contact with family members including children.
Job Centre Plus	Assist with welfare benefits, support offender in finding work.

In summary, MAPPAs have developed out of an ongoing concern to protect the public from dangerous and sexual offenders. As a result of legislation and the broader risk context, partnership arrangements have emerged that represent complex forms of managing difficult offenders. In turn, these arrangements pose questions about the extent to which they can truly demonstrate their effectiveness and provide reassurance. This leads us to the question of accountability.

Defining accountability

In its most simple definition, to be accountable is 'literally to be liable to be called upon to give an account of what one has done or not done' (Banks, S., 2004: 150). How we understand this seemingly neutral process is dependent on a number of factors. We might ask: what does it mean to be accountable in criminal justice?; who is accountable to whom?; what is offered as evidence of accountability?; to what extent might this accountability be both genuine and useful?

Whilst accountability has always been a feature of public services, attention to it has become more prominent in the past decade (Banks, S., 2004; Considine, 2005). This is in part located within a broader turn towards managerialist approaches across all public services (Canton and Eadie, this volume; Hughes, 2007), a trend representative of a wider debate about the overall role, purpose and cost of the welfare state. In probation and other criminal justice agencies, accountability became more formalized, with firmer central steer (Canton and Eadie, this volume; Morgan, 2007).

The attention to accountability has therefore taken shape in the form of increased monitoring, auditing and reporting of performance (Banks, S., 2004). There are a number of broad explanations offered for this:

- **The decline in trust** Banks calls this the 'ethics of mistrust' and identifies a 'growing loss of confidence in professional competence and professional ethics' (Banks, S., 2004: 153).
- **The pursuit of standardization** In part as a result of the loss in confidence described above, but also in some pursuit of provision equality (Newman, 2001), there has been a move towards standardized practice. Certainly in the discussion about MAPPA above, we see a move from diverse, localized sex offender risk management to a more consistent, nationally guided statutory implementation of arrangements. In various areas of criminal justice such as probation and YOTs, there is the continuous pursuit of 'what works' with offenders. All of these standard approaches, whilst not necessarily prescriptive, suggest a move away from relying solely on professional judgement (see for example Canton and Eadie, this volume).
- **The relationships between inputs, activities, outputs and outcomes** often explored in relation to Value for Money (VFM). In simple terms, VFM is defined as 'the economic acquisition of resources and their efficient utilisation' (Rouse, 1999: 77) and performance is measured in how cost effective it is (Canton and Eadie, this volume). The difficulty here is that much of what is done in terms of public services is neither easily quantifiable nor easily measured. If we think of prisons as an example, one might expect a simple VFM model to provide custodial accommodation and human resources in the form of prison staff (inputs), engaging with offenders through training programmes and treatment (activities) in order that they may be released (outputs) as more engaged and effective citizens (outcomes). Such is the simplicity of the model that we already see the multiple variables that can affect its utilization. Not all offenders are the same, not all activities will work and not all outcomes will be achieved.

- **The culture of blame** As Kemshall notes 'in a society defensive about risk, concerned with risk avoidance and the prevention of harm, the regulation of risk necessarily attracts public scrutiny and concern' (2003: 12). It is within such scrutiny that the first question asked when something goes wrong is 'whose fault?' (Douglas, 1992). A cumulative impact of the decline in trust together with the rise of risk means an imposition of regulation through increasingly prescriptive rules (Kemshall, 2003). In utilizing measures, it is hoped that risks and uncertainty can be predicted, prevented and thus avoided. This is part reflects a worship of safety (Furedi, 1997), where we, as the public, want reassurance that lessons will be learned and the same mistakes that lead to failure will not be repeated.

Approaches to accountability vary quite significantly across public services. Some models include transparency, where organizations reveal themselves to external scrutiny. External inspections, serious incident reviews, and the publication of criminal justice population data are all found to be accountability indicators. The difficulty with such measures is that, operating in the blame culture, they tend to rely on negative performance indicators. It is perhaps easier to retrospectively identify flaws and make suggestions for improvement, rather than demonstrate how and why criminal justice interventions have worked.

Understanding accountability in the MAPPA context

MAPPA poses interesting questions in relation to its accountability. In a sense, it is necessary to start by ascertaining *who* is accountable to *whom*, a task that presents numerous difficulties. MAPPA is in effect accountable to different stakeholders, for different purposes (albeit within a broader goal of protecting the public). These accountabilities can manifest as loyalties, sometimes in conflict and often resulting in a balance of competing tensions (Tyler, forthcoming).

Inter-agency accountability

As the case study above shows, MAPPA is comprised of agencies delivering various components of an overall risk management plan. This comprises *working together* (through information sharing, joint agency visiting, contributions to assessments and risk management plans) and *working independently* (to carry out agreed actions in a risk management plan). These two elements mean that accountability is differentiated. An outsider may be forgiven for thinking that accountability mechanisms should be relatively straight forward: agencies *must* provide the necessary information and *must* deliver their component of the risk management plan. However, the situation is much more complex.

The legislation underpinning MAPPA suggests that three core agencies are accountable for establishing MAPPA. These are: the National Probation Service (soon to be NOMS), the Police and the Prison Service (CJCS, 2000; Criminal Justice Act (CJA), 2003). These Responsible Authorities have a duty to put in place the arrangements for the risk assessment and management of offenders subject to MAPPA. However, as the case example shows, in these new arrangements several partners will have an input into managing offenders.

Section 325 of the CJA, 2003 names other agencies who have a duty to co-operate (DTC) with MAPPA. The Act stipulates that this duty is to be determined locally by agreement between the Responsible Authority and the agency named as such.

The Act recognises that agencies already have existing functions in relation to sexual and violent offenders and that MAPPA is a process for enabling 'each agency to discharge its duties more effectively through co-operation' (Department of Health (DoH), 2004: 2). Relationships between the key agencies named in the Act and criminal justice agencies have existed before. However, these arrangements were driven in large part by the informal relationships built across agencies. This informal accountability resulted in patchy service provision across the country, and was arguably unsustainable (e.g. key personnel move on into new roles ending the personal relationships with colleagues in other agencies).

More formal accountability measures have been employed in areas following the Act. For example, local areas have developed:

- **Memorandum of understanding** A document that outlines the relationship between the Responsible Authorities and DTC agencies based upon the determination of need in local areas.
- **Protocols for information sharing** Formalized protocols that provide the framework for local information sharing arrangements between different agencies. They provide a formal document that is jointly signed by senior agency representatives and that is ratified by the Strategic Management Board.
- **Standing membership arrangements for MAPPA Level 3** so that all agencies are consistently represented at meetings concerned with the highest risk offenders.
- **Standing membership of the Strategic Management Board (SMB).** Whilst the CJA, 2003 orders that DTC agencies are involved only in the operational aspects of MAPPA, it is now common for SMBs to comprise a standing membership of these agencies. SMB representatives are of senior grade (usually at Director level or equivalent) and are able to make resource commitments and ensure operational involvement is upheld.

(Kemshall et al., 2005; Wood and Kemshall, 2007).

Guidance from the DoH to Social Services indicates what the operational duties of a DTC agency might include (see box). In addition, the guidance suggests that whilst the function of DTC agencies is to provide 'input' into the criminal justice arrangements, they in turn may benefit from having such input.

Operational Duties of A DTC Agency

- attending case conferences where they are already involved in the case or where they have a responsibility
- providing advice (perhaps but not necessarily by attending case conferences) about cases in which they are not involved and have no direct responsibility so as to enable the Responsible Authority and the other DTC bodies involved in the case to assess and manage risk more effectively. For example, this might involve explaining how specific housing, health or social services which are not currently required in the case may be accessed or involved later

---

Continued

Operational Duties of A DTC Agency—cont'd

- advising on broader, non-case specific, issues which may affect the operation of the MAPPA more generally; and
- sharing information about particular offenders and about broader issues so as to enable the Responsible Authority and the DTC bodies to work together effectively.

(DoH, 2004: 4)

None of this actually suggests a requirement on agencies to deliver risk management in partnership with others. The DoH guidance frames the responsibility as one of information sharer, reporting on progress of interventions and giving expert advice.

Two key critical themes arise out of this development related to operational and philosophical questions about the distribution of risk.

The first area concerns operational issues. As the contextual discussion at the start of this chapter illustrates, significant changes in governmental modes (partnerships) and the increasing preoccupation with 'risk' (the new penology) have led to complex and fragmented forms of government, in which the state devolves power to locales either through statutory partnerships or more informal arrangements. This has been termed the 'adaptive strategy' to crime prevention and management comprising dispersed accountability in 'hybrid' organizations (see Kemshall, 2003: 41–3). The problem with such organizations is that they can be characterized by inconsistency based upon the local political, social and economic cultures that impact upon them despite the formalized arrangements in legislation. For example, a police force in one area may not prioritize public protection in its resource distribution, leading probation to commit additional resources.

Further difficulties may arise in the vertical nature of the partnership and its impact on delivery. MAPPA does not assume responsibility for the management of an offender, with responsibility for case management vested in the agency that referred the offender to the arrangements. This means that there is no organization known as MAPPA, rather it is an arrangement for agencies to work together. In turn, Responsible Authorities cannot direct DTC agencies to undertake work, nor are they ultimately accountable to criminal justice bodies. The extent to which legislation has indeed strengthened the input of agencies into MAPPA is subject to some dispute, with some areas experiencing poor commitment though this is not necessarily empirically supported (e.g. Kemshall et al., 2005).

The second issue is more difficult to resolve and concerns the widening net of criminal justice, and in particular how risk is understood and acted upon by the agencies involved in the MAPPA processes. There is evidence to suggest that agencies have adopted the language of risk assessment in a more systematic way as the MAPPAs have developed (cf. Maguire et al., 2001 and Wood and Kemshall, 2007) effectively sharing the burden of risk. Critical, philosophical questions arise out of these developments. To what extent might agency boundaries be blurred? Might risk come to dominate over other, equally legitimate paradigms? For example, the role of forensic mental health services in MAPPA arrangements reveals a constant tension between the public protection duty to reduce risk through information sharing, and the historical tendency towards patient rights and the protection of confidentiality.

Political and public accountability

With dangerous and sexual offenders, there can be no such thing as zero risk (Home Office guidance), since serious further offences are near impossible to prevent (Nash, 2005). Instead, criminal justice agencies must put in place measures that might help to manage the risk, but if they fail to predict or manage the risk they face the potential for blame (Nash, 2005). What follows is that criminal justice agencies seek to refine prediction and assessment, focusing on procedural processes (Banks, S., 2004) for the 'attribution of blame and fault necessarily focuses attention on accountability' (Kemshall, 2002: 9). MAPPA works in a climate of low trust in professional groups and high media scrutiny (Kemshall and Wood, 2007a) where agencies are held accountable when procedures are not adequately followed.

In such a climate, it is imperative that defensible decisions are made (Carson, 1996; Kemshall, 1998). These are decisions that 'are grounded in evidence, based on relevant information and using the most appropriate risk assessment tools' (Kemshall and Wood, 2007a: 389). For Banks, such steps reflect the growth in the 'importance of being able to demonstrate that all the required procedures have been followed and documented in order not to be blamed for a bad outcome' (Banks, S., 2004: 151). In our studies we found defensible decision making was usually manifested in:

- Consistent and appropriate approaches to the **assessment** of MAPPA offenders, including the use of standardized risk assessment tools and information sharing processes.
- Risk management plans that were **appropriately targeted** to the level of risk, taking into account the risk assessment and the resource implications involved in managing the offender.
- Documentary evidence of **decision making**, including minutes of panel meetings indicating clearly the responsibilities of agencies involved.

(Kemshall et al., 2005; Wood and Kemshall, 2007)

Such developments are in contrast with the earlier public protection arrangements that preceded MAPPA. A key feature of the new accountability is the ability of agencies to demonstrate that their inputs lead to better outcomes (Banks, S., 2004). Whilst often linked to questions about public service value for money this can also be applied to sensitive issues such as how best to manage high risk offenders. Public and political confidence depends on (1) the agencies *doing* an effective job and (2) being able to *communicate* this.

Methods for public and political communication about the effectiveness of MAPPA are limited, since more generally measures of effectiveness continue to be underdeveloped in MAPPA (Wood and Kemshall, 2007). However, two key developments signal some degree of public accountability. These are (1) the inclusion of lay advisers in the strategic management of MAPPA and (2) producing public annual reports.

The CJA (2003) set out a requirement on the Home Secretary to appoint two lay advisers to each area to assist in the review of MAPPA. The legislation is clear that this role is not an operational one, and lay advisers therefore assume membership of the Strategic Management Board.

Lay Advisers

According to the MAPPA guidance:

> The role of lay advisers is very much part-time . . . They are not expected to become experts—their value is as informed observers . . . As such their role has proved to be valuable, even when as a lay adviser they challenge professionals as a 'critical friend'.
>
> (Home Office, 2004d: para 322)

But:

> Their role is not. . . akin to that of an independent auditor. Nor is it as representative of the local community.
>
> (Home Office, 2004d: para 322).

In theory, such appointments provide a level of public involvement in the oversight of MAPPA and therefore public representation. However, as the guidance acknowledges the role is neither one that clearly provides external oversight (as auditor) nor as an operational decision maker. Further, the roles are not designed to be representative of the local community. This invites us to ask about their usefulness. In some areas, lay advisers are actively seeking further, more substantial roles that would enable them to make a meaningful contribution to the work of MAPPA (see Wood and Kemshall, 2007). In addition, they may have a role in more effectively communicating the work of MAPPA to the wider public. Perhaps the biggest problem has been the under-utilisation of lay advisers and this has led to inconsistency in their involvement. At the time of writing, this issue has been acknowledged in a recent Home Office review that commits to 'establish a defined and consistent role for MAPPA lay advisers, which will include raising public awareness' (Home Office, 2007e: 3).

Communicating the work of MAPPA to the wider public is fraught with difficulty. MAPPA works with high risk sexual and violent offenders, and is therefore subject to intense media scrutiny. This media attention is often negative, focusing on agency failures or the perceived high number of sexual offenders registered and managed in the community. Unsurprisingly, such media coverage does not detail the actual operational work of MAPPA and perhaps does little to encourage faith in public protection arrangements.

As part of a strategy for addressing this, each MAPPA area has a statutory duty to produce an annual report that:

> provide[s] a valuable mechanism for raising public awareness and understanding of public protection issues and explain[s] the multi-agency work that is undertaken through MAPPA to increase public safety.
>
> (Home Office, 2004d: para 135)

The quotation illustrates a chasm between policy objectives and empirical realities. Annual reports are published with an accompanying Home Office press release. The national and local news media focus intensively on the numbers of sex offenders subject to community management. The operational detail of MAPPA is largely unreported and annual reports fail to engage the wider public (see Kemshall et al., 2005). Again, the recent Home Office review has recognized this, with a commitment to greater

MAPPA engagement with the community, and a central point of contact for the public (Home Office, 2007e).

In summary, the methods for demonstrating accountability to the public are under-developed in MAPPA. This is evident for a number of reasons. First, the extent to which the public is meaningfully involved in the processes of public protection is limited. Second, the current models of public awareness are mediated by news media that demonstrate poor levels of engagement with the operational aspects of MAPPA, favouring instead the sensational details about numbers of sex offenders living amongst us in the community.

Accountability to victims

A marked change in policy over the past decade has been to recast the emphasis from an offender-focused criminal justice system to a victim-focused one (Tapley, 2005). Developments such as the Victims' Charter in 1990 established the duty of the Probation Service to work with victims of crime.

However it is only in subsequent years that this work has become increasingly consistent, professional and highly valued (Williams and Goodman, 2007).

More recently, victims were increasingly being characterized in policy debates as users, or even as *clients* or *consumers* (Williams, 2005) despite the false analogy that victims would rather not *choose* to engage in criminal justice services (Williams, 2005). This has led to an overwhelming rhetoric to put victims at the heart of the criminal justice system (Jackson, 2003) within a national strategy to better support victims (Home Office, 2003a).

Part of this commitment is a statutory duty for the National Probation Service to consult victims about the release of offenders in recognition that victims can contribute to the risk management of offenders and to MAPPPs (Home Office, 2003a).

MAPPA guidance (Home Office, 2004d) emphasizes that a victim focus is vital to the process of risk management. In summary:

- Risk assessment and risk management plans should reflect victim concerns and this can only be achieved through an active engagement with victims and where possible potential victims.
- Where the victim wants contact, efforts should be made to ensure the role is more than a passive one whilst recognizing the limitations of their involvement.
- Consideration of victims should include those who, whilst not being directly involved, will have been affected by the offender (e.g. family members of victims).
- Consideration of potential victims sharpens the process of risk assessment.

This may take the form of face-to-face contact with the Probation Service, the opportunity to be kept informed of developments, the opportunity to contribute to release plans and to receive information about licence conditions, all very clear requirements of the existing Victims' Charter (Williams and Goodman, 2007). However, the extent to which there is real involvement of and accountability to victims is variable across MAPPA areas. Victims are not routinely consulted on risk management planning

(Kemshall et al., 2005) but there are some key areas of good practice identified in the research, including:

- A victim liaison worker present at Level 2 and Level 3 meetings in order to report victim concerns and to ensure that adequate measures protective of the victim were incorporated into the risk management plan.
- Some evidence of victim concerns being represented at SMB level with areas indicating that victim liaison officers are members together with regular victim support involvement.
- The provision of personal alarms, rapid response police telephone numbers and restraining orders where appropriate to increase victim protection.

(Kemshall et al., 2005)

Goodey (2005) argues that with increasing victim involvement, victims are themselves 'responsible' for community safety. The reality is that, like the wider public and offenders, victims are involved in the risk management process at arm's length. We are perhaps not at a stage where they have an active, operational decision making capacity. As a result, accountability to victims is largely through contact workers providing information about the risk assessment and management decisions made. In this sense, the characterization of the passive consumer may be a fair assessment.

Accountability to offenders

For many social professions accountability to service users is integral to their core values (Banks, S., 2004). Such a statement in relation to criminal justice warrants further discussion. In what ways, for instance, are probation and police officers accountable to offenders? The relationship between offender and offender manager is not one that can be easily compared with, say, a social worker and client. Arguably, the loyalties of a probation officer may be more likely to be vested in victims as opposed to offenders. In political rhetoric, offender rights are somehow seen as counteractive to justice as if they are directly in opposition to the rights of victims (Williams, 2005).

The issue is more complex in public protection due to the necessity for restrictive conditions in community management. As a result key human rights are frequently weighed against a wider public right to safety. The latest Home Office guidance is explicit in its statement: 'the human rights of an offender must **never** override public protection' (Home Office, 2007d: p.19, original emphasis). Key failings identified by Serious Further Offence reviews have found the issue of human rights to be problematic, where decisions were made in support of the offender, perhaps at the expense of better public protection (HMIP, 2006).

Punitive and exclusionary forms of risk management are thus employed to restrict the rights of the offender. In broader terms, the community protection model emphasises the exclusion of the offender from the risk management process, suggesting limited accountability for decision making. In fact, exclusion and distancing of sexual offenders are its key functions (Kemshall and Wood, 2007b: 210). This means that there is limited evidence to suggest that offenders are actively involved in their case management

(Kemshall et al., 2005), but there is emerging evidence of a different form of accountability in relation to offenders.

Interestingly many offenders are quite pragmatic about the risk management decisions made about them but this invariably depends on how clearly they are rationalized. In our most recent study (Wood and Kemshall, 2007), there is a clear relationship between an offender's acceptance of and compliance with restrictions, and the extent to which the decisions made are clearly communicated and justified. In this respect, accountability to offenders is seen as a *justification for the public protection decisions made by professionals to the offender.*

Where this accountability is limited, offenders feel aggrieved and tend to demonstrate lower levels of co-operation with licence conditions and restrictions. Williams notes that unfair sentencing practice could lead to offenders feeling highly resentful, a situation 'not conducive to rehabilitation or reformation' (2005: 89). The same attitudes were evidenced amongst those offenders who were subjected to licence conditions that they felt were either disproportionate to their offence, or were not clearly articulated (Wood and Kemshall, 2007).

Conversely, supervisors and offenders perceived the more successful supervision relationships as those characterized by strong relationships between police, probation and offenders where a more positive construction of the offender as someone who 'can and will change behaviour in most cases' was the prevailing assumption (Wood and Kemshall, 2007: 11). The difference was observable: offenders were more likely to self-report to supervision staff where they were concerned about their own risky behaviour and they were generally more motivated to participate in programmes (Wood and Kemshall, 2007: 12–14).

Whilst the rehabilitative ideal may have fallen out of favour in probation, at the expense of the advances in public protection, promoting change in offenders remains a key task for the service (Chapman and Hough, 1998). The supervision practices that were most effective reflect those characterized as pro-social modelling (Trotter, 1999) (see box). Staff adopting this approach in their work with sex offenders felt that it was playing a key role in the prevention of further offending (Wood and Kemshall, 2007).

Pro-Social Modelling

Pro-social modelling comprises:
- Clarity about the supervisory role, including purpose and expectations of supervision, the appropriate use of authority and the role of enforcement.
- Pro-social modelling and reinforcement, involving clear expectations about required values and behaviours and their reinforcement through the use of rewards. Challenge and confrontation of undesirable behaviours and the discouragement of pro-criminal attitudes and values.
- Negotiated problem solving, clear objective setting, monitoring and accountability of the offender's progress.
- Honest, empathic relationship with an emphasis upon persistence and belief in the offender's capacity to change.

(Adapted from McNeill and Batchelor, 2002: 38; Trotter, 1999, 2000).

There are of course problems in accepting that this approach is the only qualifying factor in maintaining good risk management. For example, there is extensive research evidence to suggest that levels of motivation, acceptance of the severity of the offence and the entrenchment of offending behaviour all impact upon offender engagement with programmes and supervision. Classified as 'high-deviancy child abusers' (Fisher et al., 1999) they may hold high levels of pro-offending attitudes, seeing children as unharmed by such contact (Fisher and Beech, 2004: 31). Consequently, all risk management plans may be seen by the offender as an infringement on what is deemed to be quite normal behaviour. Changing these attitudes requires greater levels and intensity of intervention and is usually underpinned by a relationship of low trust between offender and supervisor. With treatment resources systematically below capacity, the emphasis is placed on even more restrictive measures and management (Kemshall and Wood, 2007b).

Conclusion: the challenge for applied criminologists

This chapter has examined the complexities of both partnership and accountability structures within the newly emerging Multi-agency Public Protection Arrangements. In doing so, it has considered the differing forms of partnership and the structural limits inherent within it, but also the positive achievements at individual case management level. Applied criminologists have an important role in evaluating the systems and processes for achieving effective partnerships and in assisting practitioners to move beyond 'silo management'. Accountability is no less complex, with stark differences between rhetoric and reality, particularly where accountability to public, victims and offenders is concerned. Within the MAPPA accountability can take many forms, with accountability to many different stakeholders whose interests and concerns can conflict with one another. Accountability also depends on transparency and engagement with key stakeholders, and within MAPPA this has been variable with traditionally low engagement with, and transparency to, local communities. Accountability in this context is not simply accounting for what has been done since it is beset by political sensitivities and complex social influences such as public perceptions and tolerance of risk, and there are many publics to take account of (Hughes, 2007). The task for applied criminologists is to evaluate differing accountability mechanisms and to assist practitioners and policy makers in establishing a *meaningful and balanced accountability* that can include offenders, victims, agency professionals and the wider public. Only when a more realistic and balanced approach to accountability is achieved can public protection be truly effective.

Key arguments

- The delivery of risk assessment and risk management of sexual offenders is enhanced by partnership working. Accountability, however, in these arrangements is complex and problematic.
- There are differences between rhetoric and reality, particularly in relation to accountability to offenders, victims and the wider general public. It is beset by political sensitivities and the public tolerance of risk.
- Applied criminologists must take account of these different accountabilities, and critically evaluate them.

────────────────────────── **Acknowledgements** ──────────────────────────

The authors wish to acknowledge the support of colleagues involved in the studies referred to in this chapter: Gill Mackenzie, Roy Bailey, Joe Yates, Mike Maguire and Kirsty Hudson. The responsibility for this chapter remains with the authors.

────────────────────────── **Further reading** ──────────────────────────

There are numerous key texts on risk but Denney, M. (2005) *Risk and Society* London: Sage is an entertaining and illuminating introduction. The role of risk in criminal justice is explored in Kemshall, H. (2003) *Understanding Risk in Criminal Justice*.

For an in-depth critique of public protection and the difficulties inherent within MAPPA see: Nash, M. (2006) *Public Protection and the Criminal Justice Process* Oxford: Oxford University Press. Current issues and working practices in MAPPA are detailed in Wood, J. and Kemshall, H. (2007) *The Operation and Experience of Multi-agency Public Protection Arrangements (MAPPA)*.

10

RESTORATIVE JUSTICE: THEORY, POLICY AND PRACTICE

Brian Stout and Hannah Goodman Chong

Implicit in Restorative Justice is a re-evaluation of the responsibilities of government, communities and individuals for responding to victimisation and the harms of crime. Where traditional notions of justice treated the public as the recipient of an expert service provided by criminal justice professionals, restorative justice calls upon public participation and active citizenry. Individuals and groups become reconfigured as partners in the process and coproducers of the outcome.

(Crawford and Clear, 2003: 225)

Chapter summary

- It is important to take a principled approach in measuring criminal justice against restorative standards
- Not all services for victims match up to restorative principles
- Restorative justice will play quite a minor role in the work of the National Offender Management Service.

Although restorative justice is an influence on work with young offenders in England and Wales, its influence is much less significant than in Northern Ireland.

Restorative justice has been one of the most prominent themes in the criminal justice system over the last decade. Much has been published on the subject; it has received extensive publicity and has become increasingly popular as a topic of study on university courses. Its association with meeting the needs of victims has also meant that restorative justice has proved to be an attractive term for policy makers and politicians.

What is less clear is the impact that restorative justice has had on influencing policy and practice. There has been an avalanche of legislation and policy initiatives over the last few years but in England and Wales little of it has had an explicitly restorative label. There are instances, such as in youth justice, where restorative justice has influenced policy but in other criminal justice debates restorative justice rarely figures. With relation to adult offenders, restorative justice appears to have had a minimal effect on policy. It is barely mentioned in discussions on 'rebalancing the criminal justice system' and seems to play a diminishing part in discussions relating to the development of the National Offender Management Service (NOMS) and the sentencing regime introduced by the Criminal Justice Act 2003.

This chapter will explore the influence of restorative justice on work with offenders and victims in the criminal justice system. It will consider three aspects of the criminal justice system in England and Wales, and how they have been affected by restorative justice. Attention will be given to services for victims; youth justice policy and the development of NOMS. It will be argued that although restorative justice has been an influence, and that some of the interventions could be rightly labelled as restorative, criminal justice policy debates in England and Wales have not fully engaged with the questions relating to the role of the state and the role of the community in restorative justice that are inherent to the concept. As a contrast, the example of youth justice in Northern Ireland will be covered to show where restorative justice theory has significantly influenced both policy and practice.

Is criminal justice restorative?

It is not the intention of this chapter to outline in detail the history and characteristics of restorative justice. Readers unfamiliar with restorative justice are directed to the further reading at the end of the chapter and on the associated website. However, as restorative justice has expanded in scope and popularity the term has become widely, and sometimes inconsistently, applied. It is defined differently by different writers, and the term is sometimes abused, either to refer to any process involving a victim, any process involving rehabilitation or any process originating from the community rather than from the state (Johnstone, 2003). The first box outlines some of the characteristics of restorative justice that the criminal justice interventions outlined in this chapter will be measured against.

Johnstone (2002) identifies four ideas that characterise restorative justice:
1 Crime is, in essence, a violation of a person by another person, and this is much more significant than the breach of legal rules.
2 The prime concern in responding to crime should be to respond to victims' needs and prevent further victimisation by making offenders aware of the harm that they have caused, and to prevent them repeating that harm.
3 The nature of reparation and measures to prevent reoffending should be decided collectively and consensually by offenders, victims and representatives of the community.
4 Efforts should be made to improve the relationship between the victim and the offender and to reintegrate the victim and the offender into the community.

Bazemore and Schiff (2005) suggest that those measuring criminal justice interventions against restorative standards should take a principled approach. They follow van Ness and Strong (1997) in describing what the three main principles should be:

- The first principle is the principle of repair. Restorative justice requires that we work with victims, offenders, and communities that have been injured by crime.
- The second principle suggested by the authors is that of stakeholder participation. Victims, offenders, and communities should have the opportunity for active involvement in the justice process as early and as fully as possible.

- The third and final restorative principle is that of transformation in community and government roles and relationships. Restorative justice requires a rethink of the relative roles and relationships of government and community. In promoting justice, government is responsible for preserving a just order, and community for establishing a just peace.

Alongside Johnstone's ideas, Daly (2002) raises certain points about restorative justice that can be used to analyse how restorative services for victims are. She suggests that restorative justice should be about repairing harm and promoting dialogue and negotiation between the affected parties. Miers (2004) argues that restorative justice should allow for victim participation in the system. In the next section, these principles will be applied to services available to victims of crime both within and outside of the criminal justice system.

Restorative work with victims of crime

This section will examine to what extent the criminal justice system and services for victims of crime could be said to be restorative. It will be argued that restorative justice has had a limited effect on these services, despite the wealth of evidence that it can bring benefits for offenders and victims. Services will be assessed in terms of their restorative benefits (Marshall, 1999), and not simply whether they claim to be restorative or meet the definition of a restorative method such as Victim–Offender Mediation.

Services for victims of crime can be split into two categories; services offered within the criminal justice system, and services outside of the system. Services offered by statutory agencies include Witness Care Units staffed jointly by the police and Crown Prosecution Service, victim contact work offered by the probation service, and Victim Personal Statements (VPS). Services outside of the system include agencies such as Victim Support, Rape Crisis, domestic violence agencies and smaller, local organizations.

Restorative work with victims within the criminal justice system

Victims have been referred to as forgotten players in the criminal justice system, their participation limited to that of witness in their own case (Edwards, 2004).

Victim participation in the criminal justice system is provided for by the use of Victim Impact Statements (VIS). However, take up of these has been patchy. Williams (2005) argues that although these were introduced in the UK in 2001, they were not routinely being passed on by the police. This demonstrates that even when restorative practices are introduced, they must be implemented properly to have any real effect. There is a reluctance on the part of some courts to accept VIS as they argue that the impact that a crime has on a victim should not affect the sentence passed on the offender and that these issues should in fact be kept entirely separate. Erez and Rogers (1999) argue that even where VIS have been introduced these have not had any effect on the processing or outcomes of cases. The questions could then be asked, has this restorative practice not been effectively implemented or is it sufficient that victims have the platform to have their say without this affecting their offender's sentence?

The Victims' Charter

The Victims' Charter was first introduced in 1990 and was updated in 1996. The Charter set out a series of standards of service that victims could expect to receive from agencies including the police, probation service, and Victim Support. However, these standards were not statutory duties.

The Charter introduced services such as the requirement for the Probation Service to begin to work with victims of crime for the first time.

The Charter was replaced by the Victims' Code of Practice (Home Office, 2005a) in 2006.

A copy of the Victims' Charter can be found online at http://www.homeoffice.gov.uk/documents/victims-charter?view=Binary

---

Marshall (1999) argues that the Victims' Charter was a step towards restorative services for victims although its aims were not so much to provide help as to seek to avoid secondary victimization. The Victims' Charter, and the newer statutory Victims' Code introduced by the Domestic Violence, Crime and Victims Act 2004 have not introduced a statutory basis for restorative justice to be offered to victims of adult offenders. The Victims' Code is a continuation of the restorative work provided by the earlier Victims' Charter, but no explanation is given as to why restorative justice should be offered to victims of young offenders and not adult offenders (Home Office, 2005a).

Victims may have more input into the criminal justice process through particular areas of work offered by some agencies. For example, victims may have some say through the Victim Contact scheme operated by the probation service in licence conditions that they would like to see attached to their offender's licence. However, this service is only available to victims whose offender has been sentenced to 12 months or more in custody for a violent or sexual offence. Even then the conditions can only be suggested to the prison and are not guaranteed to be attached. This is therefore another area where, for many reasons, the amount of control victims have over the treatment of their offender is limited. Thus, there is some level of dialogue between some victims and the criminal justice system, though this is not necessarily concerned with repairing the harm caused by the offence and is more focused on concerns for the victim's safety.

Restorative work with victims outside the Criminal Justice System

---

The aims of many victim agencies could be said to be supportive in nature, both in terms of emotional support and practical advice on avoiding future victimization. Their role is about repairing harm, or at least providing victims with strategies of how to cope following a crime. Apart from specialist mediation agencies, many victim agencies do not provide for mediation. Some lack the time and training, others have no contact with the offenders, making mediation difficult. Indeed, in many cases the offender will not be identified, making dialogue and negotiation impossible.

Mediation has been found to be more satisfying for participants than approaches dominated by professionals (Williams, 2005). However, it may not always be appropriate. In some cases, for example domestic violence, ensuring that cases do enter the criminal justice system is important because this highlights the seriousness with which the case is being treated and a rejection of the attitudes of the violent partner (Curtis-Fawley and Daly, 2005). In other instances, victim services within the voluntary sector work with victims who have not necessarily reported their experiences to the police. There may therefore be limits on what victims can participate in, as the offender may well not be part of any criminal justice process.

Bazemore and Schiff's (2005) first principle of restorative justice, that of repair, can be seen in the work of victim agencies as their work focuses on supporting victims in rebuilding their lives. For example, Women's Aid, a national organization supporting female victims of domestic abuse, has aims involving empowerment, challenging disadvantage and promoting cohesive responses (Women's Aid, 2007). The aims highlight the importance of repairing harm to the victim. They also meet Bazemore and Schiff's second restorative principle of stakeholder participation by stating that the service should be run by women and should be available to all women. Support for victims that is offered by the voluntary sector allows for the community to be involved in supporting victims of crime. The active participation of community members in criminal justice has also been identified as a fundamental restorative principle (Daly, 2002). Stakeholder participation can be seen in the vast number of people that volunteer their time to work for victim agencies: Victim Support alone has approximately fourteen thousand volunteers (Victim Support, 2006).

Could services for victims be more restorative?

Support for victims of crime is not always restorative in nature, and there is often good reason for this. A restorative intervention may not always be the appropriate response to certain crimes, in particular sexual violence and domestic abuse. It is important that a signal is sent, both to the offender and to wider society, that domestic violence is unacceptable and prosecution is usually the best way to send this message (Ashworth, 2002). For Curtis-Fawley and Daly (2005), a service can not be truly restorative where, such as in cases of domestic violence, women were not in safe and comforting surroundings to begin with. Restorative justice must involve the offender admitting their offences. This does not often happen in cases of domestic violence where perpetrators tend to minimize their offending.

For female victims of domestic abuse to be able to use restorative approaches, there would need to be greater awareness of the power imbalances caused by abusive relationships and recognition of the steps needed to protect victims' personal safety. Nonetheless, services could still adopt more restorative principles. The criminal justice system could allow women to tell their stories and have the actions of their offenders condemned. A more restorative approach could avoid some of the problems involved in going through the criminal justice system such as the possibility of re-victimisation and the difficulties in proving sexual assault cases (Curtis-Fawley and Daly, 2005).

There is evidence of some attempt to provide restoration to victims of crime, though not necessarily through the use of full restorative justice techniques. The next section will consider the National Offender Management Service and how, again, restorative justice has been a factor in its development, without becoming the primary influence.

Restorative justice and the National Offender Management Service

In considering work with adult offenders this section will focus on work with offenders in the community, and in particular, the changes to the role and function of the Probation Service.

Probation practice in England and Wales is going through a significant process of change. The Criminal Justice Act 2003 made changes to the sentencing regime and the introduction of the NOMS will radically overhaul the provision and organization of probation services. In this section those changes will be briefly outlined and measured against restorative principles.

The changes to probation organisation have their roots in the report *Managing Offenders, Reducing Crime* (Carter, 2003, hereafter referred to as the Carter Report) which was produced by Patrick Carter at the request of the Prime Minister. The report identified problems with prison and probation disposals being used too much with first time offenders and being poorly targeted, and with too much regional variation in sentencing. Carter proposed that a solution to this could be found in a new way of managing offenders that would reduce crime and maintain public confidence. This new approach suggested that a new role should be established for the judiciary and that sentences should be targeted and rigorous. This chapter concentrates on the third of Carter's proposals, that a new approach should be taken to managing offenders. Carter suggested that the Prison and Probation Services should be restructured into one service, the National Offender Management Service (NOMS). In this service Regional Offender Managers (ROMs) would work across prison and probation and fund the delivery of specified contracts. The system would be focused on the end-to-end management of offenders throughout their sentence, and there would be a clear separation between the role of supervising offenders and that of providing punishment and intervention.

In immediate response to the Carter Report, the government issued the paper *Reducing Crime—Changing Lives* (Home Office, 2004e) in January 2004. This paper accepted Carter's recommendations and outlined the creation of a new body, NOMS, that would bring together the prison and probation services to provide end-to-end management of offenders. The intention was that a National Offender Manager would report to the NOMS Chief Executive and manage ten ROMs. These ROMs will be responsible for sourcing prison places and community supervision through contracts with providers from the public, voluntary and private sectors.

In addition to responding to the Carter Report, the government proposals are designed to facilitate the sentencing framework created by the Criminal Justice Act 2003. Some of the sentences created by this Act require much greater co-operation between prisons and probation. The Criminal Justice Act 2003 also created a new generic community sentence that provided the courts with the maximum flexibility to tailor interventions to the particular circumstances of the individual offender. The government's view is that the NOMS reforms will allow this new sentencing regime to be implemented most effectively. Crucially, the government proposed at that stage that the new system would be accompanied by a check in the increase of numbers in custody (Home Office, 2004e). It estimated that changes in sentencing practice could ensure that the prison population in 2009 would be 80,000, rather than the projected 93,000. This target had already been exceeded by the end of 2006.

The two most significant changes that NOMS will bring to the Probation Service are related to the concepts of end-to-end management and contestability:

- **End-to-end management** It is proposed that there should be a single person responsible for each offender from the point where he enters the criminal justice system to the time when he leaves it, regardless of whether he is serving his sentence in prison, in the community, or both.
- **Contestability** The government intends to encourage the private and voluntary sector to compete to manage more prisons, and to compete to manage offenders in the community. The intention is to encourage partnerships between public sector, private sector and voluntary bodies which harness respective strengths.

The government anticipated that these changes could be introduced quickly, with a fully regionalized service introduced within five years, and invited responses to its proposals.

The proposals were followed by a process of consultation, during which it became clear that the changes would be unpopular, particularly with probation practitioners. Opposition came from the National Association of Probation Officers and the Probation Boards Association. Lord Ramsbotham, the former Chief Inspector of Prisons, speaking against the proposed changes in the House of Lords stated that out of 750 responses only ten had been in favour of the government's proposals.

The Offender Management Act, now amended to ensure that core court-related tasks such as the preparation of pre-sentence reports remain in the public sector, received royal assent in July 2007.

The nature and influence of restorative justice

Government Restorative Justice Strategy

The Government's Restorative Justice Strategy (Home Office, 2003c) makes clear that its intention is that restorative justice will play a central part in the National Offender Management Service. The strategy states that restoration will have an equivalent standing as a principal, alongside rehabilitation, punishment and public protection. It states that where restorative projects are available, there will be an expectation that offender managers will broker the involvement of suitable offenders.

Together we can reduce re-offending and increase public confidence

In this consultation document NOMS places a strong emphasis on stakeholder participation. *Together we can . . .* (Home Office, 2005b) outlines ways in which the community could be involved in the criminal justice system. These include involvement as volunteers and mentors, and partnership in reparative and unpaid work. The document contains a section on restorative justice, and it is worth considering that in some detail, to ascertain the understanding of restorative justice that, at that stage, influenced its development in NOMS.

Together we can suggests that restorative justice can meet two objectives: it can address the hurt caused to victims, and it can help offenders come to terms with their actions. It suggests that work with offenders can include sessions on victim awareness and some form of reparation. Victims can be provided with information, and possibly reparation. Face-to-face meetings between victims and offenders are mentioned as a possibility (Home Office, 2005b).

In other parts of *Together we can*, however, the attitude toward restorative justice is quite lukewarm. This is demonstrated in the assertion that the international research evidence is 'mixed' (Home Office, 2005b: 19). The document states that victims tend to be more satisfied with restorative justice interventions, but that there has been an inconsistent effect on reconviction rates. It is unclear what research evidence has been considered. The only full references are to government documents or websites, and those websites contain no further links to other external research. While mention is made of some relatively large-scale UK based research projects it remains a mystery what international research evidence is being referred to. In contrast, a subsequent independent meta-analysis of national and international research described the evidence on restorative justice as 'extensive and positive' (Sherman and Strang, 2007:5).

The document goes on to make some restorative proposals, including greater use of victim awareness material in work with offenders, providing information to victims and 'working towards' (Home Office, 2005b: 1) direct restorative approaches. Two points from this concluding section are worth highlighting. The first is this proposal:

> NOMS proposes that best practice is shared and we contribute to protecting victims by:
>
> assessing the risk of harm posed to individuals and communities and managing that risk in partnership with other agencies;
>
> (Home Office, 2005b)

The definition of restorative justice is thus drawn so widely that it includes risk assessment and management. Whilst the assessment and management of risk are clearly core functions of NOMS, it is doubtful whether such tasks would normally be considered as examples of restorative justice.

The second point worth highlighting is the suggestion that victims work: 'does not readily fit into targets and set timescales'. It is not made clear why this should be true of work with victims, when it would seem to be equally applicable to work with offenders.

The second principle of restorative justice suggested by Bazemore and Schiff (2005) is that of stakeholder participation. Victims, offenders and communities should have the opportunity for active involvement in the justice process as early and as fully as possible. *Together we can* puts stakeholder participation at the centre of NOMS but resists placing this within an explicitly restorative framework.

Responses to consultation

Together we can was a consultation document and there were a number of responses to it. The government's summary and response to the consultation were contained in an annex to a wider document on civil renewal in criminal justice and youth justice (Home Office, 2005c).

Civil renewal is the idea that government and the people should work together to improve society for everyone. The Government's Communities website identifies three ingredients to civil renewal:
• Active citizens
• Strengthened communities
• Partnerships with public bodies
(http://www.communities.gov.uk/index.asp)

This document summarized responses to the restorative justice section by describing an emphasis on ensuring that victims' needs were central and that there was a need both for practical support for restorative practitioners, and for further research. It drew particular attention to the response from the Probation Boards Association (PBA), quoting directly from its response. The PBA urged caution in treating restorative justice as a panacea, and suggested that NOMS needed to be realistic in stating what could be achieved. It further cautioned that mainstreaming restorative justice could lead to the same problems evident in the *What Works* initiative, where a promising area of work became discredited due to an over-zealous push from the top. The PBA's suggestion was that further research needed to be carried out into restorative work with adults and that the role of NOMS could be to contribute to this (PBA, 2005).

The NOMS Offender Management Model

The latest, and perhaps definitive, description of the role of restorative justice in NOMS is contained in the description of the Offender Management Model that will be adopted by Offender Managers (Home Office, 2006c). However, even at this advanced stage of planning, how much of a part restorative justice is expected to play is somewhat unclear. In the Offender Management Model, meeting the needs of victims through restorative approaches is identified as one of the objectives of offender management. However, later in the same document the contribution of restorative justice is played down. Offender managers are encouraged to pursue a restorative outcome, and to mandate such an approach if it was specified as an activity by the sentencer. It is deliberately put no higher than this (Home Office, 2006c: 34):

> There is some encouraging, if inconclusive, evidence about the rehabilitative effect of restorative measures, but the labour costs can be high. Pending more conclusive research, this encouragement stops short of an expectation that Offender Managers should seek to achieve a restorative outcome in all cases.

Offender managers are encouraged to pursue an 'indirectly restorative approach' (Home Office, 2006c: 34) such as the use of unpaid work or voluntary work in custody. The model creates an expectation that victims will be worked with by someone other than the offender manager, and that the only direct role that an offender manager will have with a victim is to pass on information about the offender.

Case Study: Probation Practice

Hindpal (19) is subject to a community order with a supervision requirement after committing an offence of theft from a disused warehouse. Hindpal's supervising officer Rebecca decides to take an indirectly restorative approach with him. Rebecca asks him to imagine a warehouse cleaner who might have discovered the break-in and write a letter of explanation and apology. Rebecca's hope is that this will help Hindpal to develop some victim empathy regarding an offence that offenders often consider to be victimless.

Applying Bazemore and Schiff's (2005) principles to the NOMS, it can be seen that although restorative justice is an influence on NOMS it is just one of many influences and is not a primary one. The first principle, that restorative justice requires that we work with victims, offenders and communities that have been injured by crime, seems to be one that is adhered to by NOMS. Although it will not be the offender manager who will work with the victim, it is established that work with victims must be done, and that work includes meeting the needs arising from the original offence and assuring future security. Williams (2005) has identified that it was the point of the Victims' Charter that it became established that probation officers would have a role in working with victims and that principle seems to be continuing into NOMS.

The third and final restorative principle is that of transformation in community and government roles and relationships (Bazemore and Schiff, 2005). Restorative justice requires a rethink of the relative roles and relationships of government and community. In promoting justice, government is responsible for preserving a just order, and community for establishing a just peace. This thinking seems to have had little influence on the development of NOMS which, despite its establishment of a regional commissioning framework is also characterized by a strong centralizing tendency. In the later section on Youth Conferencing Service in Northern Ireland the results of a criminal justice debate that also includes a consideration of the role of the state will be described. Prior to that, the influence of restorative justice on youth justice in England and Wales will be discussed.

Restorative justice in youth justice in England and Wales

Restorative justice is provided for within the youth justice system at a level that far outstrips provision within the adult Criminal Justice System. Initial moves to make the youth justice process more restorative were introduced by the Crime and Disorder Act 1998. This Act was an attempt to create a unified and structured approach to responding to youth crime (Fox et al., 2006). This Act introduced restorative methods at several stages of the youth justice system. It brought about changes in the ways in which young people were cautioned. It aimed to prevent young people receiving a number of cautions and instead to engage young people at an early stage and put in place the help needed to prevent re-offending (Fox et al., 2006).

The police can now give young people a final warning which must contain a restorative justice element. There is a range of restorative interventions that young offenders may have to undergo. A basic level of restorative work might be a meeting between the police officer, young person and their guardian. The consequences of a final warning are outlined, however the victim is not present and the views of the community also seem to be absent. Instead, this process is considered as restorative because the young offender is held to account and possible elements of the warning include mediation, reparation, or family group conferencing (Fox et al., 2006; Smith, 2007).

Case Study: Youth Justice in England and Wales

Nick (aged 15) stole his mum's car. He drove it round before eventually smashing it into Mr George's garden wall. It cost Mr George £300 to repair the wall and replace the damaged plants, including one bought for him by his children following the death of his wife.

Nick was convicted of driving offences. Police officers working within the Youth Offending Team contacted Mr George to explain about the outcome of Nick's case and to ask whether there was anything he wanted Nick to do in order to make reparation to him. Mr George wrote back that he would like for Nick to understand that whilst his costs had been mainly met from his house insurance, the plant damaged had had great sentimental value to him and that he had been deeply upset by what had happened. Nick talked about the letter with his YOT officer and decided to write a letter of apology to Mr George to explain what had led up to him taking the car (he was upset as his mum had just told him that she was leaving his dad) and that he was sorry for the damage and upset that he had caused Mr George.

Both Mr George and Nick felt better after reading each other's letters. Mr George was no longer so angry with Nick, and Nick promised that he would try to think through his actions more in the future in order to avoid upsetting anyone else.

Referral Orders were introduced by the Youth Justice and Criminal Evidence Act 1999. These are for offenders aged between 10 and 17 and are imposed where they plead guilty and are not sentenced to custody. They involve a meeting between the offender, their parent or guardian if the young person is aged under 16, a worker from the YOT and two volunteers from the community. The victim may also be present.

Those present agree a contract which outlines the order for the offender for the next 3 to 12 months. This allows for involvement by both the victim and the community. Earle et al. (2002) found that 84 per cent of young people felt that they were treated with respect by the panels and the majority also felt that the process and contract were useful. However, victims were only present in 13 per cent of panels where there was an identifiable victim.

The scale of the use of panels demonstrates transformation of existing criminal justice procedures, and there is clear evidence of involvement in panels by those involved in the offence. The rate of involvement by victims remains low, however, and this is one area that could be improved in order to make Referral Orders even more restorative. It should be recognized that the participation of victims must be voluntary and so it is unlikely that all victims will ever choose to participate.

Code of Practice for Victims of Crime

The Code of Practice for Victims of Crime (Home Office 20005a) was introduced under the Domestic Violence, Crime and Victims Act of 2004 and came into force in 2006.

This placed statutory duties on agencies for the first time and set tight deadlines for agencies to meet. The deadlines are particularly challenging where a victim has been identified as being 'vulnerable' or 'intimidated'. Agencies covered by the Code include the police, Crown Prosecution Service, Court Service, Parole Board, NOMS, Criminal Injuries Compensation Authority and Youth Offending Teams.

An example of a duty set out by this code is one placed on the police to inform victims if police bail conditions are changed within five working days, and within one working day if the victims are vulnerable or intimidated.

A copy of the Code of Practice can be found at http://www.homeoffice.gov.uk/documents/victims-code-of-practice?view=Binary

---

Under the Code of Practice for Victims of Crime (Home Office, 2005a), Youth Offending Teams must contact victims, where appropriate, to offer them the opportunity to go through a restorative process with their offender. A range of restorative measures may be carried out within Youth Offending Teams, from letters of apology to face-to-face meetings. Early research found that these measures did lead to young people being more 'responsibilised' (Gray, 2005: 945). In some cases, however, the restorativeness of these measures was questioned, for example, one young offender commented that his painting a wall had not helped his victim.

Restorative justice within the youth justice system is not without its critics. There have been accusations that new developments in the youth justice sphere, and a blanket approach to restorative justice, have increased net-widening and overly punitive sentences (Fox et al., 2006). This is because restrictions have been set on how many times a young person can come to the attention of the police before they have to go to court. Following the third contact with the police, the young person will have to go to court, regardless of the severity, or lack of severity, of the offence. This allows for the possibility that a sentence might be imposed that was more punitive than it would have been if the police had still been able to exercise discretion. It also allows for harsh penalties to come into effect if the conditions are broken, and these harsher penalties will not necessarily bring any benefit to victims.

Despite these criticisms and concerns, it is clear that a version of restorative justice has been introduced as a widely used measure with young offenders in England and Wales. The form that it has taken does seem to bear a strong resemblance to accepted definitions of restorative justice. This contrasts sharply with the attitude to restorative justice in work with adult offenders, but England and Wales is far from the only jurisdiction where restorative justice has been enthusiastically embraced in work with young offenders, but has remained peripheral to work with adult offenders. In the next section the example of Northern Ireland will be considered, where the introduction of restorative justice has been part of a fundamental rethinking of the nature of both the criminal justice system and wider society.

Restorative justice in Northern Irish youth justice

Restorative justice techniques were used in the criminal justice system in Northern Ireland during the mid-1990s, in parallel with their increased world- wide popularity.

The Northern Ireland Criminal Justice Review

It was the Criminal Justice Review of 1998, which followed the Good Friday agreement of the same year, that started the process of putting restorative justice on a statutory footing, and led to it becoming the dominant approach in Northern Irish youth justice. The Review largely accepted the recommendations of a commissioned research report into restorative justice in Northern Ireland and favoured a form of restorative justice with a strong statutory basis (Dignan, 2000; Criminal Justice Review Group, 2000). The Justice (Northern Ireland) Act 2002 created the Youth Justice Agency, and as part of that Agency, the Youth Conferencing Service.

The Youth Conferencing Service was introduced in December 2003, initially in Belfast only, with projects in other areas of Northern Ireland becoming established later. Young people who offend are dealt with by way of a youth conference. The conference will normally comprise the co-ordinator, the offender, the victim and family members or other supporters of both offender and victim. It should lead to the formulation of a plan of action for the offender, including some form of reparation to the victim. The 2005 evaluation of the Youth Conferencing Service described it as 'a radical departure from previous approaches to young offenders' (Campbell et al., 2005: 2) but acknowledged that the approach was developed within a growing climate of restorative justice. The evaluation was positive about the work of the Youth Conferencing Service, saying that the early implementation of the scheme had progressed well. The evaluation document was launched at a major international conference in Belfast in March 2006, and this conference also allowed the Youth Conferencing Service to promote the many positive achievements of its early work. Even in the short time since the Youth Conference Service was created it has become an accepted and established part of the Northern Ireland criminal justice system.

Although the Service has been favourably evaluated and has received widespread approval, the use of restorative justice in Northern Ireland has not been free of criticism.

A particular point of contention is the requirement that the police service be involved, and the exclusion of community based schemes from the new regime. This has its roots in the particular political situation in Northern Ireland, and the contentious nature of policing (see McEvoy and Mika (2002) for an account of the decision making that led to the exclusion of these schemes, and a strong argument for the appropriateness of involving them) but has meant that the Youth Conference Service has its roots very strongly in the statutory sector. However, even here, it is possible for restorative justice advocates to respond positively in that a debate regarding what sort of restorative justice should be used and what it should be like seems to be a step forward from discussing whether it should be used at all. The firm location of the Youth Conferencing Service in the statutory sector has coincided with the continuing parallel development of informal community based schemes such as Community Restorative Justice and Northern Ireland Alternatives.

Case Study: Northern Ireland Youth Justice

A young person broke into a church in Belfast with his friends, committing an offence of criminal damage by flooding the premises. He agreed in court to participate in a Youth Conference. The Youth Conference Co-ordinator met separately with the young person, his family and the clergyman. He set up a conference where all parties told their version of events. The young person apologized, donated some money to charity and agreed to carry out voluntary work in the church.[1]

The use of restorative justice in the Northern Ireland Youth Conferencing Service is probably the highest profile and most successful example of restorative justice influencing and informing the criminal justice system in the UK. It is already being held up as a world leader in restorative interventions. It is also the best, and perhaps, only example in the UK of Bazemore and Schiff's (2005) third principle being adhered to, and restorative justice processes being introduced as part of a rethink of community and government roles and relationships. Although the final decisions remain contentious, it is at least clear that the issue of community involvement in restorative justice was thoroughly considered in the discussions that ultimately resulted in the introduction of the Youth Conferencing Service (Criminal Justice Review Group, 2000; Dignan, 2000). South Africa remains the most prominent worldwide example of the introduction of restorative justice being linked to a fundamental rethink of the role of the state (see Tutu, 1999; Roche, 2002; Skelton, 2002) but Northern Ireland is probably the next most significant instance. It could even be argued that restorative justice currently plays more of a role in criminal justice in Northern Ireland than in South Africa (Stout, 2006). It remains possible that events in Northern Ireland subsequent to the Criminal Justice Review, notably Sinn Fein's acceptance of policing in 2007, could lead to the non-statutory restorative schemes such as Northern Ireland Alternatives and Community Restorative Justice building closer relationships with the statutory sector (website addresses for these schemes are provided at the end of the chapter).

---

[1]This is an abbreviated version of a real case study that appears on the Northern Ireland Youth Conference Service website http://www.youthconferenceserviceni.gov.uk/site/welcome/index.htm

Conclusion—is this as good as it gets?

It appears, then, that restorative justice has been an influence on the development of criminal justice policy and practice in England and Wales. It is particularly prominent in work with victims and restorative interventions are considered for all young offenders. Restorative interventions, despite some encouraging earlier commitments, do not appear to feature significantly in the final plans for the National Offender Management Service. However, even that is not particularly startling. Even in countries that are considered to be world leaders in restorative justice, such as Northern Ireland, South Africa and New Zealand, it is in work with young offenders that the most innovative restorative interventions have been pioneered.

So, should supporters of restorative justice in England and Wales be satisfied with what has been achieved? Compared to many other initiatives in working with offenders, it has to be acknowledged that restorative justice has been an incredible success. Some seemingly promising initiatives are never actually tried with offenders, for political or financial reasons, while others suffer from lack of funding or are withdrawn when they have barely commenced. By those criteria, restorative justice has had a very high degree of influence.

Restorative justice, however, has always had higher ambitions than this. From its early origins it has been considered as a different paradigm—an alternative to the punitive orthodoxy. Restorative justice advocates have long disparaged those who would reduce restorative justice to the level of just another sentencing option. As has been discussed throughout this chapter, Bazemore and Schiff (2005) have argued that the introduction of restorative justice should be accompanied by a fundamental rethink of the role of the state and of the community in criminal justice, and it is this that has been absent from the introduction of restorative justice in England and Wales. There does appear to be an appetite to discuss criminal justice from first principles (Blair, 2006a) and it is at this level that restorative justice should still aim to play a part. The examples of transition states of South Africa and Northern Ireland show that restorative justice can break out of merely criminological discussions and influence the whole development of a society, and it is this sort of ambition that should inspire restorative justice supporters in England and Wales.

Key arguments

- The use of the rhetoric of restorative justice is not always accompanied by the application of its key principles
- The introduction of the National Offender Management Service presents an opportunity for the greater use of restorative justice, but that opportunity has not yet been taken
- Restorative justice has had high ambitions and should hold onto those, it can play a role in discussions on the purpose and nature of criminal justice.

Further reading

For detailed introductory texts on restorative justice see McLaughlin et al. (eds.) (2003) *Restorative Justice: Critical Issues* and Johnstone, G. (2002) *Restorative Justice Ideas, Values, Debates*. There is now an increasing amount of good quality material being published on the National Offender Management Service. Gelsthorpe and Morgan (2007) *Handbook of Probation* and *Reshaping Prisons and Probation* edited by Hough, Allen and Padel (2006) provide broad and sometimes critical accounts. Williams, B (2005) *Victims of Crime and Community Justice* is a comprehensive account of victims' issues.

11

CORPORATE CRIME AND ITS VICTIMS

Steve Tombs and Brian Williams

Just like other victims of crime . . . our hearts have been torn out of our chests. The difference is, we are not seen as, not acknowledged as, and not supported as the victims of crime that we are.

(Families Against Corporate Killers, 2006)

Chapter summary

- As corporate crime is neglected in political debate, media representations of law and order, and by the discipline of criminology, then so too are its victims; but can criminology's recent focus upon victims of crime be applied to victims of corporate crimes?
- The overwhelming majority of victimology has failed to consider or investigate the impact of corporate crime upon victims.
- Victims of many forms of corporate crimes tend not to cohere with dominant representations of the 'ideal' victim—though there are exceptions.
- Many forms of corporate crimes are distinct from most forms of conventional crimes in terms of the victim–offender relations which are involved.
- Many victims of corporate crimes are unlikely even to be aware of any crime let alone their victimization to it; where they are aware, actually acting upon this is often extremely difficult.
- State approaches to corporate offending—in the enforcement of law and in responses to violations of law—further deny the existence of victims or their status as real victims of real crime.
- Criminologists should mount a critique of ideologically driven definitions of 'victims'.

'Crime' has long been at or close to the top of political agendas, in the UK as in many other advanced industrialized economies. Yet dominant understandings of what crime is and who the criminals are seem largely to be taken for granted—these are street crimes, involving property and interpersonal violence, committed largely by anti-social young people in general or by marginalized young men in particular. Such 'crimes' and criminals dominate political debate, legislative initiatives, news and fictionalized media obsessions with crime, and even criminology courses and textbooks— even if we at the same time 'know' that not all crimes fit these dominant constructions, least of all corporate crimes.

Thus the overwhelming focus of practice and rhetoric on the offences of the relatively powerless creates images and understandings which are easily recognizable, easily understood, with offenders who fit increasingly secure stereotypes. These stereotypes do not include senior executives of corporations, or organizations themselves—in fact, by contrast, business people and business life are frequently held up as role models to be emulated, rather than being exposed as the source of far greater criminal harm than any form of 'street' criminals.

If corporate crime is neglected in political debate, media representations of law and order, and by the discipline of criminology, then so too are its victims. And it is with corporate crime victimization that we are concerned in this chapter. One question to be addressed here is the extent to which criminology's recent focus upon victims of crime either has been, or might be, applied to victims of corporate crimes. In particular, we review academic work which has considered corporate crime victimization, before noting some of the peculiarities of victimization to corporate offences which actually, or apparently, make these a difficult 'fit' within victimology, as currently constructed. We find that there are various peculiarities of victimization in this area which combine to remove corporate crime further from our general experience—not least the offender–offence–victim relationships involved in corporate crime, which tend to jar when set against more conventional, or popular, understandings. Throughout the chapter we also pay close attention to the relationships between the concerns of criminology and the state's particular definitions of 'crime, law and order'—and we argue that, for the most part, applying criminological concerns with victims and victimization has hitherto meant following state definitions of who or what legitimate victims are, thus directing concern away from the victims of corporate crime.

> While corporate crime is a highly contested concept, it can be defined for our purposes as referring to:
>
> Illegal acts or omissions, punishable by the state under administrative, civil or criminal law which are the result of deliberate decision making or culpable negligence within a legitimate formal organization. These acts or omissions are . . . made in accordance with the normative goals, standard operating procedures, and/or cultural norms of the organization, and are intended to benefit the corporation itself.
>
> (Pearce and Tombs, 1998: 107–10.)

Criminology, victimology and corporate crime

Victimization and corporate crime

Although criminologists paid relatively little attention to victims of crime before the 1970s, victimology is now a healthy and growing subdiscipline. Most criminology textbooks nowadays pay at least passing attention to victims, and a good deal of research on victims and victimization has been undertaken since the first study appeared in 1948. However, that first publication, von Hentig's *The Criminal and his Victim*, created a poor precedent in a number of ways, and if many subsequent victimological studies were somewhat more rigorous, little of the early work involved victims themselves, drawing instead upon police and court records. It was only in the late 1970s that scholars, particularly feminist academics, began to challenge the positivist assumptions underlying this approach and the dubious methodology employed in some of the studies.

Despite significant contributions in the field of victimology since the shift towards more sociologically focused studies in the 1970s onwards, research on the victims of corporate crime has remained very much a minority interest among criminologists—a fact that is simply a particular instance of the general marginalization of studies of corporate offending within the discipline of criminology. However, it would be misleading to claim that there has been no criminological work around corporate crime victimization.

First, there now exist various quantitative indicators of the scale of victimization to corporate crime. Notably, in the UK, the Second Islington Crime Survey included questions relating to commercial crime, and to health and safety and pollution offences (Pearce, 1990). The findings revealed widespread victimization to corporate crime, indicating that the incidence of commercial crime is high both absolutely and relatively, that is compared to respondents' experiences of 'conventional' offending. Further, the most recent US National White-Collar Crime Survey, conducted in 2005, found widespread household victimization to the broader category of white-collar crime—though within this, corporate crime victimization was particularly prevalent, and viewed particularly harshly by respondents.

Surveying Victimization to Corporate Crime

The 2005 US National White-Collar Crime Survey, sought to measure household victimization to a variety of corporate and white –collar crimes over a twelve month period. The most frequent form of victimization, over one-third of all households, was to 'being misled as to the final price of a product or service', while over one-fifth of households reported victimization during that period as a result of a 'national corporate scandal'.

(Kane and Wall, 2006: 9)

Another way in which corporate crime victimization might be measured is through the use—or rather, given their poverty, the *reconstruction*—of official figures. Certainly reconstruction is crucial since official data of such victimization are not only scarce but, where they exist, are almost certain to be a significant underestimate of the actual level of offending. Here, for example, we might note figures on deaths at work—and while not all deaths are the result of crimes, Health and Safety Executive evidence indicates that up to 70 per cent of these are the result of violations of the criminal law on the part of employers, despite the low rates of actual prosecution following such events.

Definition: The Health and Safety Executive (HSE)

This is the body for overseeing health and safety law in England, Scotland and Wales.

But published fatality data are inadequate: they project only a *minimal* number of occupationally caused deaths in Britain on an annual basis. HSE's 'headline' figure—that trumpeted in press releases—is merely a combination of fatal injuries to workers and the self-employed required by law to be reported to and recorded by the HSE. For 2005–2006, the headline figure—for 'all workers'—is 217, while the actual figure of occupational deaths is somewhere between 1,600 and 1,700 (Tombs and Whyte, 2007). In other words, to obtain a more accurate figure of officially recorded occupational fatalities, we need to apply a multiplier of between seven and eight to the headline figure. Thus, being a victim of a work-related fatality looks much more likely than being a victim of homicide. Similarly, comparisons of recorded occupational injury data with British Crime Survey data on violent crimes produce the finding that one is more than twice as likely to be the victim of violence resulting in an injury requiring medical treatment at work than is the case for the 'real' crimes recorded by the Home Office (Tombs and Whyte, 2007). Despite these differing levels of victimization, the Home Office continues to reproduce understandings of what the 'real' crime problem is through its funding of a mass of criminological research into street crimes, their 'control', and evaluations of these controls—while it has not commissioned one single piece of research into corporate crime (Hillyard et al., 2004).

A related example further indicates the scale of victimization *and* the problems involved in such reconstruction. Even if we can reach some measurements of acute deaths and injuries, we know very little about the scale of death and disease caused by work activities, which itself tells us something about political priorities in societies where seemingly everything that *can be* recorded about populations *is* recorded. Take one category of deaths in one country—deaths from asbestos exposure in Britain. HSE has noted that in 2002 there were 1,862 deaths from mesothelioma, an asbestos-related cancer, and a further 1,800 deaths from asbestos-related lung cancers (HSE, 2004: 3). In fact, as the HSE itself recognizes, actual numbers of deaths related to asbestos exposure are far, far higher. Asbestos-related deaths continue to rise in this country (not to peak until around 2025, according to the British government), years after the apparent demise of the industry, and over 100 years after the first record of death related to asbestosis in this country (Tweedale, 2000: vii). Thus:

> excess deaths in Britain from asbestos-related diseases could eventually reach 100,000. . . One study projected that in western Europe 250,000 men would die of mesothelioma [just *one* asbestos-caused cancer] between 1995 and 2029; with half a million as the corresponding figure for the total number of West European deaths from asbestos.
>
> (Tweedale, 2000: 276)

And within this general picture, local studies can be even more revealing. For example, in Merseyside an Asbestos Victims Support Group was formed (in 1993), not only to seek justice for victims and their families, but also to record the prevalence of asbestos and its victims. Thus the Group has documented how Merseyside has a long history of asbestos use; it was widely used in local industries such as car production, garage work, building work, railway maintenance, tunnel construction and ship building and repair. Liverpool docks used to import huge amounts of asbestos: as late as 1975, 25.3 thousand metric tons of asbestos were imported exposing thousands of dockers to asbestos. Local shipyard workers have described fights using asbestos as snowballs (http://www.asbestosdiseases.org.uk/index.html).

Case Study: Estimating Victimization to Asbestos Exposure

Through the use of novel sources of data, the Merseyside Asbestos Victims Support Group has been able to compile indications of the sheer scale of victimization in Liverpool and surrounding areas. For example, it uncovered a letter by a Consultant Pathologist working in Liverpool Broadgreen Hospital in 1976 to the Asbestos Information Committee, an asbestos industry supported body. Part of that, reproduced on the Group's excellent website, states that:

> At present I am assessing the asbestos fibre lung content of the adult population of Liverpool, from post-mortem tissues and surgical tissues, in people who had no known asbestos contact. By the method I use most urban adults have between 2,000 and 7,000 asbestos fibres of dried lung. Only eight per cent of the population studied so far had a total absence of asbestos. (Merseyside Asbestos Victims Support Group, *The Scale of the Problem in Liverpool*, at http://www.asbestosdiseases.org.uk/scaleofprob.html)

In addition to this more quantitative based work, there is a solid body of qualitative evidence which attests, first, to some of the peculiarities of victimization to corporate as opposed to conventional crime and, second, to the ubiquity yet differential distribution of victimization to corporate offending. We shall discuss the former issue below; for now, we shall simply highlight some of the key dimensions of the differential distribution of victimization.

One finding that emerges from research on victims of corporate crime is that those who are already relatively vulnerable are the most likely to be victims of such offences (Walklate, 2007: 72; Croall, 1995: 242). Thus, for example, across a series of publications, Croall has set out how women, 'in their roles as workers, consumers, mothers or investors are victimised' by corporate crime (1995: 240). The peculiar vulnerability of women to certain forms of corporate crime is a function of their socially ascribed characteristics and structural location within patriarchal societies (Friedrichs, 1999: 153–4; Gerber and Weeks, 1992; Peppin, 1995; Robb, 2006; Rynbrandt and Kramer, 2001; Szockyi and Fox, 1996; Wonders and Danner, 2001).

Such claims also hold in the context of 'race' and ethnicity. Addressing the inter-connections between class–race–gender in terms of corporate crime victimization, Friedrichs, for example, notes that given that racial minorities:

> are over-represented among the socially and economically disadvantaged, they are also likely to be over-represented among victims of certain forms of [corporate] crime which disproportionately affect the vulnerable.
>
> (Friedrichs, 1999: 149)

That is, they are more likely:

> to consume lower quality, unsafe products; they are more likely to have jobs characterized by unsafe working conditions; they are more likely to live in neigh-bourhoods prone to environmental hazards.
>
> (Friedrichs, 1999: 149; see also the work of Lynch, Stretesky and colleagues on environmental racism/justice, for example Lynch, Stretesky, and McGurrin, 2002; Stretesky and Lynch, 1998, 1999; Stretesky and Hogan, 1998)

As Croall notes, further research into the structural basis of victimization to corporate crime would no doubt 'reveal other vulnerable groups' such as children or the elderly (1995: 241). She also calls for further work on the racialized dimensions of such vulnerability, and reinforces the need in particular for explorations of the intersections of race, class and gender 'in any full analysis of the victim–offender relationships' involved in such crime (1995: 243).

Finally, and within this qualitative work, academic research on corporate crime frequently uses case studies to explore its nature, aetiology, consequences and so on. Such case studies almost inevitably add to our understanding of the dynamics and consequences of falling victim to these various incidents, and within this work are uncovered some quite staggering indicators of the possible extent and enduring nature of victimization—even in the most well-known cases. Thus, for example, while the infamous gas leak at Bhopal, India, in 1984 caused, on official records, some 1,700 acute deaths, the Indian Government subsequently revised this to 3,329. Twenty years after the leak, in 2004, Amnesty International estimated that there had been over 7,000 such deaths, with 15,000 people having since died from longer-term effects. About one hundred thousand 'survivors' will never work again (Tombs and Whyte, 2007).

The invisibilities of corporate crime victimization

While we have indicated the disproportionate effects of corporate crimes on the relatively vulnerable, we should emphasise that, just as 'corporate crime' refers to a wide range of events and processes, it too is characterized by a wide range of victims. Financial crimes, crimes against consumers, crimes arising out of the employment relationship, and crimes against the environment victimize widely and at several different stages. Immediate and more remote victims can include local and national governments, other companies (again, of various types, from multinational conglomerates to small limited liability companies to the self-employed), shareholders and investors (which may include any of us who have savings or pensions linked to the stock exchange), local and national taxpayers, consumers, local communities and employees, not to mention the natural environment (and thus present and future generations of citizens). Thus, following Shichor, Friedrichs differentiates amongst three levels or categories of victims: 'primary (personal) victims, secondary (organisational) victims, and tertiary victims (abstractions such as the community at large or the public order' (Friedrichs, 1996: 59). Further, corporate crime has many *sites* of victimization, a claim borne out by even the briefest review of the evidence such as that in the previous section. Thus Croall, in recent reviews, has concluded that individuals and communities fall victim to corporate crime in the home, their local neighbourhoods, at work, as consumers, when travelling, using health and welfare services or at leisure (1998, 1999, 2001).

Images of crime and victimhood

If, popularly, politically and academically, corporate crime is rarely treated as real crime, then one of the elements and effects of this distinction is that its victims are barely represented nor treated as real victims. If the 'ideal' victim who 'deserves' support is hardly representative of victims in general, policy and services continue to perpetuate the myth, and prioritize the treatment, of this stereotypical victim. There remains, then, a 'hierarchy of victimization', both reflected and reproduced through a variety of official discourses and practices (Greer, 2007).

Yet victims of many forms of corporate crimes tend not to cohere with such representations. Workers who are victims of health and safety offences are at times deemed collusive in their victimization through the dominance of accident-prone, lazy, careless and so on discourses, classic forms of victim-blaming, or cast as having exchanged a wage for risk (Tombs and Whyte, 2007). Consumers who are victims of corporate offending are also often cast as somehow collusive in their fate, so that some generalized sense of 'caveat emptor' implies a lack of innocence or a 'contributory negligence' on the part of those wishing to make a fast return, as investors in stock or pensions, or buying cheaper cuts of meat or market stall clothing, as consumers (Croall, 1995: 242; Levi and Pithouse, 1992: 244; Friedrichs, 1996: 61; Shover et al., 1994: 95). Victims of environmental crime, such as localized pollution, often find it impossible to have their claims taken seriously on the basis of explanations in terms of lifestyles—smoking, drinking, bad diet—being ascribed to them and represented as causal factors in their ill-health. Thus, albeit perhaps with a little hyperbole, it is no coincidence that several commentators have drawn an analogy between being a victim of rape and a victim of corporate offences in terms of perceptions of personal culpability (Shover et al., 1994; Croall, 1995; Levi and Pithouse, 1992). In general, an imputed lack of innocence or credibility attached to victims of corporate crime simply reflects the general 'moral ambiguity' that some claim defines offending in this area, an ambiguity reflected in popular and many academic treatments of corporate crime, and virtually institutionalized in most state responses to these.

Of course, there are exceptions, though these tend to bear out the significance of innocence and the hierarchy of victimization referred to above—a notable recent example being the collapse of the Farepak Christmas Savings Club.

The Collapse of The Farepak Christmas Savings Club: Ideal Victims?

The collapse of the Farepak Christmas Savings Club—even if it will never be processed as a crime—contains the classic ingredients of a harm which we can all understand and which simply appears wrong, thus producing real victims—a large number of savers, the *deserving* poor, saving for an event that we all understand—Christmas—and in which many of us invest a great deal of money and emotional energy. Kids not having presents or the Christmas dinner they expected, families speaking of their devastation and loss, recognizable faces and situations appearing to be victims of what can be easily translated into a crime that we all understand, namely theft. These were victims who were propelled to the top of the media—and political—agenda: 'Here are families from the 30 per cent who own nothing, scrimping and saving to provide a Christmas for children that feels like other people's Christmases, as advertised on TV' (Toynbee, 2006). As Greer has noted, then, 'ordinary folk who are victimised by corporate "fat cats", may be seen as more deserving of 'legitimate' victim status' (Greer, 2007, p. 37).

It is important to emphasise that as well as the moral judgements regarding legitimate victim status, such status is more easily ascribed to those in situations which cohere with dominant understandings of victim–offender relationships—that is, those which are understood through the lens of conventional offending. Thus many forms of corporate crimes are distinct from most forms of conventional crimes in terms of the victim–offender relations which are involved. Crucial here is what we can best term the issue of 'proximity'. In many forms of traditional crime there is, or must at some point be, a degree of proximity between offenders and victims: this is most obviously the case with regard to personal assaults, robberies and so on; but it also applies to theft of and from motor vehicles and to burglaries, in the sense that even if absent from a dwelling or car at the time of the theft or robbery, the victim does have some proximity in time and space to these as owners, residents, drivers or passengers. By contrast, in the case of corporate crimes, there are frequently enormous distances between offender and victim, in terms of both space and time. Thus the decisions that were the source of the chain of events at the Union Carbide Corporation (UCC) plant in Bhopal were taken thousands of miles away, at corporate headquarters in Danbury, Connecticut, at an unspecified time long before the leak that caused such devastation: it is virtually certain that neither Warren Anderson, then CEO of UCC, nor any members of his board, had met any of those Indian workers and citizens whose lives were ultimately destroyed by the nature of safety training, cuts in routine maintenance and reductions in spending on safety measures over which they presided. Similarly, in the case of asbestos-caused diseases, also considered above, the slow and painful death endured by many victims is one that unfolds over years following exposure up to forty years previously. Such facets of corporate crime victimization have important implications in terms of awareness of, acting upon, and establishing 'proof' of victimization.

Victims' (lack of) awareness

This lack of fit between dominant representations of victimization on the one hand, and victimization to corporate crime on the other, means that, for many of us, corporate crime tends not to appear as crime, or as crime subject to possible control. To some extent, then, corporate crime as crime is removed from our immediate consciousness. This has important implications in terms of awareness of, and then 'proving', victimization.

First, many victims of corporate crimes are unlikely even to be aware of any crime let alone their victimization to it (Croall, 1989; Grant Stitt and Giacopassi, 1993; Meier and Short, 1995). For example, when buying a new home, or glass products, or white or other electrical goods in Britain, most of us will not have stopped to consider that these might be cheaper, or that there might be more genuine choice, were it not for price fixing or the creation of illegal barriers to market entry amongst manufacturers and retailers.

Somewhat different, but related, is an awareness of some unfavourable personal circumstance or outcome, but a lack of any awareness that we have been the victim of any type of legal offence. For example, most of us are unlikely to think of our workplace as a causal site when suffering some form of illness, and even less likely to consider unhealthy conditions in terms of illegality on the part of our employer. Where our child suffers from breathing difficulties, we may think in some generalized way about the state of our local environment (for example, poor air quality), but are unlikely concretely to consider ourselves as possible victims of illegal emissions from local taxis, buses, vans and so on.

Similarly, in the event of 'accidents'—be these major or minor—ideologies of the accident-prone worker are so prevalent that workers often routinely place blame upon themselves, as a result of their carelessness or bad luck (Tombs and Whyte, 2007). Where representations of self-blaming or collusion are resisted, victims of safety and health crimes may still be unaware of the legal status of what they have experienced—that is, they may have a sense of having suffered an injustice, or a bad employer, but not a perception of victimization to a criminal offence.

Finally, a key element in relation to corporate crime victimization is the ability, or most people's perceptions of their abilities, to seek redress. That is, where victims of corporate crimes *are* aware of their status as victims, actually acting upon this awareness is often extremely difficult (see Croall, 1989). Indeed, an informed understanding of the extent of these difficulties may act as a disincentive against reporting or acting. This might be manifest in rationalizations invoking bad luck or being more careful in the future, and uttering platitudes such as 'win some, lose some' or 'once bitten, twice shy', and so on. Yet even where victims might seek redress, either independently (via civil law, for example) or through an enforcement agency, then distances in time and space between victim and offender(s), and consequent difficulties of proving an offence has occurred even where—as is often the case—the offender is identified, are likely to prove overwhelming obstacles.

Many of these problems of both awareness and then seeking redress can be illustrated concretely if we return to the case of asbestos in the UK. It is impossible to account for the scale of the physical, emotional, and psychological harm caused by the use of asbestos—knowledge of which the industry has tried to suppress for over 100 years by co-opting the medical community, attacking critical science and funding industry-friendly research, forming apparently 'independent' lobbying groups and through quite simple and routine cover-ups, manipulation of data and lying to workers and regulators (Tweedale, 2000). But we need to bear in mind that the hazards associated with asbestos are now so well known that the substance is highly regulated and, in the UK as in some other parts of the globe, banned from use—a rarity amongst those substances to which men and women are exposed on a daily basis, the health effects of which will only really be known after generations of use/exposure.

Case Study: Asbestos Exposure—Compensation Culture?

In the case of asbestos exposure, knowledge and regulation are such that at least some financial compensation is available to victims and their families—still rare in the case of occupational disease in this country. However:

> The nature of asbestos civil claims makes it very difficult for victims to claim; in 95 per cent of the cases they are referring to asbestos exposure some 30 to 40 years ago. However a case cannot proceed without proof of employment at a place of work where the claimant was exposed to asbestos. The claimant also has to produce witnesses to that exposure. This may mean a 60 year old building worker who may have worked with asbestos in the 1950s on a small maintenance job, will have to produce eye witness accounts to his asbestos exposure from as long as 30 or 40 years ago.
> (Merseyside Asbestos Victims Support Group, http://www.asbestosdiseases.org.uk/services.html, accessed 2 February 2007)

Case Study: Asbestos Exposure—Compensation Culture?—cont'd

Indeed, the Hazards movement (a network of resource centres and campaigners on health and safety at work; see http://www.hazardscampaign.org.uk/.) recently estimated that only half of the almost 2,000 people officially recognized as:

> dying each year of the asbestos cancer mesothelioma receive industrial injuries benefit payments—despite the condition being accepted as caused by work, devastating and a guarantee of an excruciating death. Scarcely anyone suffering the even more common asbestos related lung cancers—fewer than 100 a year—receive compensation.
>
> ('A Little Compensation', *Hazards*, 90, May 2005, http://www.hazards.org/compensation/briefing.htm)

The peculiarities of corporate offending?

Many who comment upon the problematic nature of identifying corporate crime—and hence victimization to it—draw a useful contrast with many forms of conventional crimes. In the case of the latter, it is argued, the fact of a crime is rarely an issue; what is at issue, and what consumes agency (here, police) resources is identifying an offender. In the case of many forms of corporate crime, however, problems frequently arise in quite the opposite way. That is, there is very often little problem in identifying an offender (Clarke, 1990), although we should note that this is not always the case, not least given the (apparent) complexity of some forms of organizational structures (more on this below); here, the issue is actually establishing whether any offence has occurred. This involves quite a different set of problems and processes to those commonly found with respect to conventional crime.

Crimes related to occupational and environmental exposures are classic examples here. Thus if workers are aware that a skin rash, breathing problems, nausea, headaches and so on are likely to have a primary cause in working conditions, an enormous burden of proof rests with them. And proof in such instances must make reference to scientific discourses, this raising the location and role of expertise and experts, and the fact of unequal access to these, be they toxicologists, pharmacologists, epidemiologists and so on. Proof also requires that highly unequal access to legal expertise—an inequality likely to be exacerbated given the direction of legal aid reform—be overcome. Finally, also at issue here is what Becker was referring to via his notion of a 'hierarchy of credibility' (Becker, 1967), whereby he seeks to demonstrate how power is rather more significant than 'truth' in producing credible statements.

Even if one is aware that a particular condition can be caused by workplace exposures—for example, the well-known diseases associated with exposure to asbestos fibres—then there can remain enormous difficulties in locating exposures to a *particular* workplace or employer, at a *particular* time. The fact that many industrial diseases take long periods to develop—sometimes as much as forty or fifty years—makes pursuing (let alone proving) a case against a particular employer very difficult, and this is compounded where a worker has been employed by different companies over the course of a working life.

Yet even these difficulties can be further compounded. For example, some attempts to pursue legal cases against corporations must also confront one further layer of legal complexity, which arises as a result of (apparently) complex organizational structures. The existence of subsidiaries, autonomous sub-units, strategic business units and so on, creates legal difficulties in tracing lines of decision making and accountability. Thus, given the increasingly complex organization and fragmentation of businesses, as well as the increased prevalence of contracting out and 'self-employment', problems of locating causality and lines of accountability and responsibility are likely to be exacerbated (Keane, 1995; Tombs, 1995)—even more so in the case of companies organized across national borders (and thus, also, legal jurisdictions).

State responses to corporate crime and victimization

Enforcing the law?

The longstanding separation between corporate crime and 'real' crime is reflected, and institutionalized through, state responses to corporate offending, and this further excludes its victims from consideration or treatment as real victims of real crime. Most obviously this separation of corporate crime from real crime is signalled by the fact that if crime is that with which the police deal, then corporate offences are already something distinct—they are subject to regulation (not policing) by a diverse range of state and quasi-state agencies. And it is in the area of regulation that there is perhaps the most significant body of academic research around corporate crime. There are a number of studies—mostly nationally based, though with some useful cross-national comparative work—examining the practices of a whole range of regulatory bodies (for a review, see, for example, Clarke 2000: 136–61). Notwithstanding important differences in enforcement strategies across nations (Pearce and Tombs, 1998: 229–45) and across different spheres of regulatory activity (Snider, 1991), such studies allow several broad generalizations to be made about the practices and effects of regulatory enforcement agencies, one of which is crucial to our discussion: that non-enforcement is the most frequently found characteristic (Snider 1993: 120–24).

In terms of the *practice* of enforcement, the most common finding of studies of regulatory enforcement, across business sectors and discrete areas of legislation, is that a co-operative regulatory approach is dominant. In short, regulators seek to enforce through persuasion—they advise, educate, and bargain, negotiate and reach compromise with the regulated (see Pearce and Tombs 1998: 223–46). When violations become known to inspectors, they engage in a dialogue with management, prioritizing compliance with laws being violated in some areas (the most serious offences), usually on the basis of an agreed timetable, whilst accepting that others, deemed less serious, may take much longer to put right. Formal enforcement action is rare, and overwhelmingly involves the imposition of notices of varying 'severity'. Prosecution is a 'last resort', seen as a failure within the enforcement agencies themselves (Hawkins, 2002).

The effect of this general modus operandi on the part of regulators is to prevent the vast majority of corporate offending ever being recognized, recorded or treated as crime—and if there is no crime, there can be no victim of crime. So while there are 1,600 to 1,700 cases of occupationally related fatal injury in the UK each year, this figure bears little relationship to the numbers of prosecutions following these deaths. This is partly a consequence of the fact that only some 200-plus of these deaths, those within the category 'all workers', are even subject to investigation. In 2003–2004, the 255 deaths recorded to 'all workers' by the Health and Safety Executive (HSE) led to 22 'duty-holders' (employers) being prosecuted, resulting in 18 convictions (HSE, http://www.hse.gov.uk/enforce/off0405/off0405.pdf, page 50 of 63). Prosecutions and convictions following injuries are, proportionately, of course much lower.

Further, it should be noted that if the *outcomes* of criminal justice responses to work-place deaths, for example, are often felt on the part of the bereaved to represent a further victimization, so too are the actual *processes* themselves. While these experiences differ, and while there is no claim here to 'speak for' the bereaved, in general the lengthy processes of HSE investigation, the Executive's liaison with the police, the deliberations of the coronial system, the nature of decisions by the HSE and/or the Crown Prosecution Service as to whether or not to prosecute combine both to bewilder and—through their fairly systematic exclusion of the bereaved—frustrate those who have already been victimized by the death(s) in question.

Case Study: A Double Victimization

Victims of corporate crime often experience further processes of victimization through the criminal justice responses to their plight, which often deny their very status as victims. As the recently-formed campaigning group Families Against Corporate Killers has stated:

> Death by whatever means causes great sorrow and distress within families. When the death is due to someone failing to take reasonable care, failing to obey the law or callously disre-garding it, and then failing to face manslaughter charges and be punished appropriately, it is much harder for the family to recover. The repercussions of a work-related death go on for many years with spouses often unable to work again, children traumatised and failing at school, and families thrown into poverty and insecurity. Just like other victims of crime. . . our hearts have been torn out of our chests. The difference is, we are not seen as, not acknowledged as, and not supported as the victims of crime that we are.
>
> ('Families Against Corporate Killers', 2006)

In general, then, some studies of corporate crime have referred to a double victimization—that is, from the offence and then from victims' treatment by the 'official response' (Shover et al., 1994: 94). Thus, in their study of the long-term consequences of victimization to the collapse of a loan company, Shover et al. conclude that 'victims with the most extensive contact with the official system for redress of injury often emerge from the experience more disillusioned and more disheartened than when they began' (Shover et al., 1994: 95)—such official responses, deemed ultimately unfair and unjust, amount to an official denial of their status as victims of crime (Shover et al., 1994: 95). And on this point, criminologists, too, have a responsibility for the discipline's collective failure to challenge political definitions of real crimes and legitimate victims; thus 'continued neglect or indifference' by social scientists towards victims 'also may play a part in denying legitimacy to them and their suffering'

(Shover et al., 1994: 96). Unsurprisingly, studies of corporate crime victimization, then, frequently refer to the associated traumatic and enduring psychological effects associated with it (Friedrichs, 1996: 63; Grant Stitt and Giacopassi, 1993: 70), an observation common to other forms of crime victims.

Punishing corporate crime?

As the above extract indicates, the official denial of crime and thus victimization is further reinforced through the sanctions that follow successful prosecutions. By far the most common sanction is the monetary fine. Only in cases investigated by the Serious Fraud Office (SFO), unique amongst regulatory bodies in the UK in being established as part of criminal justice legislation, is imprisonment of individuals likely to be an outcome. But even here caution is needed. Fooks (2003) has noted that, after a short period in which a small number of financial crimes were subject to criminalization, the SFO has in recent years experienced retrenchment, with an increasing role being taken by the Financial Services Authority, which has an explicitly co-operative approach to regulatory enforcement (Spalek, 2001). Even during the 1990s, when the SFO received criticism for over-zealousness in terms of prosecution, it was taking an average of just fifteen cases to court per year (Fooks, 1999). Further, since the victims of serious fraud tend to be other corporations (banks and institutional investors), regulation in this sphere has been termed regulation *for* rather than *of* the City (Fooks, 2003).

More generally, following successful prosecution for corporate crime, fines are leveled at companies—and these are almost uniformly low.

Case Study: Punishing Real Crimes?

The average penalty in the 18 convictions secured by HSE following workplace fatalities in 2003–2004 was £27,876 (http://www.hse.gov.uk/enforce/off0405/off0405.pdf, 61 of 63). The average penalty following all health and safety prosecutions that year was £9,633 (ibid., page 52 of 63). In 2003, Barbara Young, the Chief Executive of the Environment Agency, criticized the 'weak' sentencing following environmental crime:

> Fines for environmental offences have struggled slowly upwards over five years but still rarely exceed £20,000. . . with irreparable environmental damage or serious risk to public health, penalties often fail to match up to the costs avoided.
>
> (Young, cited in Brown 2003)

There is widespread recognition that, in general, levels of fines for corporate offences are inadequate. Alongside calls for both higher and more sensitively determined levels of fines are many longstanding proposals for the use of other sanctions, some of which have been introduced in limited fashion, others of which remain at the proposal stage (see Croall, 2005). All have their drawbacks, none is a panacea, and each is more or less appropriate for particular types of corporation and following specific forms of offence (Slapper and Tombs, 1999). Ultimately while there are clearly enormous difficulties in developing effective sanctions in the case of corporate crime, these tend to be political rather than technical (Lofquist, 1993; Etzioni, 1993)—the key issue is again the political refusal to treat corporate crime as real crime. And the net effect is to deny those who are victims of corporate crime any sense of justice, the delivery of which represents a key rationale of criminal justice systems.

Conclusion

Corporate crime victimization is routine, with economic, physical and social effects arguably far more widespread and enduring than those associated with conventional crimes. Yet victims of corporate crime barely register on any 'crime, law and order' agendas—not on the part of Government, through its rhetoric and practices, nor, as we have indicated, those research agendas sustained by academic criminology through its research into victims.

If the criminal justice system is to be rebalanced in favour of the victim, to paraphrase Tony Blair, the category of victims to whom he and the Labour Government refer is a rather selective one (Reid, 2006: 3; Mactaggart, 2005: 2; Henry, 2004). Leaving aside the inadvisability of this rhetoric of rebalancing the system in this way (Williams, 2005), close examination of relevant policy documents reveals that victims are always framed as individual service users, much as they were by the previous government (Walklate, 2007: Chapter 1). The lists of the Government's achievements in relation to victim policy which invariably form part of such documents also, significantly, exclude any reference to corporate crime legislation or enforcement—and, as we have indicated, this is entirely consistent both with the generally de-criminalizing nature of regulatory enforcement, and with current trends towards reducing 'red tape' (which may be translated as law and its enforcement).

Thus, recent and current evidence indicates that any rebalancing is if anything less rather than more likely to include most victims of corporate crime. Indeed, the ideologically driven nature of the Government's recent and current concerns with specific classes of victims can be most clearly highlighted in relation to another area of 'business crime'—that is, understanding businesses not as offenders, but themselves as *victims* of crime. This movement to integrate the business community into a wider community of legitimate crime victims is gathering momentum: nationally and locally, where business organizations and trade associations are involved in a concerted effort to re-frame how local publics think about the process of criminal victimization; at the same time, the Home Office has been a key mover in developing a flourishing research area around crimes *against* business (Hopkins, 2002). The re-positioning of businesses as victims to rather than perpetrators of crimes has key implications in terms of the possibilities of their more effective regulation (Coleman et al., 2005).

In this context, one might argue that a task for criminologists is to mount a critique of such ideologically driven definitions of 'victims', and to confront Government in its own terms, that is, to face up to the evidence in developing the evidence-based policy that it has so often urged. But, as we have seen, for all our certainty regarding the scale of corporate crime victimization, criminological evidence attesting to this fact is relatively sparse—and this is hardly surprising, since criminology's dominant objects of research have historically and to date been dominated, some would say increasingly so, by the state's own definitions of what constitute the major 'crime, law and order' problems (Hillyard et al., 2004).

With notable exceptions, criminologists have been, and remain, complicit in the selective defining of legitimate victims. In their rush to engage with the Government's crime agenda—a rush supported through a dramatic hike in funding available for academic research within a narrow terrain defined by Government—criminologists reproduce a sterile, distorted and socially regressive view of what crime is, and of who criminals and victims are. Yet as feminist criminologists demonstrated from the 1970s onwards, uncovering hidden victimization, as part of academic work linked into a broader social movement, can have real, if still highly imperfect, effects in terms of popular understandings of, and criminal justice provision for, hitherto unrecognized groups of victims. A precondition of such a challenge now is a re-evaluation of what the discipline is for—criminology applied to a Government agenda, or criminology applied to evidence and to a more socially just criminal justice system?

Key arguments

Most victimology fails to consider the impact of corporate crime upon victims, retaining focus upon 'street' crimes and individual offences—yet there is both quantitative and qualitative evidence which allows us to construct a picture of corporate crime victimization.

Victims of many forms of corporate crimes tend not to cohere with dominant representations of the 'ideal' victim—though there are exceptions.

Many forms of corporate crimes are distinct from most forms of conventional crimes in terms of the victim–offender relations which are involved—and crucial here is the issue of 'proximity'.

Many victims of corporate crimes are unlikely even to be aware of any crime let alone their victimization to it; where victims of corporate crimes *are* aware of their status as victims, actually acting upon this awareness is often extremely difficult.

State approaches to corporate offending further deny the existence of victims or their status as real victims of real crime—in the enforcement of law and in responses to violations of law.

As Government claims to place victims ever more at the centre of the criminal justice system, criminologists could and should mount a critique of the narrow definition of 'victims' being used in this rhetoric and practice.

Further reading

There is now an extensive literature on victims of crime in general—and some of this is beginning to address issues around corporate crime. An excellent, up-to-date starting point is Davies, P., Francis, P., Greer, C., *Victims, Crime and Society* London: Sage. This text also includes an excellent overview chapter by Hazel Croall on 'White Collar and Corporate Victims of Crime'. Alongside this, required reading should also be Whyte, D. (2007) 'Victims of Corporate Crime', in Walklate, S., ed., *Handbook of Victims and Victimology* Cullompton: Willan. An excellent, if somewhat demanding, exploration of the gendered dimensions of corporate crime victimization can be found in Szockyi, E.

and Fox, J.G., eds. (1996) *Corporate Victimisation of Women* Boston, Mass.: Northeastern University Press; the contributions here both describe and theorize the various ways in which women are particularly vulnerable to certain forms of corporate crime in their socially constructed roles as bearers and raisers of children and as paid and unpaid workers. The most accessible overview of corporate crime in general can be found in Chapter 2 of Steven Box's (1983) *Power, Crime, and Mystification* London: Routledge, 16–79. Though now 25 years old, this is a highly readable, lively and provocative introduction to what remain the key concerns and debates within this area.

BIBLIOGRAPHY

Allen, P.M. (1998) 'Towards a Black construct of accessibility', in T. Modood and T. Acland (eds), *Race and Higher Education*. London: Policy Studies Institute.

Ashworth, A. (2002) 'Responsibilities, rights and restorative justice', *British Journal of Criminology*, 42: 578–95.

Bailey, R. (1994) 'Probation supervision: attitudes to formalised helping', Unpublished PhD thesis, University of Nottingham.

Bailey, R. (1995) 'Helping offenders as an element in justice', in D. Ward and M. Lacey (eds), *Probation Working for Justice*. London: Whiting and Birch.

Banks, C. (2004) *Criminal Justice Ethics*. Thousand Oaks: Sage.

Banks, S. (2004) *Ethics, Accountability and the Social Professions*. Basingstoke: Palgrave.

Barrett, L.E. (1977) *Rastafarians: The Dreadlocks of Jamaica*. London: Heineman.

Bateman, T. (2007) 'Youth Justice News', *Youth Justice: An International Journal*, 7(2).

Bazemore, G. and Schiff, M. (2005) *Juvenile Justice Reform and Restorative Justice*. Cullompton: Willan.

Becker, H.S. (1963) *Outsiders: Studies in the Sociology of Deviance*. New York: The Free Press.

Becker, H.S. (1967) 'Whose Side Are We On?', *Social Problems*, 14(3): 239–47.

Bell, A., Hodgson, M. and Pragnell, S. (1999) 'Diverting Children and Young People from Crime and the Criminal Justice System', in B. Goldson (ed.) *Youth Justice Contemporary Policy and Practice*. Aldershot: Ashgate.

Bennett, J. Crewe, B. and Wahidin, A. (2007) *Understanding Prison Staff*. Cullompton: Willan.

Bhui, S. (2003) 'Deconstructing Diversity', *Probation Journal*, 50(3): 196.

Bianchi, H. and Swaaningen, V. (1986) *Abolitionism Towards a Non-Repressive Approach to Crime*. *Proceedings of the Second International Conference*. Amsterdam: Free University Press.

Bichard, M. (2004) *An Independent Inquiry Arising from the Soham Murders*. London: The Stationery Office.

Black, J. (1997) *Rules and Regulators*. Oxford: Clarendon Press.

Blair, I. (2005) 'Dimbleby Lecture', 16th November 2005, http://news.bbc.co.uk/1/hi/uk/4443386.stm

Blair, T. (2006a) *Our Nation's Future—Social Exclusion*, available online at http://www.pm.gov.uk/output/Page10037.asp

Blair, T. (2006b) *Our Nation's Future—Criminal Justice System*. Available online at http://www.pm.gov.uk/output/Page9891.asp

Blumstein, A. (1997) 'Interaction of criminological research and public policy', *Journal of Quantitative Criminology*, 12(4): 349–61.

Bottomley, K. (1973) *Decisions in the Penal Process*. Oxford: Martin Robertson.

Bottomley, K. (1979) *Criminology in Focus*. Oxford: Martin Robertson.

Bottoms A. (1995), 'The philosophy and politics of punishment and sentencing', in C. Clarkson and R. Morgan (eds), *The Politics of Sentencing Reform*. Oxford: Oxford University Press.

Bottoms, A. (2001) 'Compliance and community penalties', in A. Bottoms, L. Gelsthorpe and S. Rex (eds), *Community Penalties Change and Challenges*. Cullompton: Willan.

Bottoms, A. (2005) 'Methodology matters', *Safer Society*, 25: 10–12.

Bottoms, A. and Stevenson, S. (1992) 'What went wrong? Criminal justice policy in England and Wales 1945–70', in D. Downes (ed.), *Unravelling Criminal Justice*. London: Macmillan.

Bowling, B. (1998) *Violent Racism, Victimisation, Policing and Social Context*. Oxford: Oxford University Press.

Bowling, B. (2005) *Bobby, Bond or Babylon: transnational police cooperation in the contemporary Caribbean?* Professorial Inaugural Lecture, King's College London. http://www.kcl.ac.uk/depsta/rel/ccjs/bowling-transnational-crimes.ppt

Bowling, B. and Phillips, C. (2002) *Racism, Crime and Justice*. Harlow: Longman.

Box, S. (1983) *Power, Crime, and Mystification*. London: Routledge.

Bradby, H. (1995) 'Ethnicity: not a black and white issue. A research note', *Sociology of Health and Illness*, 17(3):405–17.

Braithwaite, J. (1989) *Crime, Shame and Reintegration*. Cambridge: Cambridge University Press.

Braithwaite, J. (2002) *Restorative Justice and Responsive Regulation*. Oxford: Oxford University Press.

Bratton, W. and Knobler, P. (1998) *Turnaround: How America's Top Cop Reversed the Crime Epidemic*. New York: Random House.

British Council (2007) Official website: http://www.britishcouncil.org/home-diversity-areas.htm.

Brody, S. (1976) *The Effectiveness of Sentencing*. Home Office Research Study No. 35. London: HMSO.

Brown, J. (2000)'Discriminatory experiences of women police; comparison of officers serving in England and Wales, Scotland, Northern Ireland and the Republic of Ireland', *International Journal of the Sociology of Law*, 28: 91–111.

Brown, J. (2005) 'Why I study gender and policing', *The Psychologist*, 18(6).

Brown, P. (2003) 'Pollution still pays as firms shrug off fine', *The Guardian*, 31st July.

Brown, S. (2005) *Understanding Youth and Crime: Listening to Youth*. 2nd edn. Buckingham: Open University Press.

Brownlee, I. (1998) *Community Punishment. A Critical Introduction*. Harlow: Addison Wesley Longman.

Burnett, R. (2000) 'Understanding criminal careers through a series of in-depth interviews', *Offender Programs Report*, 4: 1–16.

Burnett, R. and Roberts, C. (2004) 'The emergence and importance of evidence-based practice in probation and youth justice', in R. Burnett, and C. Roberts (eds), *What Works in Probation and Youth Justice*. Cullompton, Willan. pp. 1–13.

Byrne, D. (2005) 'Complexity, configurations and cases', *Theory, Culture and Society*, 22(5): 95–111.

Cabinet Office (1999) *Professional Policy Making for the Twenty-First Century*. London: Cabinet Office.

Cabinet Office (2006) 'Penalties review rogue businesses should redress the harm they cause', Press release, 28th November, www.cabinetoffice.gov.uk/REGULATION/news/2006/061128_mr.asp

Calverley, A., Cole, B., Kaur, G., Lewis, S., Raynor, P., Sadeghi, S. et al. (2004) Home Office Research Study No. 277, *Black and Asian Offenders on Probation*. Home Office Research, Development and Statistics Directorate.

Campbell, C., Devlin, R., O'Mahony, D., Doak, J., Jackson, J., Corrigan, T. et al. (2005) *Evaluation of the Northern Ireland Youth Conference Service*. Northern Ireland Statistics and Research Agency.

Canton, R. (2005) 'Risk assessment and compliance in probation and mental health practice', in B. Littlechild and D. Fearns (eds), *Mental Disorder and Criminal Justice: Policy, Provision and Practice*. Lyme Regis: Russell House.

Canton, R. and Eadie, T. (2004) 'Social work with young offenders: practising in a context of ambivalence', in M. Lymbery and S. Butler (eds), *Social Work Ideals and Practice Realities*. Houndmills: Palgrave.

Carlen, P. (1983) *Women's Imprisonment*. London: Routledge and Kegan Paul.

Carlen, P. (1996) *Jigsaw: A Political Criminology of Youth Homelessness*. Buckingham: Open University Press.

Carlen, P. and Worrall A. (2004) *Analysing Women's Imprisonment*. Cullompton: Willan.

Carrington, K. and Hogg, R. (2002) 'Critical criminologies', in K. Carrington and R. Hogg (eds), *Critical Criminology: Issues, Debates, Challenges*. Cullompton: Willan.

Carson, D. (1996) 'Risking legal repercussions', in H. Kemshall and J. Pritchard (eds), *Good Practice in Risk Assessment and Risk Management, Vol. 1*. London: Jessica Kingsley.

Carter, P. (2003) *Managing Offenders, Reducing Crime: A New Approach*. London: Prime Minister's Strategy Unit.

Cavadino, M. and Dignan, J. (2006) 'Penal policy and political economy', *Criminology and Criminal Justice*, 6(4): 435–56.

Cavadino, M. and Dignan, J. (2002) *The Penal System: An Introduction*. 3rd edn. London: Sage.

Cavendish, C. (2007) 'The slide to invisibility must be arrested', *The Times*, 5th April.

Cawson, P., Wattam, S. and Kelly, G. (2000) *Child Maltreatment in the United. Kingdom: A Study of the Prevalence of Child Abuse and Neglect*. London: NSPCC.

Challen, M. and Walton, T. (2004) *Juveniles in Custody*. London: Her Majesty's Inspectorate of Prisons.

Chapman, T. and Hough, M. (1998) *Evidence Based Practice: A Guide to Effective Practice*. HM Inspectorate of Probation.

Chigwada-Bailey, R. (1997) *Black Women's Experiences of Criminal Justice*. Winchester: Waterside Press.

Child Poverty Action Group (1997) *Not to be Ignored: Young People, Poverty and Health*. London: Child Poverty Action Group.

Children's Rights Alliance for England (2002) *Rethinking Child Imprisonment: A Report on Young Offender Institutions*. London: Children's Rights Alliance for England.

Children's Society Advisory Committee on Juvenile Custody and its Alternatives (1993) *A False Sense of Security: The Case Against Locking Up More Children*. London: The Children's Society.

Christie, N. (1977) 'Conflicts as Property', *British Journal of Criminology*, 17: 1–15.

Christie, N. (1981) *Limits to Pain*. London: Martin Robertson.

Christie, N. (1986) 'The ideal victim', in E.A. Fattah (ed.) *From Crime Policy to Victim Policy: Reorienting the Criminal Justice System*. New York: St. Martin's Press.

Christie, N. (1998a) 'Between Civility and the State', in V. Ruggiero, N. South and I. Taylor (eds), *The New European Criminology: Crime and Social Order in Europe*. London: Routledge.

Christie, N. (1998b) 'Essai de géographie pénalé', *Actes de la Recherche en Sciences Sociales*, 124:68–74.

Christie, N. (2000) *Crime Control as Industry: Towards Gulags, Western Style*. 3rd edn. London: Routledge.

Christie, N. (2004) *A Suitable Amount of Crime*. London: Routledge.

Clair, J., Beatty, J. and Maclean, T. (2005) 'Out of Sight But Not Out of Mind: Managing Invisible Social Identities in the Workplace', *The Academy of Management Review*, 30(1): 78–95.

Clarke, M. (1990) *Business Crime: Its Nature and Control*. Cambridge: Polity.

Clarke, M. (2000) *Regulation: The Social Control of Business between Law and Politics*. London: Macmillan.

Clements, P. and Jones, J. (2006) *The Diversity Training Handbook*. London: Kogan Page.

Cloward, R. and Ohlin, E.L. (1960) *Delinquency and Opportunity: A Theory of Delinquent Gangs*. New York: Free Press.

Cohen, S. (1955) *Delinquent Boys: The Culture of the Gang*. Glencoe IL: Free Press.

Cohen, S. (1972) *Folk Devils and Moral Panics: The Creation of the Mods and Rockers*. New York: St Martins Press.

Cohen, S. (1981) 'Footprints on the sand: a further report on criminology and the sociology of deviance in Britain', in M. Fitzgerald, G. McLennan and J. Pawson (eds), *Crime and Society: Readings in History and Theory*. London: Routledge and Kegan Paul. pp. 220–47.

Cohen, S. (1985) *Visions of Social Control*. Cambridge: Polity Press.

Cohen, S. (2001) *States of Denial: Knowing about Atrocities and Suffering*. Cambridge: Polity Press.

Coleman, C. and Moynihan, J. (1996) *Understanding Crime Data*. Buckingham: Open University Press.

Coleman, R., Tombs, S. and Whyte. D. (2005) 'Capital, Crime Control and Statecraft in the Entrepreneurial City', *Urban Studies*, 42, December: 1–20.

Commission for Social Care Inspectorate, The Healthcare Commission, Her Majesty's Inspectorate of Constabulary, Her Majesty's Inspectorate of Probation, Her Majesty's Inspectorate of Prisons, Her Majesty's Crown Prosecution Service Inspectorate, Her Majesty's Inspectorate of Courts Administration, The Office of Standards in Education (2005) *Safeguarding Children: The Second Joint Chief Inspectors' Report on Arrangements to Safeguard Children*. London: Department of Health.

Community Restorative Justice (2007) Official website: http://www.extern.org/restorative/CRJI.htm

Confederation of British Industry (2006) *CBI Response to the 'Regulatory Justice: Sanctioning in a Post-Hampton World' consultation document*. London: CBI.

Connelly, C. and Williamson, S. (2000) *Review of the Research Literature on Serious Violent and Sexual Offenders*. Edinburgh: Scottish Executive.

Considine, M. (2005) *Making Public Policy*. Cambridge: Polity.

Crawford, A. and Clear, T. (2003) 'Community justice: transforming communities through restorative justice?', in E. McLaughlin, R. Fergusson, G. Hughes and L. Westmarland (eds), *Restorative Justice: Critical Issues*. London: Sage Publications.

Crawford, A. and Newburn, T. (2003) *Youth Offending and Restorative Justice*. Cullompton: Willan.

Criminal Justice Review Group (2000) *Review of the Criminal Justice System in Northern Ireland*. Belfast: HMSO.

Croall, H. (1998) 'Business, crime and the community', *International Journal of Risk, Security and Crime Prevention*, 3: 281–92.

Croall, H (1999) 'Crime, business and community safety', *Scottish Journal of Criminal Justice Studies*, 5: 65–79.

Croall, H. (1989) 'Who is the white-collar criminal?', *British Journal of Criminology*, 29(2): 157–75.

Croall, H. (1995) 'Target women: women's victimisation and white-collar crime', in R. Dobash et al. (eds), *Gender and Crime*. Cardiff: University of Wales Press. pp. 228–45.

Croall, H. (2001) 'The victims of white-collar crime', in S-Å. Lindgren (ed.), *White-Collar Crime Research: Old Views and Future Potentials*. pp 35–54.

Croall, H. (2005) 'Penalties for corporate homicide', Paper prepared for the Scottish Executive Expert Group on Corporate Homicide, 17th August, http://www.scotland.gov.uk/Publications/2005/11/14133559/36003

Crow, I. (2001) *The Treatment and Rehabilitation of Offenders*. London: Sage.

Curtis-Fawley, S. and Daly, K. (2005) 'Gendered Violence and Restorative Justice', *Violence Against Women*, 11(5): 603–38.

Daly, K. (2002) 'Restorative justice: the real story', *Punishment and Society*, 4 (1):55–79.

Daly, K. (2003) 'Mind the gap: restorative justice in theory and practice', in A. von Hirsch et al., *Restorative Justice and Penal Justice: Competing or Reconcilable Paradigms?* Oxford: Hart.

Daniels, K. and Macdonald L. (2005) *Equality, Diversity and Discrimination: A Student Text*. London: Chartered Institute of Personnel and Development.

Davies, H. T. O., Nutley, S. M. and Smith, P. C. (eds) (2000) *What works? Evidence-based policy and practice in public services*. Bristol: Policy Press.

Davies, P., Francis, P. and Greer, C. (2007) *Victims, Crime and Society*. London: Sage.

Davis, K. (1969) *Discretionary Justice: A Preliminary Inquiry*. Baton Rouge, LA: Louisiana University Press.

De Haan, W. (1990) *The Politics of Redress: Crime, Punishment and Penal Abolition*. London: Unwin Hyman.

De Haan, W. (1991) 'Abolitionism and crime control: a contradiction in terms', in K. Stenson and D. Cowell (eds), *The Politics of Crime Control*. London: Sage.

De Montfort University (2007) *Practising Diversity: The Journey from Personal Knowledge to Professional Practice – a Workbook for Trainee Probation Officers*. Leicester: De Montfort University.

Denney, D. (2005) *Risk and Society*. London: Sage.

Dell, S. and Robertson, G. (1988) *Sentenced to Hospital: Offenders in Broadmoor*. Oxford: Oxford University Press.

Department for Education and Skills (2003) *Every Child Matters*. London: The Stationery Office.

Department of Health (2004) *Multi-Agency Public Protection Arrangements and the 'Duty to Co-operate'*. Local Authority Social Services Letter (LASSL), 3.

Devlin, J. (1993) 'Class oppression, as if it mattered', *Probation Journal*, 40(2), July: 71–7.

Dignan, J. (2000) *Restorative Justice Options from Northern Ireland*. Belfast: HMSO.

Dignan, J. (2005) *Understanding Victims and Restorative Justice*. Maidenhead: Open University Press.

Dizaei, A. and Phillips T., (2007) *Not One of Us: The Trial That Changed Policing in Britain Forever*. London: Profile Books.

Dominelli, L. (2006) 'Dangerous constructions: Black offenders in the criminal justice system', in K. Gorman, M. Gregory, M. Hayles and N. Parton (eds), *Constructive Work with Offenders*. London: Jessica Kingsley.

Doob, A. (1995) 'The United States sentencing commission guidelines: if you don't know where you are going, you might not get there', in C. Clarkson and R. Morgan (eds), *The Politics of Sentencing Reform*. Oxford: Oxford University Press.

Douglas, M. (1992) *Risk and Blame*. London: Routledge.

Dowden, C. and Andrews, D.A. (2004) 'The importance of staff practice in delivering effective correctional treatment: a meta-analytic review of core curriculum practice', *International Journal of Offender Therapy and Comparative Criminology*, 48(2): 203–14.

Downes, D. (1986) 'Back to basics: reflections on Barbara Wootton's "Twelve Criminological Hypotheses"', in P. Bean and D. Whynes (eds), *Barbara Wootton, Social Science and Public Policy: Essays in her Honour*. London: Tavistock Publications.

Downes, D. and Morgan, R. (2002) 'The skeletons in the cupboard: the politics of law and order at the turn of the millennium', in M. Maguire, R. Morgan and R. Reiner (eds), *The Oxford Handbook of Criminology*. 3rd edn. Oxford: Oxford University Press.

Duff, A. and Garland, D. (eds) (1994) *A Reader on Punishment*. Oxford: Oxford University Press.

Duff, R.A. (2003) 'Probation, punishment and restorative justice: should altruism be engaged in punishment?', *The Howard Journal*, 42(2): 181–97.

Dunkel, F. (1991) 'Legal differences in juvenile criminology in Europe', in T. Booth (ed.), *Juvenile Justice in the New Europe*. Sheffield: University of Sheffield Unit for Social Services Research.

Dunkel, F. (1996) 'Current directions in criminal policy', in W. McCarney (ed.), *Juvenile Delinquents and Young People in Danger in an Open Environment*. Winchester: Waterside Books.

Dunningham, C. and Norris, C. (1996) 'The Nark's Game (Parts 1 and 2)', *New Law Journal*, 146(6736): 402–4; and 14(6737): 456–7.

Durkheim, E. (1964) *The Division of Labour in Society*. New York: Free Press.

Eadie, T. and Canton, R. (2002) 'Practising in a context of ambivalence: the challenge for youth justice workers', *Youth Justice*, 2(1): 14–26.

Earle, R., Newburn, T. and Crawford, A. (2002) 'Referral Orders: Some Reflections on Policy Transfer and "What Works"', *Youth Justice*, 2(3): 141– 50.

Edwards, I. (2004) 'An ambiguous participant: the crime victim and criminal justice decision making', *British Journal of Criminology*, 44: 967–82.

Elliott, J. and Kushner, S. (2003) *Learning Requirement for Police Probationer Training in England and Wales*. Norwich and Bristol: University of East Anglia/University of West of England (unpublished report to Home Office).

Erez, E. and Rogers L. (1999) 'Victim impact statements and sentencing outcomes and processes', *British Journal of Criminology*, 39(2): 216–39.

Ericson, R. and Carriere, K. (1994) 'The fragmentation of criminology', in D. Nelken (ed.), *The Futures of Criminology*. London: Sage.

Erikson, K.T. (1966) *Wayward Puritans: A Study in the Sociology of Deviance*. New York: Wiley.

Eriksson, A. (ed.) 'The Politicisation of Community Restorative Justice in Northern Ireland' http://www.restorativejustice.org.uk/Resources/pdf/Politic_of_RJ_in_NI.pdf

Etzioni, A. (1993) 'The US Sentencing Commission on Corporate Crime: a critique', in G. Geis and P. Jesliow (eds), *White-Collar Crime. Special Issue of the Annals of the American Academy of Political and Social Science*. 525, January, Newbury Park, CA: Sage.

Families Against Corporate Killers (2006) *FACK Briefing Paper for Committee Stage of the Corporate Manslaughter and Corporate Homicide Bill*, 18th December 2006.

Farrall, S. and Maruna, S. (2004) 'Desistance-focused criminal justice policy research: introduction to a special issue on desistance from crime and public policy', *The Howard Journal of Criminal Justice*, 4(4): 358–67.

Farrall, S., Bannister, J., Ditton, J. and Gilchrist, E. (1997) 'Questioning the measurement of the "fear of crime": findings from a major methodological study', *British Journal of Criminology*, 37(4): 658–79.

Farrall, S. (2002) *Rethinking What Works with Offenders: Probation, Social Context and Desistance from Crime*. Cullompton: Willan.

Farrington, D.P. (2000). 'Explaining and preventing crime: the globalization of knowledge—the American Society of Criminology 1999 presidential address', *Criminology*, 38(1): 1–24.

Farrington, D.P. (2003) 'Methodological quality standards for evaluation research', *The Annals of the American Academy of Political and Social Science*, 587(1): 49–68.

Farrington, D.P., Coid, J.W., Harnett, L.M., Jolliffe, D., Soteriou, N., Turner, R.E. et al. (2006) *Criminal careers up to age 50 and life success up to age 48: new findings from the Cambridge Study in Delinquent Development*. 2nd edn. Home Office Research Study No. 299. London: Home Office.

Faulkner, D. (2006) *Crime, State and Citizen: A Field Full of Folk*. 2nd edn. Winchester: Waterside Press.

Feeley, M. and Simon, J. (1992) 'The new penology: notes on the emerging strategy for corrections', *Criminology*, 30(4): 449–75.

Feeley, M. and Simon, J. (1994) 'Actuarial justice: the emerging new criminal law', in Nelken, D. (ed.), *The Futures of Criminology*. London: Sage.

Fellowes, B. (1992) 'Management and empowerment: the paradox of professional practice', in R. Statham and P. Whitehead (eds), *Managing the Probation Service: Issues for the 1990s*. Harlow: Longman.

Fielding, H. (1751) *An enquiry into the causes of the late increase of robbers*.

Fineman, S., Gabriel, Y and Sims, D. (2002) *Organizing and Organizations*. 3rd edn. London: Sage.

Finnegan, R. (1978) 'Do the police make decisions?', in J. Baldsin and A.K. Bottomley (eds), *Criminal Justice Selected Readings*. London: Martin Robertson.

Fisher, D., Beech, A.R. and Browne, K.D. (1999) 'Comparison of sex offenders to non-offenders on selected psychological measures', *International Journal of Offender Therapy and Comparative Criminology*, 43, 473–91.

Fisher, D.D. and Beech, A.R. (2004) 'Adult male sex offenders', in Kemshall, H. and McIvor, G. (eds), *Managing Sex Offender Risk*. London: Jessica Kingsley.

Fitch, K. (2006) *Megan's Law: Does it protect Children?* London: NSPCC.

Fitzgerald, M. (1993) *Ethnic Minorities and the Criminal Justice System.* Royal Commission on Criminal Justice Research Study No. 20. London: HMSO.

Fooks, G. (1999) 'The Serious Fraud Office: policing the City or policing for the City?' British Criminology Conference, Liverpool.

Fooks, G. (2003) 'Contrasts in tolerance: the peculiar case of financial regulation', *Contemporary Politics*, 9(2): 127–42.

Ford, R. (2007) 'Police want DNA from speeding drivers and litterbugs on database', *The Times*, 2nd August 2007.

Foster, J., Newburn, T. and Souhami, A. (2005) *Assessing the Impact of the Stephen Lawrence Enquiry.* London: Home Office.

Fox, D., Dhami, M. and Mantle, G. (2006) 'Restorative final warnings: policy and practice', *The Howard Journal*, 45(2): 129–40.

Fox, L. (1952) *The English Prison and Borstal Systems.* London: Routledge and Kegan Paul.

France, A., Hine, J., Armstrong, D. and Camina, M. (2004). 'The on track early intervention and prevention programme: from theory to action', Home Office Online Report 10/04. London: Home Office.

Freire, P. (1972) *Pedagogy of the Oppressed.* Harmondsworth: Penguin.

Friedrichs, D. (1996) *Trusted Criminals.* Belmont, CA: Wadsworth.

Friedrichs, D. (1999) 'White-Collar Crime and the Class–Race–Gender Construct', in M.D. Schwartz and D. Milovanovic (eds), *Race, Gender and Class in Criminology: The Intersections.* New York: Garland.

Furedi, F. (1997) *Culture of Fear: Risk-taking and the Morality of Low Expectation.* London: Cassell.

Garland, D. (1990) *Punishment and Modern Society: A Study in Social Theory.* Oxford: Oxford University Press.

Garland, D. (2001) *The Culture of Control: Crime and Social Order in Contemporary Society.* Oxford: Oxford University Press.

Garland, D. (2002) 'Of crimes and criminals: the development of criminology in Britain', in M. Maguire, R. Morgan and R. Reiner (eds), *The Oxford Handbook of Criminology.* 3rd edn. Oxford: Oxford University Press.

Garland, D. and Sparks, R. (2000) 'Criminology, social theory and the challenge of our times', in D.Garland and R. Sparks (eds), *Criminology and Social Theory.* Oxford: Oxford University Press.

Gay Police Association (2005) *Stand up and be counted: The monitoring of sexual orientation within the Police Service.* Available online: http://www.gay.police.uk/files/Stand%20up%20and%20be%20counted%20Final.pdf

Gelsthorpe, L. (2001) 'Accountability: difference and diversity in the delivery of community penalties', in A. Bottoms, L. Gelsthorpe and S. Rex (eds), *Community Penalties Change and Challenges.* Cullompton: Willan.

Gelsthorpe, L. and McIvor, G. (2007) 'Difference and diversity in probation', in L. Gelsthorpe, and R. Morgan (eds), *Handbook of Probation.* Cullompton: Willan.

Gelsthorpe, L. and Morgan, R. (eds) (2007) *Handbook of Probation.* Cullompton: Willan.

Gelsthorpe, L. and Morris, A. (1999) 'Much ado about nothing—a critical comment on key provisions relating to children in the Crime and Disorder Act 1998', *Child and Family Law Quarterly*, 11(3): 209–21.

Gelsthorpe, L. and Padfield, N. (eds) (2003) *Exercising Discretion. Decision Making in the Criminal Justice System and Beyond.* Cullompton: Willan.

Gerber, J. and Weeks, S.L. (1992) 'Women as victims of corporate crime: a call for research on a neglected topic', *Deviant Behavior*, 13:325–47.

Gibson, B. and Cavadino, P. (1995) *Criminal Justice Process.* Winchester: Waterside Press.

Goldblatt, P. and Lewis, C. (1998) *Reducing Offending: An Assessment of Research Evidence on Ways of Dealing with Offending Behaviour.* Home Office Research Study No. 187. London: Home Office.

Goldson, B. (1997a) 'Children in trouble: state responses to juvenile crime', in P. Scraton (ed.), *'Childhood' in 'Crisis'?* London: UCL Press.

Goldson, B. (1997b) 'Children, crime, policy and practice: neither welfare nor justice', *Children and Society*, 11(2): 77–88.

Goldson, B. (ed.) (1999) *Youth Justice: Contemporary Policy and Practice.* Aldershot: Ashgate.

Goldson, B. (2001) 'A rational youth justice? Some critical reflections on the research, policy and practice relation', *Probation Journal*, 48(2): 76–85.

Goldson, B. (2002) *Vulnerable Inside: Children in Secure and Penal Settings*. London: The Children's Society.

Goldson, B. (2003) 'Youth perspectives', in R. Munck (ed.) *Reinventing the City?: Liverpool in Comparative Perspective*. Liverpool: Liverpool University Press.

Goldson, B. (2006a) 'Penal custody: intolerance, irrationality and indifference', in B. Goldson and J. Muncie (eds), *Youth Crime and Justice: Critical Issues*. London: Sage.

Goldson, B. (2006b) 'Damage, harm and death in child prisons in England and Wales: questions of abuse and accountability', *The Howard Journal of Criminal Justice*, 45(5): 449–67.

Goldson, B. (ed.) (2008) *Dictionary of Youth Justice*. Cullompton: Willan.

Goldson, B. and Coles, D. (2005) *In the Care of the State? Child Deaths in Penal Custody*. London: Inquest.

Goldson, B. and Muncie, J. (eds) (2006) *Youth Crime and Justice: Critical Issues*. London: Sage.

Goldstein, H. (1975) 'Improving policing: a problem oriented approach', *Crime and Delinquency*, 25: 236–58.

Goodey, J. (2004) 'Promoting "good practice" in sex trafficking cases', *International Review of Victimology*, 11(1): 89–110.

Goodey, J. (2005) *Victims and Victimology: Research, Policy and Practice*. Harlow: Pearson Education.

Grabovsky, P. and Sutton, A. (1993) (eds) *Stains on a White Collar: 14 Studies in Corporate Crime or Corporate Harm*. Sydney: Federation Press.

Gramsci, A. (1971) *Selections from Prison Notebooks*. London: Lawrence and Wishart.

Grant Stitt, B. and Giacopassi, D.J. (1993) 'Assessing victimization from corporate harms', in M.B. Blankenship (ed.), *Understanding Corporate Criminality*. New York: Garland.

Gray, M. and McDonald, C. (2006) 'Pursuing good practice? The limits of evidence-based practice', *Journal of Social Work*, 6(1): 7–20.

Gray, P. (2005) 'The politics of risk and young offenders' experiences of social exclusion and restorative justice', *British Journal of Criminology*, 45: 938—57.

Greer, C. (2007) 'News media, victims and crime', in P. Davies, P. Francis and C. Greer (eds), *Victims, Crime and Society*. London: Sage.

Hagan, J. (1994) *Crime and Disrepute*. Pine: Forge Press.

Haggerty, K.D. (2004) 'Displaced expertise: three constraints on the policy relevance of criminological thought.' *Theoretical Criminology*, 8(2): 211–31.

Haines, K. and O'Mahony, D. (2006) 'Restorative approaches, young people and youth justice', in B. Goldson and J. Muncie (eds) *Youth Crime and Justice: Critical Issues*. London: Sage.

Hall, N. (2005) *Hate Crime*. Cullompton: Willan.

Hammersley, M. (2005) 'Is the evidence-based movement doing more good than harm? Reflections on Iain Chalmers' case for research-based policy making and practice', *Evidence and Policy*, 1(1): 85–100.

Hampton, P. (2005) 'Reducing administrative burdens: effective inspection and enforcement', London: HM Treasury, www.dti.gov.uk/files/file22988.pdf

Hannah-Moffat, K. (2002) *Punishment in Disguise*. Toronto: University of Toronto Press.

Harcourt, B.E. and Ludwig, J. (2006) 'Broken windows: new evidence from New York City and a five-city social experiment', *University of Chicago Law Review*, 73.

Hawkins, K. (2002) *Law as a Last Resort: Prosecution Decision Making in a Regulatory Authority*. Oxford: Oxford University Press.

Hawton, M., Hughes, G., and Percy-Smith, J. (1999) *Community Profiling—Auditing Social Needs*. Buckingham: Open University Press.

Health and Safety Executive (2004) 'Occupational Health Statistics Bulletin 2003/2004, HSE/ National Statistics',http://www.hse.gov.uk/statistics/overall/ohsb0304.pdf

Hearnden, I. and Millie, A. (2004) 'Does tougher enforcement lead to lower conviction?', *Probation Journal*, 51(1): 48–59.

Hedderman, C. (2003) 'Enforcing supervision and encouraging compliance', in W.H. Chui and M. Nellis (eds), *Moving Probation Forward: Evidence, Arguments and Practice*. Harlow: Pearson Longman.

Hedderman, C. and Gelsthorpe, L. (1997) *Understanding the Sentencing of Women*. London: Home Office.

Heidensohn, F. (2000) *Sexual Politics and Social Control*. Buckingham: Open University Press.

Heidensohn, F. (2006) *Gender and Justice: New Concepts and Approaches*. Cullompton: Willan.

Henry, H. (2004) Ministerial foreword, *Scottish Strategy for Victims: Progress Report 2004*. Edinburgh: Scottish Executive, www.scotland.gov.uk/library5/justice/ssvpr04–00.asp

Her Majesty's Chief Inspector of Prisons (2006) *Annual Report of HM Chief Inspector of Prisons for England and Wales, 2004–2005*. London: The Stationery Office.

Her Majesty's Inspector of Constabularies (HMIC) (2002) *Training Matters*. London: HMIC.

HMIC (2003a) *Diversity Matters*. London: HMIC.

HMIC (2003b) *Embracing Diversity*. London: HMIC.

HMIC (1997) *Winning the Race: Policing Plural Communities*. London: HMIC.

Her Majesty's Inspectorate of Prisons (2004) 'No problems—old and quiet: older prisoners in England and Wales. A thematic review by HM Chief Inspector of Prisons.' September, Anne Owers.

Her Majesty's Inspectorate of Probation (HMIP) (2004) *Towards Race Equality: Follow Up Inspection Report*. London: Home Office.

HMIP (2006) *Anthony Rice: An Independent Review of Serious Further Offences*. London: HMIP.

HMIP (2007) *Race, Disability and Gender Equality Scheme 2007–2010*. London: HMIP.

Her Majesty's Treasury (2005) *Reducing Administrative Burdens: Effective Inspection and Enforcement*. London: HM Treasury.

Hill, S. (2004) *Setting Business Free from Crime: a crime against business survey by the British Chamber of Commerce, April 2004*. London: British Chamber of Commerce.

Hillyard, P., Pantazis, C., Tombs, S. and Gordon, D. (2004). *Beyond Criminology: Taking Harm Seriously*. London: Pluto Press.

Hillyard, P. and Tombs, S. (2005) 'Beyond criminology?', in P. Hillyard, C. Polantzis, S. Tombs, D. Gordon and D. Dorling (eds), *Criminal Obsessions: Why Harm Matters More than Crime*. London: Crime and Society Foundation.

Hillyard, P., Sim, J., Tombs, S. and Whyte, D. (2004) 'Leaving a "stain upon the silence": contemporary criminology and the politics of dissent', *British Journal of Criminology*, 44(3): 369–90.

Hine, J (2006) 'Risky business', *Safer Society*, Summer: 25–7.

Hirschi, T. (1969) *Causes of Delinquency*. Berkeley CA: University of California Press.

Hirst, P. (1975) 'Marx and Engels on law, crime and morality', in I. Taylor, P. Walton and J. Young (eds) *Critical Criminology*. London: Routledge and Kegan Paul.

Hobbs, D. (2007) 'Ethnography and the study of deviance', in P. Atkinson, A. Coffey, S. Delamont, J. Loftland and L. Loftland (eds), *Handbook of Ethnography*. London: Sage.

Hogeveen, B. (2006) 'Unsettling youth justice and cultural norms: the youth restorative action project', *Journal of Youth Studies*, 9(1): 47–66.

Home Office (1985) *The Cautioning of Offenders, Circular 14/85*. London: Home Office.

Home Office (1988) *Punishment, Custody and the Community*. London: HMSO.

Home Office (1990) *The Cautioning of Offenders, Circular 59/90*. London: Home Office.

Home Office (1991) *Criminal Statistics in England and Wales*. London: HMSO.

Home Office (1997) *No More Excuses—A New Approach to Tackling Youth Crime in England and Wales*. London: Home Office.

Home Office (2000) *National Standards for Supervision of Offenders in the Community*. London: Home Office.

Home Office (2001a) *A New Choreography: An Integrated Strategy for the National Probation Service for England and Wales. Strategic Frameworks 2001–2000*. London: Home Office.

Home Office (2001b) *Making Punishments Work: Report of a Review of the Sentencing Framework for England and Wales. (Halliday Report)*. London: Home Office.

Home Office (2003a) *A New Deal for Victims and Witnesses*. London: Home Office.

Home Office (2003b) *Professionalising the Investigation Process*. London: Home Office.

Home Office (2003c) *Restorative Justice: the Government's Strategy*. London: Home Office.

Home Office (2004a) *RDS and YJB Standards for Impact Studies in Correctional Settings*. London: Home Office.

Home Office (2004b) *Building Communities, Beating Crime: A Better Police Service for the 21st Century*. London: Home Office.

Home Office (2004c) *Offender Management Caseload Statistics*. London: Home Office.

Home Office (2004d) *MAPPA Guidance: Version 2*. London: Home Office.

Home Office (2004e) *Reducing Crime: Changing Lives*. London: Home Office.

Home Office (2005a) *The Code of Practice for Victims of Crime*. London: Home Office.

Home Office (2005b) *Together We Can Reduce Re-Offending and Increase Public Confidence: NOMS Communities and Civil Renewal Strategy Consultation Paper*. London: Home Office.

Home Office (2005c) *NOMS and YJB Approach to Communities and Civil Renewal*. London: Home Office.

Home Office (2006a) *Countering International Terrorism: The United Kingdom's Strategy*. London: Home Office.

Home Office (2006b) *Race Equality: The Home Secretary's Employment Targets Report 2005 (6th Annual Report)*. London: Home Office.

Home Office (2006c) *The NOMS Offender Management Model*. London: Home Office.

Home Office (2007a) *Cutting Crime: A New Partnership 2008–2011*. London: Home Office.

Home Office (2007b) *Race Relations and the Police*. London: Home Office.

Home Office (2007c) *Police Equality and Diversity*, London: Home Office.

Home Office (2007d) *MAPPA Guidance (Draft—Version 3)*. London: Home Office.

Home Office (2007e) *Review of the Protection of Children from Sex Offenders*. London: Home Office.

Home Office (2007f) *Common Values for the Police Service England and Wales*. London: The Stationery Office.

Homel, P., Nutley, S., Webb, B. and Tilley, N. (2004) *Investing to Deliver: Reviewing the Implementation of the UK Crime Reduction Programme*. Home Office Research Study No. 281. London: Home Office.

Hopkins, M. (2002) 'Crimes against businesses: the way forward for future research', *British Journal of Criminology*, 42(4): 782–97.

Hopley, K. (2002) 'National standards: defining the service', in D. Ward, J. Scott and M. Lacey (eds), *Probation Working for Justice*. 2nd edn. Oxford: Oxford University Press.

Hough, M. and Mayhew, P. (1985) *Taking Account of Crime: Key Findings from the 1984 British Crime Survey*. Home Office Research Study No. 85. London: HMSO.

Hough, M., Allen, R. and Padel, U. (2006) *Reshaping Prisons and Probation*. Bristol: Policy Press.

House of Commons Committee of Public Accounts (2004) *Youth Offending: The Delivery of Community and Custodial Sentences—Fortieth Report of Session 2003–2004*. London: The Stationery Office.

House of Commons Science and Technology Committee (2006) *Scientific Advice, Risk and Evidence Based Policy Making: Seventh Report of Session 2005–2006*. London: The Stationery Office. Available at http://www.publications.parliament.uk/pa/cm200506/cmselect/cmsctech/900/900-i.pdf

Howard League (1997) *Lost Inside: the Imprisonment of Teenage Girls*. London: Howard League.

Howard League for Penal Reform (2006) 'Prison Numbers Out of Control and Puts Public at Risk', Press Release 29th November.

Howard, J. (1997) *The State of the Prisons in England and Wales with Preliminary Observations and an Account of Some Foreign Prisons*. Warrington.

Hoyle, C. and Young, R. (2002) *Proceed with Caution: An Evaluation of the Thames Valley Police Initiative in Restorative Cautioning*. York: Joseph Rowntree Foundation.

Hoyle, C., Cape, E., Morgan, R. and Sanders, A. (1999) *Evaluation of the 'One Stop Shop' and Victim Statement Pilot Projects*. London: Home Office.

Hudson, B. (1997) 'Social control', in M. Maguire, R. Morgan and R. Reiner (eds), *The Oxford Handbook of Criminology*. 2nd edn. Oxford: Oxford University Press.

Hudson, B. (2001) 'Punishment, rights and difference: defending justice in the risk society', in Kevin Stenson and Robert Sullivan (eds) *Crime, Risk and Justice: The Politics of Crime Control in Liberal Democracies*. Cullompton: Willan.

Hudson, B. (2003), Justice in the Risk Society: Challenging and Re-Affirming Justice in Late Modernity. London: Sage.

Hughes, G. (2007) 'The politics of crime and community', in G. Potter (ed.), *Controversies in White-Collar Crime*. Cincinnati OH: Anderson.

Jackson, G. (1972) *Blood in My Eye*. Harmondsworth: Penguin.

Jackson, J.D. (2003) 'Justice for all: putting victims at the heart of criminal justice?', *Journal of Law and Society*, 30(2): 309–26.

James, A. and Raine, J.W. (1998) *The New Politics of Criminal Justice*. Harlow: Addison Wesley Longman.

Jamous, H. and Peloille, B. (1970) 'Professions or self-perpetuating systems? Changes in the French university-hospital system', in J.A. Jackson (ed.) *Professionals and Professionalisation*, Sociological Studies 3. Cambridge: Cambridge University Press.

Jenkins, S. (2004) 'The judicial equivalent of a football hooligan', *The Times*, 23rd June.

John, T. and Maguire, M. (2003) 'Rolling out the national intelligence model: key challenges', in K. Bullock and N. Tilley (eds), *Essays in Problem Orientated Policing*. Cullompton: Willan.

Johnstone, G. (2002) *Restorative Justice Ideas, Values, Debates*. London: Willan.

Johnstone, G. (2003) 'Introduction: restorative approaches to criminal justice', in Johnstone, G. (ed.), *A Restorative Justice Reader*. Cullompton: Willan.

Jones, D. (2001) '"Misjudged youth": a critique of the Audit Commission's reports on youth justice', *The British Journal of Criminology*, 41(2): 328–60.

Jones, D. (2002) 'Questioning New Labour's youth justice strategy: a review article', *Youth Justice* 1(3): 14–26.

Jones, S. (2006) *Criminology*. 3rd edn. Oxford: Oxford University Press.

Jones, T. and Newburn, T. (2005) 'Comparative criminal justice policy making in the United States and the United Kingdom: the case of private prisons', *British Journal of Criminology*, 45(1): 58–80.

Jones, T., MacLean, B. and Young, J. (1986) *The Islington Crime Survey: Crime, Victimisation and Policing in Inner City London*. Aldershot: Gower.

Jones, T. and Newburn, T. (2001) 'Widening access: improving police relations with hard to reach groups', Police Research Series Paper 138. London: Home Office.

Joyce, P. (2006) *Criminal Justice: An Introduction to Crime and the Criminal Justice System*. Cullompton: Willan.

Judiciary of England and Wales. *Statistics—Minority Ethnic Judges in Post*. Available online:www.judiciary.gov.uk/keyfacts/statistics/ethnic.htm

Kalunta-Crompton, A. (2004) 'Criminology and orientalism', in A. Kalunta-Crompton and B. Agozino (eds) *Pan-African Issues in Crime and Justice*. Aldershot: Ashgate. pp. 5–22.

Kane, J. and Wall, A.D. (2006) *The 2005 National Public Survey on White Collar Crime*. Fairmont, WV: National White Collar Crime Center.

Kauzlarich, D., Matthews, R. A. and Miller, W. J. (2001) 'Toward a victimology of state crime', *Critical Criminology*, 10(3): 173–94.

Keane, C. (1995) 'Loosely coupled systems and unlawful behaviour: organisation theory and corporate crime', in F. Pearce, and L. Snider (eds) *Corporate Crime: Contemporary Debates*. Toronto: University of Toronto Press. pp. 168–77.

Kearns, A. and Forrest, R. (1998) *Social Cohesion, Neighbourhoods and Cities*. Paper presented at the Housing Studies Spring Conference, University of York 15th–16th April.

Keith, B. (2006) *Report of the Zahid Mubarek Inquiry*. London: The Stationery Office.

Kelling, G. (1988) 'Police and communities: the quiet revolution', in National Institute of Justice, U.S. Department of Justice, and the Program in Criminal Justice Policy and Management, John F. Kennedy School of Government, Harvard University, *Perspective on Policing, No. 1*, reprinted in W. M. Oliver, (ed.) (2000) *Community Policing: Classical Readings*. Upper Saddle River, NJ: Prentice Hall.

Kemp, V. and Gelsthorpe, L. (2003) 'Youth justice: discretion in pre-court decision making', in L. Gelsthorpe and N. Padfield (eds) *Exercising Discretion. Decision Making in the Criminal Justice System and Beyond*. Cullompton: Willan.

Kemp, V., Sorsby, A., Liddle, M. and Merrington, S. (2002) *Assessing Responses to Youth Offending in Northamptonshire*. Research Briefing 2. London: NACRO.

Kemshall, H. (1998) *Risk in Probation Practice*. Aldershot: Ashgate.

Kemshall, H. (2001) *Risk Assessment and Management of Known Sexual and Violent Offenders: A Review of Current Issues*. London: Home Office.

Kemshall, H. (2002) *Risk, Social Policy and Welfare*. Buckingham: Open University Press.

Kemshall, H. (2003) *Understanding Risk in Criminal Justice*. Buckingham: Open University Press.

Kemshall, H. and Canton, R. (2002) 'The effective management of programme attrition'. Available at http://www.dmu.ac.uk/faculties/hls/research/commcrimjustice/commcrimjus.jsp

Kemshall, H. and Wood, J. (2007a) 'High risk offenders and public protection', in L. Gelsthorpe and R. Morgan (eds) *Handbook of Probation*. Devon: Willan.

Kemshall, H. and Wood, J. (2007b) 'Beyond public protection: an examination of community protection and public health approaches to high risk offenders', *Criminology and Criminal Justice*, 7(3): 203–22.

Kemshall, H., Canton, R. and Bailey, R. (2004) 'Dimensions of difference' in A. Bottoms, S. Rex, and G. Robinson (eds) *Alternatives to Prison: Options for an Insecure Society*. Cullompton: Willan.

Kemshall, H., Mackenzie, G., Wood, J., Bailey, R. and Yates, J. (2005) *Strengthening the Multi-Agency Public Protection Arrangements*. London: Home Office.

Kitsuse, J. (1962) 'Societal reactions to deviant behaviour: problems of theory and method', *Social Problems*, 9(3): 247–56.

Kitzinger, J. (1999a) 'Researching risk and the media', *Health, Risk and Society*, 1(1): 55–70.

Kitzinger, J. (1999b) 'The ultimate neighbour from hell: media framing of paedophiles', in B. Franklin (ed.), *Social Policy, Media and Misrepresentation*. London: Routledge.

Knepper, P. (2007) *Criminology and Social Policy*. London: Sage Publications.

Law, J. and Urry, J. (2004) 'Enacting the Social', *Economy & Society*, 33(3): 390–410.

Lees, S. (1997) *Ruling Passions: Sexual Violence, Reputation and the Law*. Buckingham: Open University Press.

Leigh, A., Read, T. and Tilley, N. (1996) 'Problem-oriented policing Brit pop', Crime Detection and Prevention Series Paper 75. London: Home Office.

Lemert, E. (1951) *Social Pathology: Systematic Approaches to the Study of Sociopathic Behavior*. New York: McGraw-Hill.

Lemert, E. (1964) 'Social structure, social control and deviation', in Clinard, M. (ed.), *Anomie and Deviant Behaviour*. New York: Free Press.

Levi, M. and Pithouse, A. (1992) 'The victims of fraud', in D. Downes (ed.), *Unravelling Criminal Justice*. London: Macmillan. pp. 229–46.

Lewis, S., Raynor, P., Smith D. and Wardak, A. (2006) *Race and Probation*. Cullompton: Willan.

Liebling, A. and Price, D. (2001) 'The prison officer: HMP Leyhill', *Prison Service Journal*.

Liebling, A. and Price, D. (2003) 'Prison officers and the use of discretion', in L. Gelsthorpe and N. Padfield (eds), *Exercising Discretion. Decision-making in the Criminal Justice System*. Cullompton: Willan.

Liebling, A., Elliott, C. and Price, D. (1999) 'Appreciative inquiry and relationships in prison', *Punishment and Society: The International Journal of Penology*, 1(1): 71–98.

Lipsey, M.W. (1995). 'What do we learning from 400 research studies on the effectiveness of treatment with juvenile delinquents?', in McGuire, J. *What Works: Reducing Reoffending*. Chichester: Wiley.

Loader, I. (1999) 'Consumer culture and the commodification of policing and security', *Sociology*, 33: 373—92.

Lofquist, W.S. (1993) 'Organisational probation and the US Sentencing Commission', in G. Geis and P. Jesilow (eds), *White Collar Crime. Special Issue of the Annals of the American Academy of Political and Social Science*. 525, January. Newbury Park, CA: Sage.

Lott, J. (2000) *More Guns, Less Crime*. Chicago: University of Chicago Press.

Lucas, J. (1980) *On Justice*. Oxford: Oxford University Press.

Lynch, M., Stretesky, P. and McGurrin, D. (2002) 'Toxic crimes and environmental justice: examining the hidden dangers of hazardous waste', in Potter, G. (ed.), *Controversies in White-Collar Crime*. Cincinnati, OH: Anderson. pp. 109–136.

Macpherson, W. (1999) *The Stephen Lawrence Inquiry Report*. London: Stationery Office.

Macrory, R. (2006) *Regulatory Justice: Sanctioning in a Post-Hampton World*. Consultation Document. London: Cabinet Office, www.cabinetoffice.gov.uk/regulation/documents/pdf/macrory/pdf.

Mactaggart, F. (2005) Ministerial foreword, *Rebuilding Lives: Supporting victims of crime*. London: Stationery Office.

Maguire, M. and Kemshall, H. (2004) 'Multi-agency public protection arrangements: key issues', in H. Kemshall and G. McIvor (eds), *Managing Sex Offender Risk*. London: Jessica Kingsley.

Maguire, M. (1994) 'Crime statistics, patterns, and trends: changing perceptions and their implications', in M. Maguire et al. (eds), *The Oxford Handbook of Criminology*. 1st edn. Oxford: Oxford University Press.

Maguire, M. (2007) 'Crime data and statistics', in M. Maguire, R. Morgan and R. Reiner (eds), *The Oxford Handbook of Criminology*. 4th edn. Oxford: Oxford University Press.

Maguire, M., Kemshall, H., Noaks, L., Wincup, E. and Sharpe, K. (2001) *Risk Management of Sexual and Violent Offenders: The work of public protection panels*. London: Home Office.

Mair, G (2004) 'What works: rhetoric, reality and research', *British Journal of Community Justice*, 3(1): 5–18.

Mannheim, H. (1939) *The Dilemma of Penal Reform*. London: Allen and Unwin.

Marshall, T.E. (1999) *Restorative Justice: An Overview*. Home Office: London.

Martinson, R. (1974). 'What works?: questions and answers about prison reform', *The Public Interest*, 35(1): 22–54.

Maruna, S. (2001) *Making Good: How Ex-Convicts Reform and Rebuild their Lives*. Washington, DC: American Psychological Association.

Marx, K. and Engels, F. (1888) *Manifesto of the Communist Party: Authorised English Translation by Karl Marx and Frederich Engels*. London: Williams.

Mathiesen, T. (1974) *The Politics of Abolition*. London: Martin Robinson.

Mathiesen, T. (1986) 'The politics of abolition', *Contemporary Crises*, 10: 81–94.

Mathiesen, T. (1990) *Prison on Trial*. London: Sage.

Mathiesen, T. (2004) *Silently Silenced; Essays on the Creation of Acquiescence in Modern Society*. Winchester: Waterside Press.

Matravers, A. and Hughes, G.V. (2003) 'Unprincipled sentencing? The policy approach to dangerous sex offenders', in M. Tonry (ed.), *Confronting Crime: Crime Control Policy under New Labour*. Cullompton: Willan.

Matza, D. (1969) *Becoming Deviant*. Englewood Cliffs, NJ: Prentice Hall.

Mawby, R.I. and Walklate, S. (1994) *Critical Victimology: International Perspectives*. London: Sage.

Mawby, R.I. (2003) 'Models of policing', in T. Newburn (ed.), *Handbook of Policing*. Cullompton: Willan.

McConville, S. (1998) *The Victorian Prison: England, 1865—1965. A History of Prison Administration, Vol. 1, 1750–1877*. London, Routledge.

McEvoy, K. and Mika, H. (2002) 'The critique of informalism in Northern Ireland', *British Journal of Criminology*, 42: 534–62.

McGuire, J. (2005) 'Is research working? Revisiting the research and effective practice agenda', in J. Winstone and F. Pakes, *Community Justice: Issues for Probation and Criminal Justice*. Cullompton: Willan.

McLaughlin, E. and Muncie, J. (2006) *The Sage Dictionary of Criminology*. 2nd edn. London: Sage.

McLaughlin, E., Fergusson, R., Hughes, G. and Westmarland, L. (eds) (2003) *Restorative Justice: Critical Issues*. London, Sage.

McNeill, F. (2006) 'Community supervision: context and relationships matter', in B. Goldson and J. Muncie (eds) *Youth Crime and Justice: Critical Issues*. London: Sage.

McNeill, F. and Batchelor, S. (2002) 'Chaos, containment and change: responding to persistent offending by young people', *Youth Justice*, 2(1): 27–43.

Meier, R.F. and Short, J.F. Jnr. (1995) 'The Consequences of White-Collar Crime', in G.Geis et al. (eds), *White-Collar Crime. Classic and Contemporary Views*. 3rd edn. New York: The Free Press.

Merton, R. (1938) 'Social Structure and Anomie', *American Sociological Review*, 3: 672–82.

Merton, R. (1968) *Social Theory and Social Structure*. New York: Free Press.

Messerschmidt, J. (1997) *Crime as Structured Activity: Gender, Race, Class and Crime in the Making*. London: Sage.

Metropolitan Police Authority (2006) *Community Engagement to Counter Terrorism* http://www.mpa.gov.uk/committees/mpa/2006/060126/09.htm

Mezirow, J. (1990) *Fostering Critical Reflection in Adulthood: A Guide to Transformative and Emancipatory Learning*. Jossey-Bass Higher Education Series. San Francisco: Jossey-Bass.

Miers, D. (2004) 'Situating and researching restorative justice in Great Britain', *Punishment and Society*, 6(1): 23–46.

Miller, J.G. (1991) *Last One Over the Wall: The Massachusetts Experiment in Closing Reform Schools*. Columbus: Ohio State University Press.

Miller, J.G. (1998) *Last One Over the Wall: The Massachusetts Experiment in Closing Reform Schools*. 2nd edn. Columbus: Ohio State University Press.

Miller, S. and Blackler, J. (2005) *Ethical Issues in Policing*. Aldershot: Ashgate.

Millett, K. (1977) *Sexual Politics*. London: Virago.

Mind Fact Sheets (2007) *Lesbians, Gay Men and Bisexuals and Mental Health*. http://www.mind.org.uk/Information/factsheets/Diversity/Factsheetlgb.htm

Modood, T. and Acland, T. (eds) (1998) *Race and Higher Education*. London, Policy Studies Institute.

Mokhiber, R. (1998) *Corporate Crime and Violence*. San Francisco: Sierra Club Books.

Moore, E. and Mills, M. (1990) 'The neglected victims and unexamined costs of white-collar crime', *Crime and Delinquency*, 36(3): 408–18.

Moore, R., Gray, E., Roberts, C., Merrington, S., Waters, I., Fernandez, R. et al. (2004) *ISSP: the Initial Report*. London: Youth Justice Board.

Moore, R., Gray, E., Roberts, C., Taylor, E. and Merrington, S. (2006) *Managing Persistent and Serious Offenders in the Community*. Cullompton: Willan.

Morgan, R. (2000) 'The politics of criminological research', in R.D. King and E. Wincup (eds) *Doing Research on Crime and Justice*. Oxford: Oxford University Press.

Morgan, R. (2006) 'Race, probation and inspections', in S. Lewis, P. Raynor, D. Smith and A. Wardak (eds) *Race and Probation*. Cullompton: Willan.

Morgan, R. (2007) 'Probation, Governance and Accountability', in Gelsthorpe, L. and Morgan, R. (eds) *Handbook of Probation*. Devon: Willan.

Morris, N and Rothman, D. J. (eds) (1995) *The Oxford History of the Prison*. Oxford: Oxford University Press.

Morris, W. (2004) *The Morris Inquiry- The Case for Change: People in the Metropolitan Police Service*, London: Metropolitan Police Authority.

Moseley, A and Tierney, S (2005) 'Evidence-based practice in the real world', *Evidence and Policy* 1/1: 113–119.

Muncie, J. (1999) 'Institutionalized Intolerance: Youth Justice and the 1998 Crime and Disorder Act', *Critical Social Policy*, 19(2): 147–175.

Muncie, J. (2002) 'A new deal for youth? Early intervention and correctionalism', in Hughes, G., McLaughlin, E. and Muncie, J. (eds) *Crime Prevention and Community Safety: New Directions*. London: Sage.

Muncie, J. (2002) 'Policy Transfers and What Works: Some reflections on comparative youth justice', *Youth Justice*, 1(3): 27–35.

Muncie, J. (2008) *Youth and Crime*. 3rd edn. London: Sage.

Muncie, J. and Goldson, B (eds) (2006) *Comparative Youth Justice: Critical Issues*. London: Sage.

Murray, C. (1990) *The Emerging British Underclass*. London: Institute of Economic Affairs.

NACRO (1986) *Black People in the Criminal Justice System*. London: National Association for the Care and Rehabilitation of Offenders.

NACRO (1991) *Black People's Experience of Criminal Justice*. London: NACRO.

NACRO (1992) *Black People Working in the Criminal Justice System*. London: NACRO.

NACRO (1993) *Race and Criminal Justice: Training*. London: NACRO.

Nash, M. (2005) 'The Probation Service, public protection and dangerous offenders', in Winstone, J. and Pakes, F. (eds) *Community Justice: Issues for probation and criminal justice*. Devon: Willan.

Nash, M. (2006) *Public Protection and the Criminal Justice Process*. Oxford: Oxford University Press.

National Black Police Association (2007) Official website: http://www.nationalbpa.com/.

National Offender Management Service (2007) *Prison Population and Accommodation Briefing*. London: NOMS.

National Policing Improvement Agency (NPIA formerly CENTREX) (2007) *Professionalising the Investigation Process* available online at http://www.npia.police.uk/.

Nelken, D. (Ed.) (1994) *The Futures of Criminology*. London: Sage.

Newburn, T. (2003) *Handbook of Policing*. Cullompton: Willan.

Newburn, T. and Souhami, A. (2006) 'Youth Diversion', in N. Tilley (ed.) *The Handbook of Crime Prevention and Community Safety*. Cullompton: Willan.

Newman, J. (2001) *Modernising Governance*. London: Sage.

Neyourd, P (2003) 'Police and Ethics', in Newburn, T. (ed.) *Handbook of Policing*. Cullompton: Willan.

Nicholas, S., Povey, D., Walker, A. and Kershaw, C. (2005) *Crime in England and Wales 2004 / 2005* Home Office Statistical Bulletin 11/05 Appendix Two: available online at http://www.homeoffice. gov.uk/rds/pdfs05/hosb1105append.pdf.

Norfolk, Suffolk and Cambridgeshire Strategic Health Authority (2003) '*Independent Inquiry into the Death of David Bennett,* Department of Health.

Northern Ireland Alternatives (2007) http://www.extern.org/restorative/Alternatives.htm

Nutley, S and Webb, J (2000) 'Evidence and the policy process', in Davies, H T O, Nutley, S M and Smith, P C (2000). *What Works? Evidence-Based Policy and Practice in Public Services*. Bristol: Policy press.

Oakley, A (1999) 'People's way of knowing: gender and methodology', in Hood, S, Mayall, B and Oliver, S (Eds) *Critical Issues in Social Research: Power and Prejudice*, Buckingham: Open University Press.

Oettmeier, T. N. (1992) 'Matching Structure to Objectives', in L. T. Hoover (ed.) *Police Management: Issues and Perspectives*,. Washington, D.C.: Police Executive Research Forum.

Oliver, M. (1996) *Understanding Disability: from Theory to Practice*. Basingstoke: Macmillan.

Owers, A. (2006) 'Report on an unannounced short follow up inspection of HMP Leicester (21–23 August 2006)', Her Majesty's Inspectorate of Prisons, London.

PA Consulting Group (2001) Diary of a Police Officer. *Police Research Series Paper 149*. London: Home Office.

Padfield, N. (ed.) (2007) Who to Release?: parole, fairness and criminal justice. Cullompton: Willan

Parekh, B. (2002) *The Future of Multi-Ethnic Britain*. Runnymede Trust.

Parsons, W (2002) 'From Muddling Through to Muddling Up—Evidence Based Policy Making and the Modernisation of British Government', *Public Policy and Administration* 17/3: 43–60.

Pawson, R (2006) *Evidence-based Policy: A Realist Perspective*. London: Sage Publications.

Pawson, R and Tilley, N (1997) *Realistic Evaluation*. London: Sage.

Pearce, F. (1990) *Second Islington Crime Survey: commercial and conventional crime in Islington*, Middlesex: Middlesex Polytechnic.

Pearce, F. and Tombs, S. (1998) *Toxic Capitalism: corporate crime and the chemical industry*. Aldershot: Ashgate.

Peppin, P. (1995) "Feminism, Law and the Pharmaceutical Industry", in Pearce and Snider, eds., *Corporate Crime: Contemporary Debates*. Toronto: University of Toronto Press.

Pitts, J. (1988) *The Politics of Juvenile Crime*. London: Sage.

Pitts, J. (1990) *Working with Young Offenders*. London: Macmillan.

Policeman's Blog 1/1/06 *And I thought I had problems* http://coppersblog.blogspot.com/search?q=paper+work.

Posen, I (1994) *Review of Police Core and Ancillary Tasks*. Home Office: London.

Pragnell, S. (2005) 'Reprimands and Final Warnings', in T. Bateman and J. Pitts (eds) *The RHP Companion to Youth Justice*. Lyme Regis: Russell House Publishing.

Pratt, J. (1987) 'A revisionist history of intermediate treatment' in *British Journal of Social Work* 17(4): 417–435.

Press for Change (2007) http://www.pfc.org.uk/.

Prior, V., Glaser, D. and Lynch, M.A. (1997) 'Responding to Child Sexual Abuse: The Criminal Justice System', *Child Abuse Review*, 6: 128–140.

Prison Reform Trust (2006) Bromley Briefing Paper, Prison Fact File, November, London: Prison Reform Trust.

Prison Reform Trust (2007) *Information Book for Disabled Prisoners*: http://www.prisonreformtrust.org.uk/standard.asp?id=507.

Probation Boards Association (2005) *The NOMS Communities and Civil Renewal Strategy—Response on behalf of the PBA*, available online http://www.probationboards.co.uk/.

Punch, M. (1996) *Dirty Business: Exploring Corporate Misconduct; Analysis and Cases*. London: Sage.

Purwar, N. (2003) *Pilot Research Project on the Barriers facing BME Female Police Personnel*, British Association of Police Women. http://www.bawp.org/New/Documents/BSAResearch1%5B2%5D.doc

Putnam, R.D. (1993) *Making Democracy Work. Civic Traditions in Modern Italy*. Princeton NJ: Princeton University Press.

Putnam, R.D. (2000) Bowling Alone: The Collapse and Revival of American Community. New York: Simon and Schuster.

Raine, J.W. and Willson, M.J. (1993) *Managing Criminal Justice*. Hemel Hempstead: Harvester Wheatsheaf.

Rawlings, P. (1999) *Crime and Power: A History of Criminal Justice 1688–1998*. Harlow: Addison Wesley Longman.

Raynor, P. and Vanstone, M. (2002) *Understanding Community Penalties: Probation, Change and Social Context*. Buckingham: Open University Press.

Reform Website (2007) http://www.reform.co.uk/website/crime/abetterway/middlesbroughand hartlepool.aspx

Reid, J. (2006) Foreword by the home secretary, *Rebalancing the Criminal Justice System in Favour of the Law-Abiding Majority*. London: Home Office, www.cjsonline.gov.uk/downloads/application/pdf/CJS_Review.pdf

Reid, K. (1997) 'The abolition of cautioning? Juveniles in the "last chance" saloon', *The Criminal Lawyer*, 78: 4–8.

Reiner, R. (1992) 'Policing a postmodern society', *The Modern Law Review*, 55(6): 761–81.

Reiner, R. (2000) *The Politics of the Police*. 3rd edn. Oxford: Oxford University Press.

Restorative Justice Consortium (2006) *'Regulatory Justice: Sanctioning in a Post-Hampton World'—A Response from the Restorative Justice Consortium*, www.restorativejustice.org.uk/Better_Regulation/MacroryRegulationConsult_Final_Aug06.pdf

Rex, S. (1999) 'Desistance from offending: experiences of probation', *The Howard Journal of Criminal Justice*, 38(4): 366–83.

Rex, S. (2005) *Reforming Community Penalties*. Cullompton: Willan.

Robb, G. (2006) 'Women and white-collar crime. Debates on gender, fraud and the corporate economy in England and America, 1850–1930', *British Journal of Criminology*, 46(6): 1058–72.

Roberts, R (2006) 'Uses of research: editorial', *Criminal Justice Matters*, 62: 3.

Roche, D. (2002) 'Restorative justice and the regulatory state in South African townships', *British Journal of Criminology*, 42: 514—33.

Rock, P. (1990) *Helping Victims of Crime: The Home Office and the Rise of Victim Support in England and Wales*. Oxford: Clarendon.

Rock, P. (1994) *History of Criminology*. Aldershot: Dartmouth Publishing.

Rock, P. (2004) *Constructing Victims' Rights: The Home Office, New Labour, and Victims*. Oxford: Oxford University Press.

Roshier, B. (1989) *Controlling Crime*. Milton Keynes: Open University Press.

Rouse, J. (1999) 'Performance Management, Quality Management and Contracts', in S. Horton (ed.), *Public Management in Britain*. Basingstoke: Palgrave.

Rowe, M. and Garland, J. (2007) 'Police diversity training: a silver bullet tarnished?', in M. Rowe (ed.) *Policing Beyond Macpherson*. Cullompton: Willan.

Rutherford, A. (1986) *Growing Out of Crime*. Harmondsworth: Penguin.

Rutherford, A. (1992) *Growing Out of Crime: The New Era*. Winchester: Waterside Books.

Rutherford, A. (1995) 'Signposting the future of juvenile justice policy in England and Wales', in Howard League for Penal Reform (eds), *Child Offenders: UK and International Practice*. London: The Howard League for Penal Reform.

Rynbrandt, L. and Kramer, R.C. (2001) 'Corporate violence against women', in C. Renzetti and L. Goodstein (eds), *Women, Crime and Criminal Justice*. New York: Oxford University Press.

Said, E. (1994) *Representations of the Intellectual: The 1993 Reith Lectures*. London: Vintage.

Sanderson, I. (2002) 'Evaluation, Policy Learning and Evidence-based Policy Making', *Public Administration*, 80(1): 1–22.

Satter, G. (2004) 'Prisoner-on-prisoner homicide in England and Wales', Home Office Research Findings 250. HMSO: London.

Savin-Baden, M. (2000) *Problem-Based Learning in Higher Education: Untold Stories*. Buckingham: Open University Press.

Savin-Baden, M. and Howell-Major, C. (2004) *Foundations of Problem-Based Learning*. Maidenhead: Society for Research into Higher Education and Open University Press.

Schön, D. (1987) *Educating the Reflective Practitioner: Towards a New Design for Teaching and Learning in the Professions*. Jossey-Bass Higher Education Series. San Francisco: Jossey-Bass.

Schön, D. (1991) *The Reflective Practitioner: How Professionals Think in Action*. Aldershot: Ashgate.

Schön, D. (1993) 'Generative metaphor: a perspective on problem-setting in social policy', in Ortonry, A. (ed.), *Metaphor and Thought*. 2nd edn. Cambridge: Cambridge University Press.

Scarman, L. (1981) *The Scarman Report: The Brixton Disorders*. London: HMSO.

Schur, E. (1973) *Radical Non-Intervention*. New York: Prentice-Hall.

Scraton, P. (ed.) (1997) *'Childhood' in 'Crisis'?* London: UCL Press.

Sebba, L (2001) 'On the relationship between criminological research and policy: the case of crime victims', *Criminal Justice*, 1(1): 27–58.

Security Industry Authority (2007) *The Security Industry—Aims*. http://www.the-sia.org.uk/home/security/police_family.htm

Shearing, C.D. and Stenning P.C. (1983) 'Private security: implications for social control', *Social Problems*, 30(5): 493–506.

Sheptycki, J. (2006) 'Marxism' in E. McLaughlin and J. Muncie, *The Sage Dictionary of Criminology*. 2nd edn. London: Sage.

Sherman, L.W. (2005) 'The use and usefulness of criminology, 1751–2005: enlightened justice and its failures', *Annals of the American Academy of Political and Social Sciences*, 600: 115–35.

Sherman, L. and Strang, H. (2007) *Restorative Justice: The Evidence*. London: Smith Institute.

Shover, N., Litton Fox, G. and Mills, M. (1994) 'Long-term consequences of victimization by white-collar crime', *Justice Quarterly*, 11(1): 75–98.

Shute, S., Hood, R. and Seemungal, F. (2005) *A Fair Hearing? Ethnic Minorities in the Criminal Courts*. Cullompton: Willan.

Sim, J. (1990) *Medical Powers in Prison*. Oxford: Oxford University Press.

Sim, J. (1994) 'The abolitionist approach: a British perspective', in A. Duff et al. (eds), *Penal Theory and Practice: Tradition and Innovation in Criminal Justice*. Manchester: Manchester University Press.

Sim, J. (2002) 'Abolitionism', in E. McLaughlin and J. Muncie (eds), *The Sage Dictionary of Criminology*. London: Sage.

Sim, J. (2004) 'Thinking about imprisonment' in J. Muncie and D. Wilson (eds) *Student Handbook of Criminal Justice and Criminology*. London: Sage.

Sim, J., Scraton, P. and Gordon, P. (1987) 'Crime, the State and critical analysis: an introduction', in P. Scraton (ed.), *Law, Order and the Authoritarian State: Reading in Critical Criminology*. Buckingham: Open University Press.

Skelton, A. (2002) 'Restorative justice as a framework for juvenile justice reform—a South African perspective', *British Journal of Criminology*, 42: 496—513.

Skolnick, J. (1966) *Justice Without Trial*. New York: Wiley.

Slapper, G. and Tombs, S. (1999) *Corporate Crime*. London: Longman.

Smart, C. (1977) *Women, Crime and Criminology*. London: Routledge and Kegan Paul.

Smith, D. (1995) *Criminology for Social Work*. Basingstoke: Hampshire.

Smith, R. (2006) 'Actuarialism and early intervention in contemporary youth justice', in B. Goldson and J. Muncie (eds), *Youth Crime and Justice: Critical Issues*. London: Sage. pp. 92–109.

Smith, R. (2007) *Youth Justice: Ideas, Policy, Practice*. 2nd edn. Cullompton: Willan Publishing.

Smith, S.M., and Aamodt, M.G. (1997) 'The relationship between education, experience, and police performance', *Journal of Police and Criminal Psychology*, 12(2): 7–14.

Snider, L. (1991) 'The regulatory dance: understanding reform processes in corporate crime', *International Journal of the Sociology of Law*, 19: 209–36.

Snider, L. (1993) *Bad Business: Corporate Crime in Canada*. Toronto: University of Toronto Press.

Social Exclusion Unit (1999) *Bridging the Gap*. London: Cabinet Office.

Solomon, E. and Rutherford, M. (2007) *Community Sentences Digest*. London: Centre for Crime and Justice Studies.

Spalek, B. (1999) 'Exploring victimisation: a study looking at the impact of the Maxwell scandal upon the Maxwell pensioners', *International Review of Victimology*, 6: 213–30.

Spalek, B. (2001) 'White collar crime and secondary victimisation, an analysis of the effects of the closure of BCCI', *Howard Journal of Criminal Justice*, 40(2):166–79.

Spalek, B. (2002) *Islam, Crime and Criminal Justice*. Cullompton: Willan.

Spalek, B. (2006) *Crime Victims: Theory, Policy and Practice*. Basingstoke: Palgrave Macmillan.

Sparks, R. (1996) 'Penal "Austerity": The Doctrine of Less Eligibility Reborn?', in R. Matthews and P. Francis (eds), *Prisons 2000*. Basingstoke: Macmillan.

Sparks, R. (2003) 'States of insecurity: punishment, populism and contemporary political culture', in S. McConville (ed.), *The Use of Imprisonment*. Cullompton: Willan.

Sparks, R., Bottoms, A.E. and Hay, W. (1996) *Prisons and the Problem of Order*. Oxford: Clarendon Press.

Spierenburg P.C. (1991) *The Prison Experience: Disciplinary Institutions and their Inmates in Early Modern Europe*. New Brunswick, NJ: Rutgers University Press.

Stern, V. (1987) *Bricks of Shame: Britain's Prisons*. Harmondsworth: Penguin.

Stonewall (2007) Official website: http://www.stonewall.org.uk/

Stout, B. (2006) 'Is diversion the appropriate emphasis for South African child justice?', *Youth Justice*, 6(2): 129–42.

Stretesky, P. and Hogan, M. (1998) 'Environmental justice: an analysis of superfund sites in Florida', *Social Problems*, 45: 268–87.

Stretesky, P. and Lynch, M. (1998) 'Corporate environmental violence and racism', *Crime Law and Social Change*, 30: 163–84.

Stretesky, P. and Lynch, M. (1999) 'Environmental justice and the predictions of distance to accidental chemical releases in Hillsborough County, Florida', *Social Science Quarterly*, 80: 830–46.

Sutherland, E. and Cressy, D. (1955) *Principles of Criminology*. Chicago: Lippincott.

Sykes, G.M. (1958) *The Society of Captives: The Study of a Maximum Security Prison*. Princeton, NJ: Princeton University Press.

Szockyi, E. and Fox, J.G. (eds) (1996) *Corporate Victimisation of Women*. Boston, MA: Northeastern University Press.

Tapley, J. (2005) 'Improving confidence in criminal justice: achieving community justice for victims and witnesses', in J. Winstone and F. Pakes (eds), *Community Justice: Issues for Probation and Criminal Justice*. Devon: Willan.

Taylor, I., Walton, P. and Young, J. (1973) *The New Criminology*. London: Routledge and Kegan Paul.

Temkin, J. (2002) *Rape and the Legal Process*. 2nd edn. Oxford: Oxford University Press.

Thomas, J. and Boehlefeld, S. (1991) 'Re-thinking abolistionism: "What do we do with Henry?"', *Journal of Social Justice*, 18(Fall): 239–51.

Thompson, N. (2003) *Promoting Equality: Challenging Discrimination and Oppression*. 2nd edn. Basingstoke: Palgrave Macmillan.

Times Higher Education (2006) 'Evidence against policymakers', 1 December, p. 7.

Titus, R., Heinzelmann, F. and Boyle, J. (1995) 'Victimization of persons by fraud', *Crime and Delinquency*, 41(1): 54–72.

Tombs, S. (1995) 'Corporate crime and new organisational forms', in F. Pearce and L. Snider (eds), *Corporate Crime: Contemporary Debates*. Toronto: University of Toronto Press. pp. 132–146.

Tombs, S. (2002) 'Understanding regulation?', *Social and Legal Studies*, 11(1): 113–33.

Tombs, S. and Whyte, D. (2004) 'Why bad news is no news and crime is big business', available online at http://www.catalystmedia.org.uk/issues/misc/articles/bad_news.htm

Tombs, S. and Whyte, D. (2006) 'Community safety and corporate crime', in P. Squires (ed.), *Community Safety: Critical Perspectives on Policy and Practice*. Bristol: Policy. pp. 155–68.

Tombs, S. and Whyte, D. (2007) *Safety Crimes*. Cullompton: Willan.

Tomsen, S. (2002) 'Victims, perpetrators and fatal scenarios: a research note on anti-homosexual male homicides', *International Review of Victimology*, 9 (3): 253–71.

Tonry, M. (1996) 'Racial politics, racial disparities, and the war on crime', in B. Hudson (ed.) *Race, Crime and Justice*. Aldershot: Dartmouth.

Tonry, M. (2003) 'Evidence, elections and ideology in the making of criminal justice policy', in M. Tonry (ed.) *Confronting Crime: Crime Control Policy Under New Labour*. Cullompton: Willan.

Tonry, M. (2004) *Punishment and Politics: Evidence and Emulation in the Making of English Crime Control Policy*. Cullompton: Willan.

Towl, G. and Crighton, D. (2000) 'Risk assessment and management', in G. Towl, L. Snow and M. McHugh (eds), *Suicide in Prison*. Oxford: Blackwell.

Toynbee, P. (2006) 'The Farepak scandal lays bare a gross inequality', *The Guardian*, 14th November, http://www.guardian.co.uk/commentisfree/story/0,,1947219,00.html

Trasler, G. (1986) 'Innovation in penal practice', in P. Bean and D. Whynes (eds) *Barbara Wootton, Social Science and Public Policy: Essays in her Honour*. London: Tavistock Publications.

Trotter, C. (1999) *Working with Involuntary Clients: A Guide to Practice*. London: Sage.

Trotter, C. (2000) 'Social work education, pro-social modelling and effective probation practice'. *Probation Journal*, 47: 256–61.

Tutu, D. (1999) *No Future Without Forgiveness*. London: Rider Books.

Tweedale, G. (2000) *Magic Mineral to Killer Dust: Turner and Newall and the Asbestos Hazard*. Oxford: Oxford University Press.

Tyler, M. (forthcoming) 'Managing the tensions', in J. Wood and J. Hine, (eds) *Work with Young People: Developments in Theory, Policy and Practice*. London: Sage.

Tyler, T. (1990) *Why People Obey the Law*. New Haven: Yale University Press.

Umbreit, M. and Zehr, H. (2003) 'Restorative family group conferences: differing models and guidelines for practice', in McLaughlin, E., Fergusson, R., Hughes, G. and Westmarland, L. (eds) *Restorative Justice: Critical Issues*. London: Sage.

Van Ness, D. and Strong, K.H. (1997) *Restoring Justice*. Cincinnati, OH: Anderson.

Vanstone, M. (1995) 'Ethics in social work', *Vista Perspectives on Probation* 1(1): 49–58.

Victim Support (2006) Official website: www.victimsupport.org.uk.

Von Hentig, H. (1948) *The Criminal and his Victim: Studies in the Sociobiology of Crime*. New Haven: Yale University Press.

Wacquant, L. (2005) 'The great penal leap backward: incarceration in America from Nixon to Clinton', in J. Pratt, D. Brown, M. Brown, S. Hallsworth and W. Morrison (eds) *The New Punitiveness: Trends, Theories, Perspectives*. Cullompton: Willan.

Waddington, P. (1999) 'Police (canteen) sub-culture: an appreciation', *British Journal of Criminology*, 39(2): 286–309.

Wahidin, A (2002) *Older Women in the Criminal Justice System: Running Out of Time.* London: Jessica Kingsley.

Wahidin, A (2006) 'Managing the Needs of an Older Prison Population', Unpublished Report.

Wahidin, A. (2007), '"Senior citizens": Growing old in prisons'. Liverpool University: Unpublished Paper.

Wahidin, A. and Cain M. (2006) *Ageing, Crime and Society.* Cullompton: Willan.

Wakefield, A. (2004) *Selling Security: The Private Policing of Public Space.* Cullompton: Willan.

Walker, N. (1991) *Why Punish?* Oxford: Oxford University Press.

Walklate, S. (1989) *Victimology: The Victim and the Criminal Justice Process.* London: Unwin Hyman.

Walklate, S. (1990) 'Researching victims of crime: critical victimology', *Social Justice*, 17(2): 25–42.

Walklate, S. (2005) *Criminology: the basics.* London: Routledge.

Walklate, S. (2007) *Imagining the Victim of Crime.* Maidenhead: Open University Press.

Walmsley, R. (2003) *World Prison Population List.* 4th edn. London: Home Office.

Walters, R. (2003) *Deviant Knowledge: Criminology, Politics and Policy.* Cullompton: Willan Publishing.

Walters, R. (2006) 'Boycott, resistance and the role of the deviant voice', *Criminal Justice Matters*, 62: 6–7.

Ward, D, and Crisp, A. (2004) *Audit of the Initial Police Learning and Development Programme.* Leicester: De Montfort University (unpublished report to Home Office).

Ware, S. (2007) 'Age Concern services—a social care model for older people in prison and ex-offenders in the community: service users' perspectives'. Unpublished paper.

Weiss, C.H., Murphy-Graham, E. and Birkeland, S. (2005) 'An alternate route to policy influence: how evaluations affect D.A.R.E.', *American Journal of Evaluation*, 26(1): 12–30.

White, D. (2006) 'A conceptual analysis of the hidden curriculum of police training in England and Wales', *Policing and Society*, 16(4): 386–404.

Whitfield, D. (ed.) (1991) *The State of the Prisons 200 Years On.* Howard League. London: Routledge.

Whyte, D. (2004a) 'Leaving a stain upon the silence: contemporary criminology and the politics of dissent', *British Journal of Criminology*, 44(3): 369–90.

Whyte, D (2004b) 'All that glitters isn't gold: environmental crimes and the production of local criminological knowledge', *Crime Prevention and Community Safety*, 6(1): 53–63.

Whyte, D. (2007) 'Victims of corporate crime', in S. Walklate (ed.), *Handbook of Victims and Victimology.* Cullompton: Willan

Wilcox, A. (2003) 'Evidenced-based youth justice? Some valuable lessons from an evaluation for the Youth Justice Board', *Youth Justice*, 3(1): 19–33.

Wilkins, L. (1964) *Social Deviance.* London: Tavistock.

Williams, B. (1999) *Working with Victims of Crime: Policies, Politics and Practice.* London: Jessica Kingsley.

Williams, B. (2005) *Victims of Crime and Community Justice.* London: Jessica Kingsley.

Williams, B. and Goodman, H. (2007) 'Working for and with victims of crime', in L. Gelsthorpe, and R. Morgan (eds), *Handbook of Probation.* Cullompton: Willan.

Williams, R. (2004) 'The management of crime scene examination in relation to the investigation of burglary and vehicle crime', Home Office, http://www.homeoffice.gov.uk/rds/pdfs04/rdsolr2404.pdf

Wilson, J. and Kelling, J. (1982) 'The police and neighbourhood safety: broken windows', *Atlantic Monthly online.*

Wolfgang, M.E. (1958) *Patterns in Criminal Homicide.* Montclair, NJ: Patterson Smith.

Women's Aid (2006) Official website: http://www.womensaid.org.uk/landing_page.asp?section=0001000100190002

Wonders, N. and Danner, M (2001) 'Globalization, state-corporate crime and women: the strategic role of women's NGOs in the new world order', in G. Potter (ed.), *Controversies in White-Collar Crime.* Cincinnati OH: Anderson. pp. 165–184.

Wood, J. and Kemshall, H. (2007) *The Operation and Experience of Multi-Agency Public Protection Arrangements (MAPPA).* London: Home Office.

Worrall, A. (1997) *Punishment in the Community: the Future of Criminal Justice.* Harlow: Longman.

Worsley, R. (2007) *Young People in Custody 2004–2006.* London: HM Inspectorate of Prisons and the Youth Justice Board.

Wright Mills, C. (1959) *The Sociological Imagination.* New York: Oxford University Press.

Yates, J. (2004a) 'Evidence, group work and the new youth justice' *Groupwork*, 14(3): 112–32.

Yates, J. (2004b) 'Criminological ethnography: risks, dilemmas and their negotiation', *British Journal of Community Justice* 3(1): 19–31.

Yates, J. (2006a) *An Ethnography of Youth and Crime in a Working Class Community*. Unpublished PhD Thesis. Leicester: De Montfort University.

Yates, J. (2006b) '"You just don't grass": youth crime and "grassing" in a working class community', *Youth Justice*, 6(3): 195–210.

Young, J. (2003) 'In Praise of Dangerous Thoughts', *Punishment and Society* 5(1): 97–107.

Young, J. (1979) 'Left idealism, reformism and beyond', in National Deviancy Conference (ed.), *Capitalism and the Rule of Law*. London: Hutchinson.

Young, J. (1986) 'The Failure of Criminology: The Need for Radical Realism', in J. Young and R. Mathews (eds), *Confronting Crime*. London: Sage.

Young, K., Ashby, D., Boaz, A. and Grayson, L. (2002) 'Social science and the evidence based policy movement', *Social Policy and Society*, 1(3): 215–24.

Youth Justice Board (2007a) *Annual Report and Accounts 2005–2006*. London: Youth Justice Board.

Youth Justice Board (2007b) *Improving Practice: A Risk-based Approach to Interventions*, http://www.yjb.gov.uk/en-gb/practitioners/ImprovingPractice/Risk-basedApproachtoInterventions/

Youth Justice Board (2007c) *The Youth Justice System: Intensive Supervision and Surveillance Programme*, http://www.yjb.gov.uk/en-gb/yjs/SentencesOrdersand Agreements/IntensiveSupervisionAnd SurveillanceProgramme/

Zedner, L. (2002) 'Victims', in M. Maguire, R. Morgan and R. Reiner (eds), *The Oxford Handbook of Criminology*. 3rd edn. Oxford: Oxford University Press.

INDEX

Diagrams are given in italics